Researching Paganisms

THE PAGAN STUDIES SERIES

SERIES EDITORS
Wendy Griffin (California State University, Long Beach)
and Chas S. Clifton (University of Southern Colorado)

The label "Pagan studies" marks the movement of scholarly inquiry into a diversity of religious expressions formerly considered new religious movements. The definition of paganism advocated by sociologist of religion Michael York—"an affirmation of interactive and polymorphic sacred relationships by individual or community with the tangible, sentient, and nonempirical"—emphasizes what these spiritual traditions have in common: a feeling for "the sacred" that is non-monotheistic, based on relationship rather than revelation and scripture, and often includes an immanent dimension for landforms, plants, and animals.

The traditional approach to the study of religions assumes that formal religious traditions are normative, and so misses religious sects that are inherently more fluid and more ambiguous. The approach taken by Pagan studies permits examination of highly dynamic and mutable religious communities within a hypermodern society, and demonstrates the increasing religious pluralism of our times. This shift in perspective will be a welcome addition to the intellectual endeavor to understand and give meaning to a wide variety of religious experience.

The Pagan Studies Series is interdisciplinary in nature and aims to include both junior scholars who seek to turn strong dissertations into publishable monographs and senior scholars who are looking for the kind of attention a small academic press can give their work. The most exciting feature of the series is that it will take the lead in building Pagan studies into a legitimate field by focusing research on this unexplored topic.

BOOKS IN THE SERIES

Researching Paganisms, edited by Jenny Blain, Douglas Ezzy, and Graham Harvey

FORTHCOMING BOOKS

Her Hidden Children: The Story of American Neopaganism, by Chas S. Clifton

Researching Paganisms

Edited by
Jenny Blain, Douglas Ezzy,
and Graham Harvey

ALTAMIRA
PRESS

A Division of Rowman & Littlefield Publishers, Inc.
Walnut Creek ● Lanham ● New York ● Toronto ● Oxford

ALTAMIRA PRESS
A division of Rowman & Littlefield Publishers, Inc.
1630 North Main Street, #367
Walnut Creek, CA 94596
www.altamirapress.com

Rowman & Littlefield Publishers, Inc.
A wholly owned subsidiary of The Rowman & Littlefield Publishing Group, Inc.
4501 Forbes Boulevard, Suite 200
Lanham, MD 20706

PO Box 317
Oxford
OX2 9RU, UK

Copyright © 2004 by AltaMira Press

British Library Cataloguing in Publication Information Available

Library of Congress Cataloging-in-Publication Data

Researching paganisms / edited by Jenny Blain, Douglas Ezzy, and Graham Harvey.
    p. cm. — (The Pagan studies series)
    Includes bibliographical references and index.
    ISBN 0-7591-0522-7 (hardcover : alk. paper) — ISBN 0-7591-0523-5 (pbk. : alk.
paper)
    1. Religion. 2. Paganism. I. Blain, Jenny. II. Ezzy, Douglas. III. Harvey,
Graham. IV. Series

    BL85.R397 2004
    299'.94'072—dc22
                                                            2004004654

Printed in the United States of America

♾™ The paper used in this publication meets the minimum requirements of American
National Standard for Information Sciences—Permanence of Paper for Printed Library
Materials, ANSI/NISO Z39.48–1992.

CONTENTS

CONTENTS

PREFACE

T he appearance of this book, the first in this series in Pagan studies, is an exciting introduction to the new field of Pagan studies.

As a discipline, Pagan studies exists because Paganism lives—not as "irreligion" or even as Wordsworth's "creed outworn," but both as a mode of religious expression concealed within other religious traditions and as a self-conscious set of religious traditions themselves. In that sense, it might be more accurate to write "Paganisms," since Paganism is the farthest thing from monolithic, but we will stay with the customary usage here. Nevertheless, multiplicity is a key idea in Pagan studies: multiple concepts of the divine, multiple local forms of religion, and a sacred relationship with the multiple forms of the material world as they are experienced by Pagans.

The first international conference in contemporary Pagan studies was held at the University of Newcastle-upon-Tyne, UK, in 1993. Organized by Charlotte Hardman and Graham Harvey, one of the editors of this anthology, it brought together academic scholars and teachers in the Pagan community to present papers and discuss future directions for the field. Thus, from its inception, Pagan studies has taken a unique approach to academic inquiry, weaving together both etic and emic perspectives and being profoundly interdisciplinary in nature. In that spirit, we conceive of this series as multiple and interdisciplinary, for Pagan studies avoids the common approach to the study of religions, one that assumes that formal religious traditions are normative. Instead, its unique approach permits examinations of highly dynamic and mutable religious communities within

contemporary society, ones that demonstrate the increasing religious pluralism of our times. Likewise, we believe that rethinking definitions of
contemporary Paganisms will facilitate reexamination not only of the
movements that preceded it but of the Pagan religions of the ancient
world as well.

Contemporary Paganisms, the beliefs, practices, and "traditions," are
still in and of themselves taking shape, redefining and creating a discourse
about what it means to see Divinity as polymorphic and immanent in the
context of the twenty-first century. The fluidity within Paganisms com-
bines with the fluidity inherent in methods used by researchers in the field
as they negotiate what Graham Harvey calls the "areas of becoming." This
fluidity and flexibility permits new kinds of questions to be asked and new
answers to be discovered by the innovative field of Pagan studies.

Because of this approach, we believe that it is particularly appropriate
that *Researching Paganisms* is the first book to appear in AltaMira's new
series in Pagan studies. It brings together a group of thirteen successful researchers who demonstrate the significance of reflexivity, integrity, and
courage, as they explore the challenges of doing liminal research in a fluid
field. The results of their work will not only help give shape to the field of
Pagan studies, but will be of interest to any researchers who do fieldwork.
With its publication, the discourse on methodological inquiry takes a
large step forward.

Wendy Griffin
Chas S. Clifton
Series Editors

INTRODUCTION

Jenny Blain, Douglas Ezzy, and Graham Harvey

T he need for a sophisticated understanding of contemporary spirituality is perhaps one of the most pressing issues of our time. New
trends are emerging; older ones are changing and taking on renewed importance. Increasingly identities are constituted around not
only explicit religious affiliations or agnosticism or atheism, but also
more diffuse accumulations of spirituality. There are growing levels of religiously linked violence, and rapid transitions in contemporary society
lead to the marginalization of values and ethical orientations traditionally
linked to religious traditions. We are convinced, both as academics and
practitioners, that religious traditions still have an important role to play
in contemporary society, and that the study, by practitioners and nonpractitioners, of such traditions and the meanings and identities generated within them is a crucial and central part of not only academic, but
political and pragmatic engagement with the complexities of today's
changing societies. This book, while specifically about contemporary Paganisms, is also part of a more general debate about the role of academics in contemporary religious traditions, and the relevance of religion to
contemporary society.

This is a book about how researchers of Paganism have both been
changed by (or at least been forced to rethink methodology because of experiences) and been parties to the evolution of pagan spiritualities and religions. The book examines current developments in research
methodologies and epistemologies within a variety of disciplines that will
interest researchers in those disciplines engaged in research about a variety of religious and nonreligious phenomena. In particular it highlights

1

the relationships of researchers with the communities researched, "owner-ship" of knowledge so created, and problems in presenting a nonmain-stream, and seemingly "nonrational," area within academic discourses across discipline boundaries.

Being Changed by Cross-Cultural Encounters (Young and Goulet 1994) examined the issues of how ethnographers within anthropology deal with spiritual or "extraordinary" experience, and concomitant experience of "be-ing changed" thereby. It raised questions about the extent to which ethno-graphers become part of what they experience, and suggested that conventional understandings of the separation of researcher and re-searched were inadequate. It also suggested that even where people who were seen as "other" (than mainstream Westerners) were enabled to dis-cuss and theorize those "extraordinary" experiences, problems still existed within academia for researchers who drew on "native theory" in present-ing the "nonrational."

Today many researchers in many disciplines draw on understandings and paradigms that stress the importance of the researcher's own experi-ences and the situated nature of the knowledge s/he constructs. Such de-velopments include recognition that both participation and distancing include experiences that change the researcher and (potentially, at least) the researched. At the same time, developing Paganisms draw on aca-demic scholarship, and researchers contribute directly and indirectly to understandings within the communities they study. Yet today, Paganisms within Western society are still seen as marginal, and those who research them may feel pressure to "objectify" communities and practices re-searched and distance themselves from their experiences.

Western Paganisms therefore provide opportunity to examine re-search relationships, and changes resulting therefrom, across a number of disciplines, and thereby create a major contribution to theory and practice of research within pluralized postmodernity.

Aims of the Book

The book and individual chapters within it have three major aims. First, the authors discuss developments in each discipline that affect or are af-fected by experiencing Paganism or Pagan experiences. Second, challenges to the researcher's experience, worldview, and lifeway from researching Pa-ganism are examined. As a consequence, Pagan researchers have had to deal, at some level, with contradictions and tensions between being an academic researcher, and their participation in the experiences of that which is being researched. Third, the chapters examine ways in which not only the researcher, but also the communities in which s/he works and practices spiritually, is changed by these interactions.

Most chapters do not simply "reflect" in the third person, but provide personal accounts that illustrate the author's engagements with spiritual practices studied and/or their own spiritual path. This enables a discussion of how their spiritual practice and understanding has shaped both the topics and epistemology/methodology of their academic research, critical reflection on interactions between their academic research and their own spiritual journey, and critical reflection on how their research forms part of the development of the communities researched, or of the more general Pagan movement.

Chapters and Organization

The contributors to this book come from a wide variety of academic disciplines: their work is both informed by and informs current academic practice. Each presents, in their chapter, something of themselves and their experiences, and how these contribute to their understandings and analyses of the western Pagan spiritual practices with which they are engaging. Some, not all, considered themselves "Pagan" at the outset of their research, but all have, in some sense, been changed by their experiences, and all are striving for ways to present these changes and their reflexive impact on the research and communities studied.

Their writing is not simply about Paganisms, but about academia and its disciplines, theoretical approaches, epistemologies, methodologies, and methods. Thus the intended audience for these chapters, and this book, is not restricted to those already interested in Paganisms, but includes colleagues interested in developments in academic research. In short, we consider that the study of Paganisms has import for other academic areas, particularly those in which identity (of researcher and/or researched) and reflexivity are key.

It is worth saying, at the outset, that Western Paganisms are not all the same either in practices, worldviews, or derivations, although there are substantial overlaps and similarities. Contributors engage with Druidry, Wicca, Goddess spirituality, Thealogy, Eco-Paganism, Heathenry, and Western Shamanism, as well as a more generic "Paganism," which is coming to understand itself as separate from any of those. The range both of contributors and Paganisms is deliberate. Much research still focuses on "Wicca" and still attempts to give "objective" description, even when it is undertaken by insiders. Those who profess "insider" knowledge, at academic conferences or in academic journals, may be regarded with suspicion. Furthermore, within the communities studied the myth of academic detachment still, to some extent, persists. The chapters in this book and knowledges presented therein are situated not only by each researcher's particular engagements, but also by academia and its disciplines, and by the sense of Paganisms as interlopers to the cultural, political, and religious environments of (variously in this book) Britain, Norway, Australia, and the United States.

Topics in this book include:

1. performing Paganisms, the reflexivity of understanding oneself as "Pagan," and implications for the community;

2. dealing with the remnants of positivism and the worship of "objectivity," the need to take Pagan research seriously, and challenges of insider research for "Pagan studies," comparable with those for feminist and antiracist research;

3. embodying relationships between research into Paganisms, environment, and community;

4. re-locating the researcher, and moving beyond the critique of ethnography to research as located political practice.

Part I includes two accounts of how researchers undertaking Ph.D. work found themselves having to deal with issues of participation, "going native," their own critical understandings of their "performances" of Paganisms, and the reception of their work by the communities in which they were researchers and practitioners. A third chapter discusses various transitions and performances in the biography and career of a researcher. Andy Letcher's account explores tensions between the "performance" of Paganisms and the "performance" of research, and how each performance has its repercussions on community, individual, and indeed discipline. As a Bard he was an active participant within the communities he studied: in undertaking a Ph.D. study of Bardism he was in part moving from pagan to academic performance—a term that he unpacks within the chapter. In reflexively discussing his own location within the development of "Bardism," he draws on performance theory and "neotribal" theory, introducing these as major contributors to Pagan studies. But he comments on the tensions within his own self-understanding that have ensued from his move to theoretical academia.

Jone Salomonsen describes fieldwork with the "Reclaiming" witches of San Francisco, exploring how her experiences led her to new ways of conceptualizing her relationship to the research. After findings from her initial empirical/textual analysis approach were rejected by her "informants," she adopted a participant/anthropological approach where she was defined as participant/apprentice within the Reclaiming Witches—a group identifying as feminist mystics. Salomonsen points to anthropology's ambivalence about mysticism/magic: whereas participation in other areas of life is lauded, engaging with mysticism, taking it seriously is still often seen as "going native." She describes her solutions, introducing a theme that will recur throughout this book, that of being "one's own informant," and points to the difficulties of "staying," to some extent, a compassionate "native" while conducting critical analysis of her field material. Another theme raised by this chapter is that of how communities studied are themselves consumers of the academic research we produce.

Wendy Griffin provides a rich and sensitive account of the transitions in her life and career as researcher, academic, parent, performer, and more. She does so in order to demonstrate not only that subjectivity cannot "be left hanging at the door like a raincoat wet with experience," but also that objectivity and subjectivity are necessarily entangled. She discusses the dilemmas that a researcher faces in establishing herself within the communities researched: her performance as a drummer has given her access and insights, but there are issues of how the "performance" locates the researcher as both within and apart from the community, and, for Griffin, issues of data validity when her participation—as drummer, or even as survey researcher undertaking an "objective" questionnaire study—changes the experiences of those around her and hence their responses. This issue of "data contamination" is one that has been extensively debated among followers of both qualitative and quantitative methodologies and epistemologies, and will be addressed in various ways in successive chapters: the specific and moving examples of Griffin's own experiences give insight into issues faced by many people, particularly postgraduate students, researching in fields outside the sociology of religion. How researchers might negotiate the various pulls and tensions generated by engaging with other people (whether they be single mothers, priestesses, or communities) is powerfully explored in this chapter.

In part II, four contributors engage with challenges to and from objectivity and subjectivity. They provide different perspectives on how they negotiate the demands for the classical goal of academic objectivity and the seductive enticement of experiential subjectivity in relation to their research. The fact that their research interests and disciplinary positions were quite distinct is only part of the variation presented in these chapters.

Melissa Harrington examines problems and possibilities of working within a discipline that is still largely positivist and rationalist—psychology—while conducting research within experiential and nonrationalist Paganisms. The focus of her research on male Wiccan experiences and narratives of "conversion" (or "coming home") tested the value of previous uses of explanations and theories arising from psychology. She argues that a greater familiarity with the more-or-less normative approaches and writings of the discipline would greatly benefit the study of Paganisms and other religious traditions. Reference to a previous researcher's limited knowledge of psychology illustrates the pitfalls of a too facile interdisciplinary research. But, even as she reiterates the necessity of producing work that is "representative but unbiased, theoretically well informed, and methodologically rigorous," Harrington demonstrates the value of long-term and intense "insiderly" participation. The model she offers for understanding the process by which people identify as Pagans (with specific reference to male Wiccans) benefits both from rigorous academic training and reflexivity and from her thirteen-year membership of a Wiccan coven. Not every researcher will replicate these qualifications, but they may, at least, see benefits available from some fusion of classic "outsider" and "insider" roles.

Chas S. Clifton turns the focus from "acceptability" within academia to "acceptability" within Paganisms. In discussing development of the infant "Pagan studies," he points to tensions between Paganisms and the academy, particularly over the kinds of material that many Pagans will produce and read. For instance, nonacademic Pagans may see pagan scholars as occupying an archetypal ivory tower, distant from those who are simply getting on with being Pagan: At least one of the editors has repeatedly been told on various e-mail lists that sociological research is only about counting heads and is of little use to practitioners, unless, of course, they want to know numbers of Pagans. So-called "reconstructionists" are rather more keen on research, but may not want to know about current theories or have favorite ideas—for instance about "the Celts"—challenged. However, Clifton sees much of the writing printed by "Pagan" presses as dealing only in safety, reassurance, avoidance of critical awareness or engagement with current theories, or topics that may challenge the public presentation of Paganisms as "respectable." Research on shamanic ecstasy, particularly when associated with the use of entheogens, is a case in point; and Clifton has "begun to find the writing of Pagan academics more provocative, more 'edgy,' and more grounded in experience than much of what is produced by . . . publishers catering to the Pagan market." He uses the term *excursus*— i.e., "going out"—not only in Timothy Leary's sense of "turn on, tune in and drop out," but also as a means to examine movement between pagan and academic communities, and in general as a metaphor for pushing the bounds of the possible as well as the "acceptable."

Sarah M. Pike addresses dilemmas in analyzing personal experiences within the discipline of religious studies, where these have been disregarded as sources of "data." She describes herself as a researcher not identifying as "pagan" and yet, with hindsight, as much "pagan" as anyone she so labelled, and identifies a need within religious studies for recognition of reflexivity. Her chapter argues for the inclusion of personal reflections about bodily and emotional experiences and relationships during research, not only in field notes but also in published scholarly accounts of religious practice. Pike not only demonstrates the considerable value of such experiences, feelings, and reflections in reaching a deep understanding of the religion in question, but she also demonstrates that the effacement of subjectivity (including change and relationships) diminishes the value of research outcomes.

Finally, Douglas Ezzy argues that spiritual realities should be taken at face value, in contrast to traditional research methodologies that primarily aim to explain away practitioner accounts of spiritual experiences. He argues that reported spiritual experiences should be treated as both real and socially constructed. Ezzy draws together a theoretical context for moving beyond traditional research and its reporting, within a sociological/ethnographic research context, advancing postmodern critiques of traditional methodologies to problematize the position of researchers caught between the pressures of a "secular modernist scientific worldview" and their own needs to make sense of the subjectivity of their own experiences.

Part III provides contexts—physical as well as theoretical—for some of these subjectivities. Sylvie Shaw's chapter examines the embodied relationships of researched and researcher with earth and environment. Her research draws on descriptions of individual, embodied relationships, and deconstructions of the insider/outsider debate, to further a quest for the "dimensions of the 'ecoerotic' body, the body that has lain dormant in the socially constructed postmodern world." Her writing, especially by including excerpts from those among whom she researched, is full of a passion and engagement suitable to her subject matter. It might, then, serve as an encouragement to find means of communication that resonate more fully with the feel and flavor of that which researchers attempt to convey to those who could not be present in the encounter and action of research.

Ruth Mantin's work with the "Goddess-talk" of feminist thealogy arises within the context of her relationships with the sister-women whose discourse she explores. Her research is therefore a journey with others to explore embodied spiritualities, which becomes a journey to find ways to conduct those explorations. In common with other feminist theorists, researchers, and activists, she finds it necessary to coin and/or use reformations of seemingly familiar terms to draw attention to the "different layers of meaning, reclamation, and exclusion" in particular discourses and activities. Among the most significant of these turns of phrase (and approach) for the dissemination of research results are "dis-cover," "re-member," and "de-monstrate." But Mantin's most important contribution to consideration of research methods, relationships, positions, and situatedness is her elaboration of "inter-viewing" as a more fully dialogical and conversational engagement in research.

Ronald Hutton describes the changing context of writing and reception of studies in this area, and explores how research becomes part of the context of the study, with inherent obligations. His attempt "to become the first person to write the history of one of the most sensational and radically countercultural of the world's mystery religions, which had taken to itself the glamour and fear associated with the traditional stereotype of the witch" was firmly rooted in commonplace academic interests and reasons. However, the pursuit of that research and the reception of the resulting publications have caused Hutton to reflect further on issues of reflexivity and reactivity. In this chapter he writes more about the former, the double-sided problem of the preconceptions a researcher brings to a project and the changes that familiarity invites in a researcher.

Part IV examines attempts to challenge dominant perspectives through exploration of explicit practitioner/researcher positions. Can Pagan studies provide impetus for change within disciplines, and new ways of conceptualizing self, other, and society? What is the location of the researcher, not only as a broker between the researched and academia, but within and between disciplines, and how and in what ways does this location shift? Robert J.

Wallis draws on his double "insider" position (within archaeology and Paganisms) and on new directions within postmodernist ethnography to indicate challenges for archaeology posed by "autoarchaeology" and neoshamanic engagements with monuments and research. He describes challenges to his "insider" status as a "neo-Shaman" posed by his academic involvement, his need to negotiate practice within Pagan and academic milieus, and subsequent move toward a queer theory approach that challenges both insider and outsider perceptions and enables multiple understandings and analyses—while emphasizing that were a researcher/practitioner position to become hegemonic within Pagan studies, the ability of such research to produce new and different insights would be compromised.

Jenny Blain presents herself as researcher-practitioner multiply located by specifics of practice and cultural landscapes and attempting to outline a politics of postmodern spirituality. She describes a trajectory in which personal, political, and pagan understandings result in new directions in ethnography and discourse analysis and in constructions of "self," and she raises issues about "authenticity" as a construct of some Pagan reconstructionist religions—one which is immensely problematic for a postmodernist-leaning researcher. In discussing her own involvement as a practitioner of seidr (Northern shamanistic practice) and a researcher of meanings at sacred sites, she also questions the ethnicisms that may be inherent in some pagan discourses, and raises issues about the obligations of the researcher/practitioner in problematizing dimensions or issues within communities studied.

Graham Harvey questions the duality conventionally inculcated in new researchers and demanded of "acceptable" scholars: "insider" or "outsider" location. He finds "participant observation" only a partial solution, as revealed by the continuing accusation that some researchers have "gone native" (i.e., participating more fully than they ought even after returning from "the field") or become "advocates" or even "insiders." In his own discipline, religious studies, this is couched in terms of a separation from and delegitimation of theology as a academic discipline. Resisting the allure and authority of the choice proffered between two options (theology or religious studies, subjectivity or objectivity, insider or outsider, participation or observation, native or academic, and so on), he argues that another position (not a resolution of or compromise between those choices) has always been available, that of "guesthood." Apart from anything else, this is intended as a celebration of the plurality of ways in which scholars engage with Paganisms and other religions.

Conclusion: Toward a Narrativized Pagan Studies

This book is not simply a narrative about various contemporary Paganisms. It is also a set of stories about how some academics engage with one or more of those Paganisms.

Ruth Mantin (this volume) writes of how "Catherine Kohler Riessman explains the 'narrative turn' taken by all the social sciences in terms of the realization that 'individuals become the autobiographical narratives they tell about their lives'" (citing Riessman 1993, 20). Here, since some of these academics are also Pagans, and all of them have participated in religious activities (certainly in the course of their research, but most often they are much more involved), the book includes stories of how they have come to make sense of their own spiritual practice and experiences. In narrating their attempts to "make sense," the authors illustrate various engagements with reflexive research and issues of representation and epistemology. Additionally, all of the contributors discuss ways in which they have benefited from, struggled with, and contributed to the academic disciplines within which they work. The book, then, becomes an example of what Alvesson and Sköldberg (2000) discuss as a "play of interpretative levels," moving between autobiography, hermeneutics, discourse analysis, and critical ethnography/autoethnography, to illustrate and begin to resolve the situations and tensions inherent in researching Paganisms for today.

Further, the book as a whole is a narrative, however fragmented, partial, and contradictory, about what we hope the study of contemporary Paganisms, and other religious traditions, will "become."

The issues discussed in this book cut to the heart of contemporary religious life. Fundamentalist responses to both rapid social change and new interpretive theological practices are common in the monotheistic religions. Politics, of course, is deeply embedded in the social conflicts shaped by these fundamentalist religious traditions. The Paganisms discussed in this book are still small in comparison to the dominant global religions, and marginal also with respect to secular/agnostic society and academia. It is precisely this liminal status, both politically and demographically, that provides the authors of this book with the freedom to examine the religious and spiritual practices of the various Paganisms that is both insightful and innovative. At the same time, the contemporary Paganisms discussed in this book are growing rapidly. Many are of quite recent origin. These factors alone make the study of contemporary Paganisms exciting and provide a rare opportunity to study religious movements in their formative moments. Further, the role of academics in these movements is also increasingly important. The development of a sophisticated intellectual understanding of contemporary Paganisms will facilitate, we hope, the maturing of these religious traditions into valued and vibrant facets of contemporary social life.

We anticipate and intend, however, something even more ambitious than this. It is our understanding that the study of Paganisms has much to offer academic colleagues, whether or not they are at all interested in Paganisms. The contributors to this book are at the forefront of developments in research methodologies and interdisciplinary dialogues that promise considerable advances in academic approaches to religions and religious cultures. In one way or another, to one degree or another, they all proffer modes of engagement in research that takes place far from the now-decayed ivory tower of objectivist academia. They negotiate the more exciting territory in which religions and academia are continuously "becoming" and requiring the telling of new stories. Some contributors label their approaches "practitioner" or "insider" research, others insist on various forms of dialogical encounter and relationship, often combined with high levels of reflexivity. The recognition and even celebration of the fact that both the researcher and the researched are changed by the entanglement of academic (however "objective" or "subjective" they may be) and religionist (however critical or naïve they may be), establishes more honest and ethical foundations for research than some of those established by some of our predecessors.

This will certainly not be the last word in the study of Paganisms or in academic reflection on improving research methods, positions, and relationships. The notes and references of each chapter point to significant works that deserve further consideration as the story continues. In particular, readers might follow up suggestions made in this volume that elaborate ideas and arguments initiated in exemplary books such as Young and Goulet's *Being Changed* (1994), Griffin's *Daughters of the Goddess* (2000), and Spickard, Landres, and McGuire's *Personal Knowledge and Beyond* (2002). In the end, however, research is an action toward and with other people and, thus, is best learned in doing. This book, then, may find its chief role in initiating enthusiasm for, and aiding reflection on, experiences arising in the encounter between academics and those among whom they research.

In short, *Researching Paganisms: Religious Experiences and Academic Methodologies* offers people interested in religions enriching narratives about a set of religions (Paganisms), a series of academic practices (research positions, methods, and relationships), and an incitement to re-view the implications hinted at by labeling academic work as "humanities" and/or "social sciences." Simultaneously, it offers people interested in research methods and epistemologies across a wide range of these "humanities" and "social sciences" the example of researchers who, because of the complexities and challenges of their subject matter, must engage with the "cutting edge" of reflexive methodologies and critical autobiographical research. To all such people, academic or practitioner, we offer the following chapters.

References

Alvesson, M., and Sköldberg, K.
2000 *Reflexive Methodology.* London: Sage.

Griffin, W.
2000 *Daughters of the Goddess: Studies of Healing, Identity and Empowerment.* Walnut Creek, Calif.: AltaMira.

Riessman, C. K.
1993 *Narrative Analysis* (Sage University Paper series on Qualitative Research Methods, Vol. 30). Newbury Park, Calif.: Sage.

Spickard, J. V., Landres, J. S., and McGuire, M. B., eds.
2002 *Personal Knowledge and Beyond: Reshaping the Ethnography of Religion.* New York: New York University Press.

Young, D. E., and Goulet, J.-G., eds.
1994 *Being Changed: The Anthropology of Extraordinary Experience.* Peterborough, Ontario: Broadview Press.

Part One
PERFORMANCE AND REFLEXIVITY

CHAPTER ONE

BARDISM AND THE PERFORMANCE OF PAGANISM: IMPLICATIONS FOR THE PERFORMANCE OF RESEARCH

Andy Letcher

It is nearly midnight and in a corner of the festival marked out as the "Pagan Space," among the assorted tents, benders, and marquees, a large fire has been lit. About fifty people, mainly adults with some children, are sitting round chatting quietly, waiting for the stories to start. At last the storyteller begins, dark tales for the dark moon at midnight. Unusually dressed, though not out of place here, he has long hair, a d'Artagnan beard, and colorful clothes, and sports an outrageous woolly hat topped with a long feather. He stands, illuminated only by the flames. His performance lasts for nearly an hour, an eclectic mix of stories from indigenous cultures and British legend interspersed with songs accompanied with a mandolin, which he keeps slung across his back. As the stories unfold he takes his audience on an emotional journey through tales of horror, humor, and desire. Later he concedes that this was one of his best-ever performances, that he felt as if the stories were "telling themselves" and that he "had" the audience. He says that he was inspired.

Introduction—Hear the Voice of the Bard

The opening vignette describes an example of an emerging type of Pagan performance known as Bardism. The figure of the Bard, as divinely inspired poet, musician, and storyteller, is one that has fired the Western poetic imagination from Homer to the present day, animating groups along the way as diverse as medieval Welsh poets and nineteenth-century Romantics from Wordsworth to Blake. In its current Pagan manifestation, as distinct from the "cultural" Bardism of the Welsh and Cornish Eisteddfodau[1] (about which see Davies 1998; Hale 2000), Bardism is of particular significance within contemporary Druidry, where the bardic search for inspiration underpins Druidic practice. Bardism is also found within Eco-Paganism, albeit in a less-structured form, and in the contemporary storytelling revival (about which see Heywood 1998). It may also be found, as described above, at the plethora of alternative camps and festivals that now feature throughout the English summer.

Bardism as a stylistic genre is the performance of poetry, story, song, and instrumental folk music, from memory. Poetry and songs are often composed by the performer, typically on Pagan-related themes, but may also, like the stories and music, come from "traditional" British sources. Stories are usually taken from the Celtic vernacular literature (about which see Hutton 1996) and from Arthurian romance, but may be supplemented by stories appropriated or borrowed from indigenous or other world cultures. Folk musical forms are favored (Irish, Scottish, English, French, and Breton), and instruments typically include lap harps (the iconic instrument of the stereotypical Bard), mandolins, whistles, bagpipes, and guitars. The instruments played, the material recited, and the ambience of the performance are all connotative of, or are culturally constructed as signifying, a catchall ahistoric past; a Celtic, medieval, Tolkienesque, once-upon-a-time enchanted world. Contemporary events—the struggles of, say, ecoprotesters to prevent the construction of roads—may well be related, but in a form which places them into this mythic realm. Similarly the Bardic mode of delivery involves the use of archaic words, (e.g., "t'was," "thence," "deeds"), and a "grandiose" manner of intonation that signifies "greatness" or "import" (on the use of archaic language in ritual settings, see Bell 1997). In significant ways contemporary Bardism differs from the narrative performance of genuinely preliterate cultures that it seeks to emulate, most notably in the absence of panegyric, satire, and formulaic or repetitive narrative devices (see Lord 1960; Finnegan 1970). It represents rather a romanticization of our preliterate ancestors, an anomic longing for an enigmatic and utopian world that, by virtue of its distance in time, provides a suitable canvas for the projection of modern desires.

Bardic performance rarely takes place in theaters or other conventional Western performance venues. It occurs rather in opportunistic spaces at camps and festivals, or at ritual gatherings at prehistoric sites, in yurts or benders, or perhaps around the fire (as above). In Druidry, rituals often end with an *eisteddfod*, a semiritualized platform for Bardic performance, either where selected individuals perform or where everyone present is encouraged to participate.[2] At Eco-Pagan protests, performance can occur in more unusual spaces: in treehouses or across lines of security guards. Wherever they are held, performances may entertain, but primarily they enchant audiences. Perhaps the most important feature of contemporary Bardism is that Bards should be divinely inspired, an attribute linking them directly back to Homer.

Contemporaneously with the emergence of this relatively unstudied form of Pagan performance, scholars have been increasingly drawn to "performance" per se as an analytical category with which to understand aspects of culture and religion. The use of a theatrical analogy has proved insightful, so much so that the performance approach is currently in vogue within religious studies, sociology, anthropology, ritual studies, and gender studies. It has, for example, moved scholarship away from regarding social life as a "text" to be interpreted to an appreciation of the actual embodied physicality of "doing," say, religion and ritual, and to the way that such activities are "framed" (Bell 1997). Thus it places "emphasis on agency, intentionality, and active constructions of meaning, whereas earlier functionalist and structural analyses privileged a static 'culture' or 'society'" (Blain and Wallis 2001, 2). Most importantly, it has allowed scholars to engage with that intangible increase in intensity, the "something which happens" during performances and rituals across many different cultures, and in a wide range of contexts (Bell 1997; Schechner and Appel 1990).

The insights afforded by the performance approach are not unproblematic. That scholars perceived an analogous relationship between ritual and Western theater provided the hope that the "unknown other" could be explained by means of reference to something "known" in our own culture: in fact it is not at all clear that Western theater *is* known (Szerszynski, personal communication). The tendency to universalize all human activities as "performance" fails "to account for the way in which most cultures see important distinctions between ritual and other types of activities" (Bell 1997, 56). Some of the most trenchant criticism of the approach has come from within Paganism itself, both from practitioners and reflexively positioned Pagan scholars. The term "performance" has several meanings, but the typical connotation of "pretence" or "make-believe" is what is problematic here: Pagans do not believe that what they do is pretend, but that the alternative realities with which they interact are "real, very real indeed" (Wallis 1999, 13). The performance approach has therefore been criticized as another yet cognicentric form of reductionism.

17

"Performance" also refers to how well a task is undertaken, and the approach has implications, therefore, for the performance of research. Given the success of postmodern critiques of alleged scholarly objectivity (see Hufford and other contributors to McCutcheon 1999; Wallis 2003), the revelation that the Bard in the opening vignette was *myself* should not cause the shockwaves that once it might. Given that "there is no position of luxurious all knowing or neutral narration" (McCutcheon 1999, 9), the scholarly approach to the study of the other has now become dialogical (Harvey 2003), with especial headway being made here in the fields of Pagan studies and the study of indigenous religions (see Salomonsen 1999; Wallis 1999, 2003; Greenwood 2000; Harvey 2000; Pearson 2001; Letcher 2001a; Blain 2002). With increasing numbers of academics "coming out" as Pagans (and Pagans as academics) that dialogue is increasingly becoming an internalized one. Research is now routinely undertaken across the emic/etic boundary (indeed, if ever such a boundary existed), and the negotiation of subjective ontological tensions, such as those raised by adopting a performance approach, has created a particularly fruitful line of inquiry.

In this chapter, then, I evaluate performance theory from the perspectives of Pagan, Bardic insider, and scholar. I begin by reviewing the main strands of performance theory, before illustrating how the approach may be used to explain the process by which subjects come to be identified as Bards. I go on to situate myself within the research, describing how my adoption of the performance approach was influenced by my Bardic practices. Unusually for a Pagan I find performance theory a tenable bridge between my subjective Pagan and scholarly selves, and therefore I address and answer Pagan criticisms of "performance," drawing upon the work of Richard Schechner and Judith Butler and developments in cognitive science. Finally I examine the effect that the research process has had upon those studied, including myself, before widening the focus and suggesting the implications of the performance approach for Pagan studies and the academic project more generally.

Performance Theory: A Review

The performance approach emerged from the work of sociologist Erving Goffman and anthropologist Victor Turner, giving rise to two streams of thought.[3] Firstly, Goffman famously developed a dramaturgical model in which he viewed everyday life, everyday interaction, as a type of performance. "All the world is not, of course, a stage," he remarked, "but the crucial ways in which it isn't are not easy to specify" (Goffman 1959, 72). In day-to-day life we may not think of ourselves as performing, but we pay great attention to the way we publicly present the self. An ordinary event, such as queuing at a supermarket or passing in the street, masks a highly complex and culturally determined set of interactions consisting of bodily cues, responses, dispositions, and movements.

The drama of passing someone in the street usually involves no physical contact, but should it occur participants' response will depend on how the situation is "framed" (Goffman 1975). Thus, according to the frame of reference, unexpected physical contact will be interpreted as accidental or deliberate, as threatening or amicable. If the performance of everyday life is always framed, this is principally because we have been socialized into acting out certain roles. Typically these include "father, mother or child . . . worker, salesman or manager . . . priest, physician, or politician . . . neighbour, spectator, host or guest" (Burns 1992, 107), and they form the "basic unit of socialisation" (Goffman 1972, 75), imposed from the top down. Consequently "a self . . . virtually awaits the individual entering a position; he need only conform to the pressures on him, and he will find a *me* ready made for him" (Goffman 1972, 77).

Goffman's acutely observed model may well have been apposite for the 1950s America in which it was formulated, but it has come to be regarded as too simplistic an explanatory framework for late/postmodernity. Everyday life may yet be performed, but in a climate of detraditionalization (see Heelas 1996) roles are no longer imposed rigidly from the top down; rather identities, not roles, are reflexively constructed. Identities, once imposed by the class, religion, or gender categories into which one was born, are no longer seen as fixed but as fluid, discursive formations with unstable boundaries, shaped as much through resistance as legitimation (Hetherington 1998). Goffman allowed some contestation or negotiation into his model through "role distance," whereby individuals may resist the constraints of their imposed role (Goffman 1972, 95), but his formulation of a fundamental tension between top and bottom is what has come to be regarded as simplistic: contemporary social space is seen as being far more topologically fractured and complex (Hetherington 1998).

This less certain social space has begun to be filled by various postmodern theories of identity and here I describe two which draw upon Goffman's legacy: neotribal theory and Judith Butler's formulation of gender as *performative*. Neotribal theory originated with the French sociologist

Michel Maffesoli and has been developed and popularized by Zygmunt Bauman (Maffesoli 1991, 1996; Bauman 1992, 1993; see also Lury 1996; Shields 1996; Hetherington 1998). In the move to the postmodern, identities are no longer shaped by the top-down forces of socialization, but by the bottom-up sociality, or *puissance*, of the people. Neotribes are temporary associations, expressions of sociality typically drawn together over single issues. Examples might include attendees of a yoga class, ecoprotesters at a protest encampment, or a gathering of Druids at a stone circle. Unlike "classic" tribes, neotribes are theorized to be short-lived, not lasting longer than the lifespans of their members. Moreover, unlike classic tribes membership is not prescribed by birth, but is elective and affectual, with individuals contemporaneously part of many neotribes. Neotribes provide therefore a series of temporary, expressive identifications (Shields 1996), and people are driven to seek this form of collective identification by the emotional need to belong and the need to express, to display, indeed to *perform* that sense of belonging (see Hetherington 1998).

The notion of performativity is central to Judith Butler's theorization of gender formation and presentation. Drawing on Goffman, Freud, and Foucault, Butler suggests that gender is a discursive formation inscribed upon the surface of the body (Butler 1999). Gender, she argues, always "proves to be performative—that is, constituting the identity it is purported to be. In this sense, gender is always a doing, though not a doing by a subject who might be said to pre-exist the deed" (Butler 1999, 25). I shall return to this point below, for one of the principal criticisms leveled at the performance approach is that it implies a subject, a knowing actor, behind outward performance, and that therefore performances are characterized by "pretence." Butler rejects this, stressing the distinction between performance and performativity with regards to gender: "whereas performance presupposes a pre-existing subject, performativity contests the very notion of the subject" (Salih 2002, 63). For Butler there "is no gender identity behind the expressions of gender; that identity is performatively constituted by the very "expressions" that are said to be its results" (Butler 1999, 25).

The second stream of performance theory derives from the work of the anthropologist Victor Turner. Turner perceived social life as being punctuated by "social dramas," wherein, say, "a village falls into factions, a husband beats a wife, a region rises against the state" (Geertz 1983, 28). In his model these dramas follow a set sequence. Initially a "breach" occurs whereby "a person or subgroup breaks a rule deliberately or by inward compulsion, in a public setting" (Turner 1990, 8). A period of "crisis" ensues, followed by socially determined "redressive action." This "is often ritualised, and may be undertaken in the name of law or religion" (Turner 1990, 8). Two outcomes are possible, a successful reintegration back into society, or the recognition by all that there now exists an irreparable schism.

Here Turner was drawing and expanding upon the earlier work of Arnold van Gennep and his three-stage model of rites of passage: separation, liminality, and aggregation (van Gennep 1960). Turner emphasized the importance of the liminal phase, arguing that societies exist in two states, *societas* (structure) and *communitas* (anti-structure). In communitas, the liminal phase, normal social relations are softened, melted, inverted, and broken down, only to be reformed again in the transition back to societas (van Gennep's aggregation) (Turner 1990). His contribution was therefore to break with the Durkheimian model of ritual as reflecting, structuring, and binding society, and to adopt a processual model in which ritual, enabling the transition through "structure → anti-structure → structure," is the mechanism which facilitates structural change (Deflem 1991).

Turner searched for evidence of liminality in postindustrial society but found only remnants, in theater and particularly in festival, which he termed liminoid. This, coupled with Mikhail Bakhtin's carnivalesque theory, paved the way toward the study of carnival and festival as large-scale societal performances (see Schechner 1993). For Bakhtin, Russian dissident and literary critic, the often grotesque humour found in Rabelais' sixteenth century novel *Gargantua and Pantagruel* (Rabelais 1955) was symptomatic of a folk or carnival humor, or mode of being (Bakhtin 1984; Stallybrass and White 1986). The great medieval carnivals were a time of inversion, of mockery of authority, of ritualized transgression, a celebration of excess and of the low, and of the body with all its appetites and unpalatable functions. Like Turner with his reading of festival as liminoid, Bakhtin regarded the "grotesque realism" of carnival as creating renewal and the possibility for social change.[4]

This rather utopian vision has been challenged, not only for its ahistorical basis (Humphrey 2001), but over the question of whether carnival actually causes structural change or simply acts as a safety valve, thereby serving to legitimate the power of those in authority (Gluckman 1963; Schechner 1993). Nevertheless, contemporary theorists have drawn upon the idea of the liminoid and the carnivalesque to reveal the ways in which the meanings of spaces are discursively constituted and how they can form temporary arenas of resistance to power and authority: I am referring here to Hakim Bey's pirate utopias, or "temporary autonomous zones," and Michel Foucault's "heterotopias" (Bey 1991; Foucault 1998). Likewise in the field of Pagan and related studies, these ideas have informed empirical research: for instance Pike's (2000) study of California's Burning Man festival; Szerszynski's (1999) reading of radical environmental protest as a form of civil religion; and my own studies of ecoprotest camps and British festivals (Letcher 2001a, 2001b, 2003).

These two theoretical streams, from Goffman and Turner, which have given rise to the performance approach, have been largely synthesized in the work of the experimental theater director/performer Richard Schechner. Schechner, who worked with Turner in the years before the latter's death, shares Turner's search for "universals of performance." Unlike Turner, however, Schechner rejects the notion, derived from the Cambridge anthropological "myth and ritual" school, that Western theater has evolved, ultimately, from ancient Greek Dionysian ritual. Instead he regards ritual, theater, and the performance of everyday life as existing on a continuum, related horizontally, not vertically (Schechner 1988, 6). In Schechner's view human performance extends across a range of magnitudes of space and duration, from the almost subliminal movements of facial muscles called kinemes, to the presentation of the self, to ritual and theater, to sporting events, to international "dramas" (Schechner 1990). There is little, in fact, that does not count as performance in Schechner's view.

This last point is certainly not unproblematic (see Bell 1992, 1997, 1998), but Schechner refines this rather generalized view through a reappraisal of Goffman's frames, categorizing performances according to how they are framed by subjects and observers. "The main question one asks is whether a performance generates its own frame, that is, is reflexive (self-conscious, conscious of its audience, the audience conscious of the performer being conscious of being a performer, etc.); or whether the frame is imposed from the outside" (Schechner 1990, 28).

In the first of three categories an action, or set of actions, is framed as performance by an external observer—participants do not see themselves as performing. In this category we would include Goffman's presentation of the self and Butler's performativity of gender. In the second category the frame is "hidden," that is, the "actor" knows that they are performing, but the audience remains unaware. Schechner suggests that the activities of a con artist fall into this category, but we could also include the presentation of television news, in which the discursive construction of what constitutes "news" is masked by the stylized intonation, gestures, facial expressions, and dress codes of the presenters, which are used to signify "objectivity" and "impartiality." In the third and final category the frame is upfront and acknowledged by both actors and audience, as it is in Western theater. By developing Goffman's frames, Schechner creates a model in which a great variety of human activities, from Goffmanesque presentation to Turneresque social dramas, can be categorized and understood as related "performances." What distinguishes them is the degree to which active subjects are reflexively aware that they are performing. "The evidence is accumulating that the only difference between 'ordinary behaviour' and 'acting' is one of reflexivity: professional actors are aware that they are acting" (Schechner 1990, 30).

Drawing on the insights of theatrical performance, Schechner also stresses the need to look beyond the actual performance instance itself. Performance necessitates "training, rehearsal (and/or workshop), warm-up, the performance, cool-down, and aftermath" (Schechner and Appel 1990, 5). Similarly audience preparations include "deciding to attend, dressing, going, settling in, waiting" (Schechner 1988, xiii). He also pays attention to the intangible "something which happens" during performances. "While performing, a certain definite threshold is crossed—that moment when spectators and performers alike sense a 'successful' performance is taking place" (Schechner and Appel 1990, 4). The anthropologist Edward Schieffelin refers to this "something which happens" as "emergence," which "comes about when the performance 'works.' It is that aspect of socially produced reality, which cannot be reduced to any of its means (text, structure, or symbolic manipulation)" (Schieffelin 1996, 64). More typically Cszikszentmihalyi's concept of "flow" has been used, having achieved a kind of prominence within the performance literature (see for example Lindquist 1997). In this psychological model flow is accessed through "those activities which provide opportunities for action which a person can act upon without being bored or worried" (Cszikszentmihalyi 1977, 49), and results in "the holistic sensation that people feel when they act with total involvement . . . in the flow state, action follows upon action according to an internal logic that seems to need no conscious intervention by the actor" (Cszikszentmihalyi 1977, 36). It can be experienced in any number of activities, with examples given such as rock climbing, performing surgery, or playing chess. However, whether "flow" really does offer insights into the "something which happens," or whether it simply universalizes and psychologizes a range of different but not necessarily commensurable activities, remains a moot point (for a fuller discussion see Letcher 2001a).

This concludes the review of performance theory, and I turn now to an example of how the approach may be used empirically, detailing an examination of the process by which practitioners become "Bards."

Pagan Performance: Becoming a Bard

Bardism, as an explicit form of performance and one which has emerged from Western stage genres, lends itself to a performative analysis (for a more comprehensive account see Letcher 2001a). Such an analysis of the contemporary Bardic repertoire reveals the ways in which Bards skillfully distill, enunciate, and reinforce neotribal identities. It draws attention to the "axiom of frames" (Schechner 1988) within which Bards perform: from the large-scale setting of autonomous zones, heterotopias, and carnivalesque festival spaces, to the small-scale opportunistic appropriation of "stages" and the physical arrangement of performers and audience. It notes the connotative meanings of the musical styles and the instruments played (e.g., harps as "spiritual"). It investigates the "something which happens" during successful performances that practitioners refer to as inspiration, and inquires how the experience of inspiration comes to be legitimated.

Furthermore the attention to process rather than structure focuses attention upon the uptake or conferment of identities. Here, summarizing the results of a more detailed analysis (Letcher 2001a), I describe the process of how subjects come to be identified, and thereby identify themselves, as Bards within contemporary British Druidry. The role of the Bard does not exist, in a Goffmanesque sense, in wider society beyond being a figure of speech or a posthumous label of poetic genius. Within some contemporary Druid Orders,[5] however, mirroring the three degrees of Wiccan initiation, the Bard forms the first of three grades (Bard, Ovate, Druid) into which the aspiring Druid is typically initiated. Bards are concerned with creativity and with finding inspiration; Ovates with "tree-lore," divination, and healing; Druids with priesthood.[6] Thus at any one time there are those within Druidry who may legitimately call themselves Bards. However, there are certain individuals, skilled performers, who are truly labelled and may identify themselves as such, and who stand apart from ordinary members of the Bardic grade. Although several of the larger Druid orders run teaching courses (especially the Order of Bards Ovates and Druids, OBOD, and the British Druid Order, BDO), which include exercises and techniques for accessing one's latent creativity, there is no systematic training in performance techniques. How then do subjects learn to perform and thereby come to be identified as truly being Bards?

Given that we are dealing with a neotribal arrangement—Druidry is disembedded (*sensu* Giddens 1990) and membership is elective and affectual (Hetherington 1998; Sutcliffe and Bowman 2000)—we would not expect the rites of passage model to hold here. Neotribes do not conform to the above Turnerian model of "structure → anti-structure → structure," for they consist rather of structure condensing *out of* a semipermanent antistructure (Bauman 1993; Letcher 2001a). Correspondingly initiation into the Bardic grade marks entry into the Druidic neotribe, not an accumulation or change of status within it. Initiation does not confer a Bardic identity, which is rather bestowed upon individuals who have overcome four obstacles.

Firstly, would be Bards must be competent poets, musicians, or storytellers. This naturally requires the hours of dedication and practice required to master any complex skill. The hours "practicing in the bedroom" or "woodshedding" are private events leading up to a performance, and audiences are often unaware of just how much time is required to achieve competency, and for performers to obtain and learn a repertoire.

Secondly, Bards must generate their own performance frame. The physical layout of stage and auditorium in traditional Western theaters creates a frame whereby individuals on stage are identified as performing (Schechner's third frame). The theater is "that arrangement which transforms an individual into a stage performer, that latter in turn being an object that can be looked at in the round and at length without offence, and looked to for engaging behaviour by persons in an 'audience role'" (Goffman 1975, 124). Bardic performance typically does not take place in theaters but in opportunistically appropriated spaces within the heterotopias of festivals or camps. Moreover Bards are often located as part of the audience before and after performing. Consequently as they cross an imaginary line between "stage" and audience, they must generate their own frame and consciously make what Hymes calls the "breakthrough into performance" (Hymes cited in Schieffelin 1996). In "breaking through one moves from the expressiveness of everyday interactional performativity [*sensu* Goffman] to an expressiveness that calls attention to itself as a genre, or an object of appreciation. The shifts in behavioural and linguistic features (or "cues") that bring this about convey the metamessage 'I am performing'" (Schieffelin 1996, 61). In other words the onus is on the individual to confidently create, establish, and maintain Schechner's third frame, in which both performer and audience are aware that performance is occurring.

Thirdly, so as to make this breakthrough confidently, Bards must be able to overcome the fear associated with presenting the self in public, for "we all have a universal phobia of being looked at on stage" (Johnstone 1989, 30). One of my informants, "Jason," told me that "most people in society are saying 'Don't look at me, don't look at me,' but if you are doing stories or music you're going 'Look at me, listen to this.' You're actually calling out to everyone to look at you, or listen to you, but most people don't want to be looked at or listened to by a vast number of [other] people. I can see why people don't want to do it on a confidence level . . . it's bloody hard work."

The final point relates to this phobia of being looked at, in that performances are inherently risky and may "fail" (Schieffelin 1996), a situation accentuated when the performance contains a degree of improvisation. Bards do not adhere to a script, but recite stories from memory, or improvise around a remembered "core." They must decide which song, story, or poem to draw from their repertoire, judging which is the most appropriate given the mood, expectations, and inclinations of the audience. Failure is a failure to engage the audience.

Successful Bards are therefore those individuals who have overcome these obstacles. Initially inspired by their peers, individuals begin to acquire a repertoire and technical competence. As they overcome the risks of failure and the fear of being looked at, they begin to generate a convincing frame and so are able to make the breakthrough into performance. They learn to tailor their choice of material to the mood of the audience (or to successfully negotiate the risk of consciously departing from audience expectations) and in doing so they begin to fulfill the expectations of the genre and come to be labeled by audiences as Bards, perhaps even as inspired. Contemporaneously, a shift in self-identity occurs such that individuals, feeling that they have earned the title, confidently name themselves as such.

"Daniel," an OBOD member, is a performer who has only recently come to identify himself as a Bard. His preferred identity was as "a teacher first, and then a storyteller, and then a performer." Unusually Daniel came into Druidry having had considerable acting experience—he is by profession a drama teacher. Like many others he described his first experience of Druidry as one of "coming home," but it was the figure of the Bard that captured his imagination, particularly as he had been involved in storytelling for some time. He described to me how he began to regard himself as a Bard after attending the OBOD retreat on the Scottish island of Iona. Here, during an intense week of meditations and workshops based around the story of Taliesin,[7] he built strong relationships with the other participants. Although he was already in a long-term relationship, he found himself falling in love, and consequently the end of the retreat proved to be a particularly harrowing emotional experience. Here he describes the ferry journey home.

> Everyone was feeling really desolate. I certainly was, it's not an exaggeration to say that. One of the party saw a seal, just one seal floating behind the boat. I had worked for a while with the Druid Animal Oracle,[8] and I knew that [within the oracle] the seal represents loss. When I got home I was in a terrible state.

The poignant sighting of the seal seemed to symbolize, or represent, the loss he was feeling. On returning home, he felt in such turmoil that he arranged to cancel a long-standing storytelling engagement. However, the organizer persuaded him to continue, at which point Daniel chanced upon a Scottish story about a seal who turns into a woman.

> I picked up a story . . . called the Woman from the Sea. . . . I remember saying [by way of introduction] "This story I'm about to tell comes from the west coast of Scotland. It probably comes from the Hebrides, but I'm going to pretend that it comes from a place called Iona, which I left a week ago, and which I miss desperately." Now I'd read that story once, maybe twice, which [for me] is unheard of [9] but it just came out. . . . I was deeply moved by what I was saying . . . [and] . . . I was aware I had my audience absolutely spellbound. . . . At that point I suddenly realised that the Bard [in me] was born. It was very moving at the time.

Several factors led to this shift in his identity. Firstly, the event (a storytelling evening for Beltaine), but more particularly, the story, fitted perfectly with the expectations of the Bardic genre: a Celtic-inflected story dealing with the themes of love and loss. Secondly the performance was successful, with the audience "spellbound." Owing to the resonance between real events and the story's narrative, he was able to give a commanding and moving performance,[10] which in turn helped him to express and resolve his own emotional predicament. Thirdly, and most importantly, in telling the story so eloquently he felt that he had become a "vessel" or a "conduit" through which the story was being channelled. In short he felt that he had accessed the inspiration which separates a "Bard" from a mere "storyteller."

Reflexive Considerations

Having explored some of the ways in which "performance" as an analytical category is instructive in the understanding of Bardism, I now turn to a reflexive account of my involvement in the research. When I undertook this research I had a well-established identity as a Bard and was heavily involved with Druidry and road-protesting: I was "Andy the Bard." Trained initially as a scientist I had studied ecology to doctoral level, but then renounced academic life in favor of the more practical ecology of direct action, a decision also motivated by a desire for alterity and the more liminal existence promised by protesting and playing in a psychedelic folk band.

However, it was through my involvement with Druidry, and particularly with OBOD, that I met both Graham Harvey and Ronald Hutton, who were to become my (second) Ph.D. supervisor and external examiner, respectively (both are frequently invited to address Pagan audiences). Graham Harvey, having secured research funding, invited me to return to academic life, this time studying Bardism toward a Ph.D. in Religious Studies. After five years of liminality the lure of scholarly inquiry, and aggregation, proved compelling.

Initially I experienced a great resistance to this new identity and its concomitant demands. In part this was due to a deeply conditioned disregard for the humanities, engendered by an instilled scientific disdain, but also by the often seemingly impenetrable language and, dare I say, "self-referential intertextuality" of academic discourse.[11] But more significantly this was due to the disjuncture between my beliefs and experiences as a Pagan, and the modernist assumption of the academy that they, and indeed religion more generally, were phenomena in need of explanation or understanding (see for example Wiebe 2000). Faced with the ontological broadsides to my beliefs delivered by a consideration of Durkheim, Marx, Freud, and Foucault (to name a few), performance theory proved positively appealing, reflecting as it did my own experience and understanding of the world as a Bard. Goffman's observations on the presentation of everyday life, Schechner's performance frames, and carnivalesque theory all "made sense," the latter giving a theoretical legitimacy to my time invested at protest camps and free festivals. Furthermore the approach privileged the research position of the performer: "performers from different cultures are more likely to understand each other . . . than they can understand, and be understood, by people within their own culture who have not themselves either been performers or who have gone out of their way to understand what performers experience. Performance experience . . . is something the outsider has to specifically go out of her/his way to get from the inside" (Schechner 1990, 28).

Unusually for a Pagan, therefore, performance theory was a body of academic knowledge with which I *could* relate, and so provided an avenue back into the academy from whence I was then able to appreciate the insights of Durkheim, Marx, and so on. Ultimately my choice of performance theory as the basis upon which to conduct my research was made not so much out of a rational decision about which approach might contribute most to an understanding of the phenomenon (although it is clearly pertinent in the case of Bardism), but out of a subjective predisposition toward it. This, I would suggest as a challenge to the notion of academic "objectivity," is not unusual for the theoretical inclinations of scholars, and the phenomena they choose to study must always reflect autobiographical interests and dispositions.

From the perspective therefore of being Pagan and academic, I contend that the performance approach remains an instructive tool for the understanding of Paganism more generally, in which there is a significant performative dimension. Public rituals (as at Stonehenge, Avebury, and Glastonbury Tor) and Pagan fairs (such as the annual London "Beltaine Bash," or "Megalithomania" 2002) are occasions where neotribal identities are clearly paraded: Druids in white robes, Wiccans in black velvet or more gothic/fetish-inspired regalia. The analysis above can easily be extended into a discussion of how subjects become Pagans per se, for as yet the majority of practitioners are not born into Pagan families, and must elect membership (but see Berger 1999). Invoking spirits of the watchtowers or entering *seidr*, unlike queuing or passing in the street, are not culturally bestowed behaviors: practitioners must learn how to perform them. In very similar ways to Bards, practitioners must overcome the fear of being looked at and the fear of failure, and generate a convincing frame. They must learn how to correctly perform Paganism. However it is this point that many Pagans and Pagan scholars have disputed, and it is to a discussion of this that I now turn.

Pagan Criticisms of "Performance"

"Performance" has a multiplicity of meanings. Jenny Blain, for example, describes how as a dancer "performance" meant "the real thing," requiring a more complete involvement than when in rehearsal (Blain and Wallis 2001). More typically in Western discourse however the term implies pretence, make-believe, or acting (Schechner and Appel 1990; Blain and Wallis 2001). The implication of deceit is inherent in Schechner's model of performance frames, wherein he situates someone in trance as falling between frames one and two (framed as performing, and performing without the audience knowing), and a shamanic exorcism as falling between frames two and three (hidden performance and performance explicitly acknowledged by all) (Schechner 1990). By contrast Pagan and neo-Shamanic practitioners, such as Jonathon Horwitz, deny that they are acting, and reject any accusation of pretence.

> I define the shamanic rite as any action or series of actions made by the shaman with the definite purpose of bringing the power of non-ordinary reality (the world of the spirits) to ordinary reality (the material world). It is the bridge the shaman builds between our world and the world of the spirits. The ritual is not the source of power, but the vehicle for bringing the power to the recipient(s). It is the means, not the goal. In other words, that which is really going on in the shamanic rite is going on in non-ordinary reality. The ritual is the form. The power and spirit are the content. (Horwitz, n.d., cited in Blain and Wallis 2001, 16)

Put differently, for "indigenous and neo-shamans in their 'spirit worlds' this *is* reality. Showmanship may be involved, to invoke the mood and spirits, and stir the community gathered, as well as, of course, the shaman; but the experience is a vitally real one: some practitioners recount it as 'more real' than the 'everyday.' From this practitioner standpoint, the term 'performance' is inappropriate and may be considered by some insulting, racist even (the exotic 'other' is merely 'acting'); at least certainly cognicentric" (Blain and Wallis 2001, 19).

That said, and even allowing for the existence of spirits or other-than-human-persons (Harvey 2003)—which as a Pagan I most certainly do—there remain some thorny questions. Why is it, for example, that interaction with spirits requires the use of "shamanic paraphernalia"? If shamanic ritual is the means, not the end, why does it always take recognisably "shamanic" forms; why can't interaction with spirits occur while queuing at the supermarket? Is the paraphernalia for the benefit of the shaman (to put them in the mood so that they can access the spirit world), for the benefit of the spirits (who require a certain kind of deference), or to fulfil the culturally constituted expectations of the audience? Goffman himself noted that a person in trance will be "able to provide a correct portrayal of the god that has entertained him [because of all the contextual knowledge and memories available; that] the person possessed will be in just the right social relation to those who are watching; that possession occurs at just the right moment in the ceremonial undertaking, the possessed one carrying out his ritual obligations" (Goffman 1959, cited in Schechner 1990, 26). Given that he also noted that participants "in the cult believe that possession is a real thing and that persons are possessed at random by gods whom they cannot select" (Goffman 1959, cited in Schechner 1990, 26), this would seem to suggest an irreconcilable cognitive break between the emic and the etic. Such tensions or dissonances are typical of those that Pagan scholars are "forced to resolve on a day-to-day basis" (Wallis 2003, xiii). As a Pagan insider, performer, and scholar, I believe both that spirits exist *and* that performance is an insightful category for understanding what I, and others like me, do. Here I suggest that these positions are not hopelessly irreconcilable.

A "weak" response would be to bracket the question of whether the spirits, or other supernatural entities with whom Pagans routinely interact, exist. "Performance" in this instance becomes just one of many different analogies that scholars use to illuminate certain aspects of the phenomena they study, others being the analogy of the "game" or the "text" (Geertz 1983). "Performance" is used connotatively, that is, a connotative resemblance between indigenous or Pagan ritual and Western theatre is established, by which the known (theater) is used to shed light on the unknown.[12] Connotation does not imply denotation: ritual may resemble performance but that does not mean that it can be reduced to being simply performance.

Here I suggest a stronger response, drawing on the work of Ray Birdwhistell, Richard Schechner, Judith Butler, and Larry Weiskrantz. Schechner (following Fischer) suggests that while Western stage actors may obtain a range of moods, from the quietened (trophotropic) to the excited (ergotropic), they never entirely lose a sense of "normal-I" (Schechner 1990). So when an actor playing Othello reaches for a pillow with which to smother Desdemona, he remains conscious of his actions and does not in actuality harm the actress. Subjects in trance differ in that they temporarily lose their sense of normal-I, only to regain it at the end of the ceremony; while some, construed as mad or schizophrenic, may lose their normal-I entirely (Schechner 1990).

The implication is that when the normal-I is temporarily suspended, subjects are still unconsciously performing. How is this possible? Birdwhistell filmed human interaction, slowing down the tape to identify the minutest of facial expressions, occurring across milliseconds, that he called kinemes (cited in Schechner 1990). Kinemes, he found, are not under conscious control but are culturally constructed, culture-specific. Thus there "is an American way of flashing the eyebrows" (Schechner 1990, 29). Judith Butler arrives at a remarkably similar conclusion but from a completely different epistemological trajectory. Her understanding of gender as discursively constituted, inscribed upon the body, and performative but with no subject choosing or performing the "script," no way "out of the box," suggests that that most fundamental of bodily dispositions, one's gender identity, is unconsciously enacted (Butler 1999).

Interestingly there is potential corroboration from the scientific epistemology of cognitive science. Researchers have found that individuals with certain kinds of damage to the visual cortex, who are subsequently blind, "report an inability to see objects, but if pressed to guess at their location they display a capacity to point at them with reasonable accuracy" (Grobstein and Butoi n.d). This phenomenon, termed "blindsight" (Weiskrantz 1986), is "one of the more dramatic of a number of lines of evidence suggesting that being aware of doing something is distinguishable from doing something, that areas of the brain underlying the experience of doing at least some things are distinct from those needed to actually do those things" (Grobstein and Butoi n.d.).

While referring to one particular aspect of human cognition, blindsight, in principle at least, allows for a separation of consciousness, what Weiskrantz calls the "commentary system" (Weiskrantz 1986, 168–71) and perhaps what Schechner refers to as normal-I, from unconscious bodily activity. If so, this would enable a shaman's normal-I to venture to whatever other or spirit worlds may exist, to interact with gods or spirits, and at the same time to unconsciously perform and enact those utterances, expressions, actions, and physical dispositions discursively constructed and kinematically embodied as marking the subject as shaman, as female or male, as teenaged or middle-aged, as possessed or whatever. Clearly there is something of a leap of faith between the observed phenomenon of blindsight and this sort of conclusion, and one must tread carefully to avoid reducing the "something which happens" to brain functioning, but even so this fascinating area of research may yet provide evidence in support of the analytical conclusions of the performance approach.

Reactivity—The Consequences of Undertaking This Research

Given that my methodological approach has been dialogical, what has been the outcome of that dialogue? I am currently gauging the impact of my research on those studied: having circulated my thesis I await feedback, which I intend to include in future publications. Within Druidry I anticipate discussion regarding my work on the invention of tradition (the construction of an imagined Celtic/Druidic past), and my observation that inspiration, which is supposed to be "neutral" and thereby available to all, is actually socially constituted and legitimated. Within Eco-Paganism, one informant found my thesis deeply moving, not for its academic content, which I suspect he found largely inaccessible, but for the recounting of highly emotionally charged events—the struggles, triumphs, and failures of protesting, together with the nonordinary experiences which together form the Eco-Pagan lifeworld—in such a manner that they demand to be taken seriously. Interestingly, I have heard from informants (I should more honestly say, from friends) that since I made my inquiries, many Eco-Pagans have begun to call themselves Bards where they did not before. As they fulfilled the expectations of the genre, often more convincingly than many Druids, it struck me as interesting that the identity was not adopted more frequently. It seems, however, that I may have inadvertently, though by no means regrettably, created the very category that I sought to examine.

If I am not yet able to assess the full impact of my research on others, I can at least relate the impact it has had upon myself. On the one hand scholarship gave me a language, a framework, and a platform with which to address the questions that had always troubled me but that I had not been able to articulate clearly. On the other hand, as mentioned above, the academic project of the humanities came directly to challenge my faith in ways that my scientific training never had.[13] I came to doubt the existence of spirits, gods, the supernatural, and whether the wondrous otherworldly encounters related by my peers were nothing short of delusory, the product of mental instability, not inspiration. Something of a crisis of faith ensued, whereby I distanced myself from the self-adopted role of Bard: the long hair, the beard, the colorful clothes, and the outrageous hat all went in an attempt to see what, or whom, lay beneath. In hippy/protest culture the ultimate heresy, comparable to that of the anthropologist "going native," is "straightening out." Unquestionably the changes I went through led to a distancing of myself from my former peers, one of whom once accused me of looking like a policeman, the worst possible insult! Neotribal identities aside, becoming a scholar not only distanced me cognitively from my former world, but also spatially and temporally, by imposing structures upon my time which made it impossible to, say, stay up all night playing music.

At time of writing I find myself in a rather unusual position. I have not fully let go of my past identity to embrace structure and academic life, yet neither have I been fully able to leave academia (again) and return to being the person I once was. If at times I would rather simply *be* a Pagan rather than endlessly questioning what it is to be a Pagan, then at others I find that questioning stimulating and fulfilling. If at times I would rather go back to playing in a band and indulging the luxury of time, then at others I enjoy the status and sense of purpose, not to mention regular income, that academic life provides. This then is a tension that I have yet to resolve, a drama that has yet to play out. Recently I have been relieved to find my faith returning. In keeping with the times my spirituality remains impeccably elective, affectual, and syncretic; but where once I combined elements of Druidry, Wicca, Anglo-Saxon Heathenism, Bardism, and sixties psychedelia into my personal bricolage, I now include Aristotlean metaphysics, animism, performance, romanticism, Foucauldianism, phenology, and *flâneurisme:* terms, theories and concepts derived from academic discourse.[14] Nevertheless, while I have used academic terminology herein to describe my own experiences (my search for "liminality" and so on), that part of me does not quite have the upper hand, for I regard the outcome of my personal drama to be, quite literally, in the lap of the Gods.

Performance and Pagan Studies—The Next Act?

The performance approach has recently become popular, and while it has much to offer Pagan studies it brings with it a fresh set of problems that come to the fore particularly when undertaking research "at home," where the "other" more clearly has a voice. While unarguably appropriate for an investigation of an overt form of performance such as Bardism, extension of the analogy to other aspects of Paganism may create a cognitive break with the experiences and understandings of insiders. Such breaks form part of the challenge of postmodern research, part of the internal negotiation that the insider-scholar must routinely undertake. Negotiation does not preclude asking difficult questions of both sides, but it does avoid sweeping denotative moves in favour of constructive dialogue. But while I have been able to find a compatibility between "performance" and what I do as a Pagan, others have not, and this may simply be an inevitable and unavoidable consequence of the academic epistemological trajectory.

One of the most fruitful outcomes of the performance approach has been the attention given to process over structure. Performance of all kinds causes change, whether temporary, as with "an audience struck into a kind of wonder by the elocutionary force of a . . . poem" (Bloomfield and Dunn 1989, 24) or during carnival, or more permanently as with a rite of passage, the uptake of neotribal identities, or when carnival becomes revolution. But perhaps most significantly the performance approach has helped to collapse the emic/etic boundary. Performers across many cultural genres have noted the impact that the audience has upon any particular performance. "When a performance moves to a new place encountering new audiences (on tour, for example), even if everything is kept the same, the performance changes. The same happens when an audience is imported, as when tourists or anthropologists see 'the real thing'" (Schechner and Appel 1990, 4). To observe then *is* to participate, to affect that which we see; and as there is no panoptical vantage point, no ultimate position of neutrality, we are all, insiders or not, involved in that we research. It is this final nail in the coffin of "scholarly objectivity" that is perhaps the approach's most significant contribution to the future development of Pagan studies, and more widely, the academic project itself.

Notes

1. The Eisteddfod was a form of poetry competition in Wales, dating back to the middle ages. It was revived by Edward Williams (1747–1826) and incorporated into his version of Druidry, which still forms part of the proceedings of modern Welsh National Eisteddfod. Primarily, though, the Eisteddfoddau of Wales and Cornwall are celebrations of regional culture and identity.

2. The Secular Order of Druids has reinstated the traditional competitive element to the eisteddfod, with the introduction of annual competitions for Bardic chairs of Bath, Bristol, and Winchester.

3. For other accounts of performance theory see Bell 1992, 1997, 1998; Csordas 1996; Blain and Wallis 2001.

4. For this reason Bakhtin's work may be regarded as a thinly veiled attack on the Stalinist regime under which it was written.

5. Reflecting its origins in the eighteenth- and nineteenth-century Druid revival, in which Druid orders functioned as "secret societies" and/or "friendly societies" based on a model provided by Freemasonry, contemporary Druidry tends to be structured into "orders." See Hutton 1999; Letcher 2001a.

6. For a fuller account of the classical origins of these three grades, and the meanings they hold for practitioners, see Letcher 2001a.

7. The Welsh story of Taliesin is a central myth within Druidry. Taliesin is regarded as the archetypal inspired Bard, whom practitioners seek to emulate.

8. The oracle, written by Philip and Stephanie Carr-Gomm of OBOD (Carr-Gomm and Carr-Gomm 1996), is a set of cards depicting various animals, mostly indigenous to Britain. Each animal represents some essential quality of

human experience, and the cards may be used for divination and meditation rather like a deck of tarot cards.

9. Normally he would have rehearsed the story many times over.

10. "This reliving a past emotional experience is the classic acting exercise from the turn-of-the-century, called 'emotion memory' or 'affective memory' by the Russian theatre director Konstantin Stanislavski" (Schechner 1990, 30).

11. The novice experiences something of the classic hermeneutical dilemma: individual works cannot be understood without reference to the whole canon of academic thought, but the whole can only be understood through knowledge of its parts. The tendency to use "shorthand" in academic discourse, assuming a common level of knowledge, meant that for the first eighteen months of my Ph.D., terms such as "signify," "discourse," "postmodernism," and "intertextuality" remained irritatingly obscure. Eventually I completed enough reading to make the hermeneutic breakthrough. This marked something of a cognitive break with my former Pagan self.

12. As mentioned above, it is not entirely clear that Western theater *is* known.

13. As an undergraduate I was taught that the question of the existence of "God" was untestable, and therefore lies beyond the limits of scientific inquiry: it was bracketed off.

14. In itself this is nothing new—contemporary Paganism is founded on the discarded theories of academics.

References

Bakhtin, M.
    1984 *Rabelais and His World.* Bloomington: Indiana University Press.

Bauman, Z.
    1992 *Intimations of Postmodernity.* London: Routledge.

———.
    1993 *Postmodern Ethics.* Oxford: Blackwell.

Bell, C.
    1992 *Ritual Theory, Ritual Practice.* New York: Oxford University Press.

———.
    1997 *Ritual: Perspectives and Dimensions.* Oxford: Oxford University Press.

———.
    1998 Performance. In *Critical Terms for Religious Studies,* edited by M. Taylor. Chicago: University of Chicago Press.

Berger, H.
    1999 *A Community of Witches. Contemporary Neo-Paganism and Witchcraft in the United States.* Columbia: University of South Carolina Press.

Bey, H.
1991 *T.A.Z. The Temporary Autonomous Zone, Ontological Anarchy, Poetic Terrorism.* New York: Autonomedia.

Blain, J.
2002 *Nine Worlds of Seidr-Magic: Ecstasy and Neo-Shamanism in North European Shamanism.* London: Routledge.

Blain, J., and R. Wallis
2001 Ritual Reflections, Practitioner Meanings: Disputing the Terminology of Neo-Shamanic "Performance." Paper delivered at the British Sociological Association Study Group on Religion Conference, Oxford, UK.

Bloomfield, M., and C. Dunn
1989 *The Role of the Poet in Early Societies.* Cambridge, UK: D. S. Brewer.

Burns, T.
1992 *Erving Goffman.* London: Routledge.

Butler, J.
1999 *Gender Trouble: Feminism and the Subversion of Identity.* New York: Routledge.

Carr-Gomm, P., and S. Carr-Gomm
1996 *The Druid Animal Oracle.* London: Connections.

Csordas, T. J.
1996 Imaginal Performance and Memory in Ritual Healing. In *The Performance of Healing,* edited by C. Laderman and M. Roseman. London: Routledge.

Csikszentmihalyi, M.
1977 *Beyond Boredom and Anxiety. The Experience of Play in Work and Games.* San Francisco: Jossey-Bass.

Davies, C.
1998 "A Oes Heddwch?" Contesting Meanings and Identities in the Welsh National Eisteddfod. In *Ritual, Performance, Media,* edited by F. Hughes-Freeland. London: Routledge.

Deflem, M.
1991 Ritual, Anti-Structure, and Religion: A Discussion of Victor Turner's Processual Symbolic Analysis. *Journal for the Scientific Study of Religion* 30: 1–25.

Finnegan, R.
1970 *Oral Literature in Africa.* Oxford: Oxford University Press.

Foucault, M.
1998 Different Spaces. In *Aesthetics, Method and Epistemology.* Vol. 2 of *Essential Works of Foucault,* edited by James Faubion. Harmondsworth, UK:

Allen Lane.

Geertz, C.
1983 Blurred Genres: The Reconfiguration of Social Thought. In *Local Knowledge. Further Essays in Interpretive Anthropology*, 19–35. London: Fontana.

Giddens, A.
1990 *The Consequences of Modernity*. Cambridge, UK: Polity Press.

Gluckman, M.
1963 *Order and Rebellion in Tribal Africa*. New York: Free Press.

Goffman, E.
1959 *The Presentation of Self in Everyday Life*. Garden City, N.Y.: Doubleday.

———.
1972 *Encounters. Two Studies in the Sociology of Interaction*. London: Penguin.

———.
1975 *Frame Analysis. An Essay on the Organisation of Experience*. Harmondsworth, UK: Penguin.

Greenwood, S.
2000 *Magic, Witchcraft and the Otherworld. An Anthropology*. Oxford: Berg.

Grobstein, P., and B. Butoi
n.d. "Seeing What You Don't See?" http://serendip.brynmawr.edu/bb/blindsight.html, accessed on November 3, 2003.

Hale, A.
2000 "In the Eye of the Sun": the Relationship between the Cornish Gorseth and Esoteric Druidry. In *Cornish Studies* 8, edited by P. Payton. Exeter, UK: Exeter University Press.

Harvey, G., ed.
2000 *Indigenous Religions. A Companion*. London: Cassell.

———.
2003 *Shamanism. A Reader*. London: Routledge.

Heelas, P.
1996 Introduction: Detraditionalization and Its Rivals. In *Detraditionalization*, edited by P. Heelas, S. Lash, and P. Morris. Oxford: Blackwell.

Hetherington, K.
1998 *Expressions of Identity. Space, Performance, Politics*. London: Sage.

Heywood, S.
1998 The New Storytelling: A History of the Storytelling Movement in

England and Wales. *The Society for Storytelling Papyrus Series 2.* Coombe Martin, UK: Daylight Press.

Hufford, D. J.
[1995] 1999 The Scholarly Voice and the Personal Voice: Reflexivity in Belief Studies. In *The Insider/Outsider Problem in the Study of Religion. A Reader,* edited by R. McCutcheon. London: Cassell.

Humphrey, C.
2001 *The Politics of Carnival. Festive Misrule in Medieval England.* Manchester, UK: Manchester University Press.

Hutton, R.
1996 Who Possesses the Past? In *The Druid Renaissance,* edited by P. Carr-Gomm. London: Thorsons.

———.
1999 *The Triumph of the Moon: A History of Modern Pagan Witchcraft.* Oxford: Oxford University Press.

Johnstone, K.
1989 *Impro. Improvisation and the Theatre.* London: Methuen.

Letcher, A.
2001a *The Role of the Bard in Contemporary Pagan Movements.* Unpublished Ph.D. thesis. King Alfred's College, Winchester, UK.

———.
2001b "The Scouring of the Shire: Fairies, Trolls and Pixies in Eco-Protest Culture." *Folklore* 112: 147–61.

———.
2003 "Gaia Told Me to Do It": Resistance and the Idea of Nature within Contemporary British Eco-Paganism. *Ecotheology.*

Lindquist, G.
1997 *Shamanic Performances on the Urban Scene. Neo-Shamanism in Contemporary Sweden.* Stockholm: Stockholm Studies in Social Anthropology.

Lord, A.
1960 *The Singer of Tales.* Cambridge, Mass.: Harvard University Press.

Lury, C.
1996 *Consumer Culture.* Cambridge, UK: Polity Press.

Maffesoli, M.
1991 The Ethic of Aesthetics. *Theory, Culture and Society* 8: 7–20.

———.
1996 *The Time of the Tribes: The Decline of Individualism in Mass Society.* Translated by D. Smith. London: Sage.

McCutcheon, R., ed.
1999 *The Insider/Outsider Problem in the Study of Religion: A Reader.* London: Cassell.

Pearson, J.
2001 "Going Native in Reverse": The Insider as Researcher in British Wicca. Paper presented at BASR (British Association for the Study of Religion) Annual Conference "Religion and Community," Faculty of Divinity, University of Cambridge, UK.

Pike, S.
2000 "The Burning Man Festival: Pre-Apocalypse Party or Postmodern Kingdom of God?" *The Pomegranate* 14: 26–37.

Rabelais, F.
[1534] 1955 *The Histories of Gargantua and Pantagruel.* Harmondsworth, UK: Penguin.

Salih, S.
2002 *Judith Butler.* London: Routledge.

Salomonsen, J.
1999 Methods of Compassion or Pretension? Anthropological Fieldwork in Modern Magical Communities. *The Pomegranate* 8: 4–13.

Schechner, R.
1988 *Performance Theory.* London: Routledge.

———.
1990 Magnitudes of Performance. In *By Means of Performance. Intercultural studies of Theatre and Ritual,* edited by R. Schechner and W. Appel. Cambridge: Cambridge University Press.

———.
1993 *The Future of Ritual: Writings on Culture and Performance.* London: Routledge.

Schechner, R., and W. Appel, eds.
1990 *By Means of Performance: Intercultural Studies of Theatre and Ritual.* Cambridge: Cambridge University Press.

Schieffelin, E.
1996 On Failure and Performance: Throwing the Medium Out of the Séance. In *The Performance of Healing,* edited by C. Laderman and M. Roseman. London: Routledge.

Shields, R.
1996 Foreword to *The Time of the Tribes. The Decline of Individualism in Mass Society*, by M. Maffesoli. Translated by D. Smith. London: Sage.

Stallybrass, P., and A. White
1986 *The Politics and Poetics of Transgression*. Ithaca, N.Y.: Cornell University Press.

Sutcliffe, S., and M. Bowman, eds.
2000 *Beyond New Age. Exploring Alternative Spirituality*. Edinburgh: Edinburgh University Press.

Szerszynski, B.
1999 Performing Politics: The Dramatics of Environmental Protest. In *Culture and Economy after the Cultural Turn*, edited by L. Ray and A. Sayer. London: Sage.

Turner, V.
1990 Are There Universals of Performance in Myth, Ritual, and Drama? In *By Means of Performance. Intercultural Studies of Theatre and Ritual*, edited by R. Schechner and W. Appel. Cambridge: Cambridge University Press.

van Gennep, A.
[1904] 1960 *The Rites of Passage*. Chicago: University of Chicago Press.

Wallis, R. J.
1999 *Autoarchaeology and Neo-Shamanism. The Socio-Politics of Ecstasy*. Unpublished Ph.D. thesis, Department of Archaeology, University of Southampton, UK.

———.
2003 *Shamans/Neo-Shamans. Ecstasy, Alternative Archaeologies and Contemporary Pagans*. London: Routledge.

Weiskrantz, L.
1986 *Blindsight*. Oxford: Oxford University Press.

Wiebe, D.
2000 Modernism. In *Guide to the Study of Religion*, edited by W. Braun and R. McCutcheon. London: Cassell.

CHAPTER TWO

METHODS OF COMPASSION OR PRETENSION? THE CHALLENGES OF CONDUCTING FIELDWORK IN MODERN MAGICAL COMMUNITIES

Jone Salomonsen

Classical anthropology is famous for having developed a notion of fieldwork in which the role of the "participant observer" is crucial. An intended goal when entering this research position is to be able to study an ethnographic field horizontally, in solidarity with an indigenous point of view, not vertically and from externally applied norms. If, however, the field is religious studies, an ethnographer will soon confront paradoxical and conflicting professional claims, which all revolve around whether to take "indigenous" beliefs seriously or not, and if so, to what extent. On one hand, there is an ideal that an anthropologist should study her ethnographic field from the inside, with an empirical, inductive approach. On the other, there is still fear within the discipline of scholars "going native," that is, adopting the values, practices, and beliefs of those studied to such an extent that one loses the ability to be reflexive about them. Also, to complicate the matter, when it comes to religion, the anthropologist should pay homage to the lineage of Feuerbach and deductive, philosophical claims that religion is *only* a human, social construction.

In this chapter[1] I shall examine some of these paradoxes, in particular how the warning against "going native," especially in the wrong community, is entangled with unacknowledged normativity and a positivist, hierarchical view of the relation between observer and observed. I encountered these paradoxes during fieldwork among feminist Witches in San Francisco for a doctoral thesis, while trying to fit the research position of a "participant observer" (in 1988–1989, partly in 1990 and 1994).[2] Very quickly this position became too narrow for the goals set, which was to get to the inside of Witches' claims of having reconstructed an ancient mystery religion centered on the worship of "the Great Goddess" and re-installed a plausible foundation for magical practices in Western culture. In order to build a deep account of Reclaiming people's sacred cosmology, ritualizing practices, and female agency I needed entrance of a different kind than what is usually provided through "participant observation," and was promptly—for reasons to be explained later—confronted with the necessity of becoming "my own informant." Alas, the empirical field "forced" me to elaborate on a more *compassionate* methodological approach, and in the following I shall present the processes and reflections that made me develop an alternative.

In this connection it is important to point out that my primary training is as a theologian, while my secondary one is as an anthropologist. My initial (and predoctoral) studies of Witchcraft started while I was a student in systematic or constructive theology, and it was not until I had "indulged" in the material long enough to experience the shortcomings of the primarily deductive methods of this theological discipline that I (also) became an anthropologist. This article, therefore, not only questions the sufficiency of the methods of classical anthropology in terms of studying religion and modern magical communities; it also questions those of theology. At the same time I hope to display how these two very different academic traditions have supplemented and challenged each other in the actual research process, and that this, in itself, is an argument for why a new interdisciplinary approach in the study of complex social phenomena *and* metaphysical discourses—such as magical practices and religious beliefs—may be regarded as most fruitful.

From Theology to Anthropology

I discovered Witchcraft when I (in the early 1980s) was searching for a topic for my MA thesis in systematic theology at the University of Oslo that could pass as "feminist theology." I wanted to profile my thesis with empirical knowledge and textual analysis of one of the branches of the emerging goddess spirituality in Western culture, but nothing of this kind was yet manifesting in Norway or Scandinavia. After having been given a one-year student grant from the Norwegian Research Council to be able to pursue my interests, I ended up enrolling at the Graduate Theological Union in Berkeley, while at the same time hoping to meet and be included in the community I wanted to study.

San Francisco is across the bridge from Berkeley and my chosen community, Reclaiming, is located in its Mission district. This Witchcraft community was founded in 1979 by a well-known Jewish author, feminist, and political activist named Starhawk and her circle of friends. When I arrived in 1984 they offered workshops, classes, and large public rituals. A large majority were also active in direct political action, some form of social work, and experimental, collective living.[3]

After a patient process (at least to me) I was finally accepted in the community and could begin a more systematic study of its esoteric teachings and ritual symbolism. However, as a theologian I had no methodological or theoretical training in studying "lived life," and even less so Witchcraft as a "lived religion." I only knew about texts, piled up in libraries, museums, and bookstores, waiting to be picked out as precious objects of study. I knew how to study "this book thing," an object I could hold between my two hands. I did not know how to study communities or people—their various beliefs, ritualizations, or claims of personal transformation. Consequently, I was only looking for a consistent narrative, a general belief system that could be represented and made accessible to some kind of semiotic analysis. Everything I learned and experienced with the Witches was therefore reduced and converted into "text," understood as a symbolic system of meaning.

I developed a general narrative of Reclaiming, which, I claimed, contained two systems of meaning: feminist *symbols of belief* on one hand and *ritual symbolism* on the other. I perceived these systems to be in ideological conflict, and that Reclaiming Witches' ritual symbolism and magical practices derived more or less from the occult heritage of male secret societies around the turn of the twentieth century. Not very feminist, not very progressive. Indeed, I argued, feminist Witches were perpetuating the heavy patriarchal burden of romantic gender essentialism, reducing "woman" and "goddess" into feminine counterimages of the essential masculine. My findings, however, were the result of an approach that was highly *deductive*: I already had a constructionist, feminist theory at hand and, as I read Reclaiming, I *applied* the latest fads in French feminist theory and semiotics onto the representations made.

Just before returning to Norway in the summer of 1985, I enthusiastically put forth the preliminary results of my research for a group of Reclaiming people. They were eager to hear; some even brought tape recorders so that those absent could also have a part in the sharing. I summarized the findings of my deductive research, spelled out the tacit patriarchal notions of the pillars of correspondence in Western occultism inherent in their symbol system, and stated that Reclaiming Witches were not as radical as they claimed to be. In fact, to a large extent they were only replacing one patriarchal tradition (Jewish and Christian religions) with another (Western occultism).[4]

When I finished there was complete silence. Nobody shared my enthusiasm over these findings. They were just staring at me, confused and sad. Finally, one male member started to talk. He said that my analysis sounded great, logical, and convincing, except that it made him completely depressed. A woman agreed with him and asked: How could it be that feminist Witchcraft was only a reproduction of patriarchal trends in Western esotericism and spirituality when in fact this religious path had changed her life and given a completely new meaning to what it meant to be religious, and what it meant to be a woman and have "a life"?

I was struck by her comment. What was the revitalizing power of feminist Witchcraft that I was not able to catch with my symbolic, textual analysis? Retrospectively I will say it had something to do with the transformative potentials of ritual and the ways in which the self was ritualized, respected, and integrated into this community. To focus my study entirely upon the reinvention of the divine feminine and of magical symbols was missing the point, although "goddess" and "magic" were the headlines through which feminist Witchcraft often drew new people.

To this day I claim that feminist Witchcraft, in terms of its favorite symbols, is burdened with heavy biological essentialism.[5] But this observation only holds a partial truth. If we are concerned with understanding the modus operandi of this religion and why it continues to appeal to and "change people's lives," we must enter its study from a somewhat different angle. A feminist theologian and theoretician must also become an anthropologist (and vice versa) and be willing to study this phenomenon from the inside—not from the inside of books but from the inside of "lived reality." I had, of course, already touched upon the profoundly communal and ritualizing aspects of Witchcraft, but not really used them to elicit knowledge and deep understanding.

To be able to change the scope of her research so radically it was necessary for the theologian to learn to listen to "the other" without having to reach consensus or state disagreements, that is, to learn the methods of participant observation and gain the competence required to study living communities, not only texts. For the anthropologist then coming into being, it was important that she discarded reductionist and biased approaches to religion and regarded feminist Witchcraft as a genuine and qualified religious (and theological) expression.[6]

Methodology and the Problem of "Insider" versus "Outsider"

This was my pledge when I, in 1988, was admitted to the Ph.D. program at the University of Oslo and to the training program for ethnographic fieldworkers at the Department of Anthropology (I already had a major in anthropology from my BA). I wanted to learn the ethnographic skills of an anthropologist and return to Reclaiming for a new period, with the intent of conducting fieldwork. I also wanted to give up my former deductive approach and conform to the empirical aim in anthropology of interpreting a phenomenon horizontally, in solidarity with the indigenous points of view and conceptual frameworks and not from a priori theoretical assumptions or claimed philosophies. In other words, I wanted to use an *inductive* methodological strategy, consistent with an almost exegetical approach to reading. This approach moves from text to theory and back to text, assuming that careful reading and listening will eventually disclose from the text its implicit theory about itself: how it "asks" to be read to make sense. From this epistemological stance it is not primarily interesting to apply external theoretical models, that is, models established on the basis of having read "another text" to explain textual meaning in "our text." It is more interesting to *extract* implicit theory and models from the data and discuss these "extractions" with adequate, already established theoretical discourse.[7]

It was then that I confronted the paradoxical structures of anthropology. As already mentioned, a serious student in anthropology first must subscribe to the empirical aim of interpreting ethnographic phenomena horizontally, from the inside out. Second, she must agree with the prohibition against indulging the inside *too much* and promise not to "go native." Third, she must recognize that, in terms of religion, the a priori theoretical assumption of her field is that religion is a human projection onto the supernatural of originally social and perfectly natural phenomena. Religion is not *also* a symbolization of "spiritual phenomena" but always of something else. Religious beliefs are therefore inferior, cognitive representations that, in the era of modernity, both can and should be substituted for superior ones. By subscribing to this thesis, American anthropologist Katherine P. Ewing claims that anthropology participates in an "atheist hegemonic discourse" (Ewing 1994). This theoretical position prevents the anthropologist from effectively utilizing an inductive analytical approach when confronting magical religion.

Thus, anthropologists are permitted to "go native" behaviorally ("participant observation"), even emotionally ("empathy"), but not cognitively. This prohibition cannot be explained merely with reference to the necessity for analytical distance to the object studied. The prohibition it-self has a normative foundation because the anthropologist is already a native: she has been socialized into the dominant values and cognitive worldviews of Western, scientific culture. To question the values of this culture, such as its fundamental articles of atheist belief, has until recently been a sign of no longer being able to do social anthropology (Berger 1970, 12).

From a classical and descriptive anthropological point of view, any community or culture is interesting, adding to the complexity of human life. Cultures are not "better" or "worse" and none may be said to hold beliefs that are more truly founded than another. Therefore, as a *descriptive* discipline, anthropology has a great archaeological interest in religion and magic, but as a *normative* discipline it represents the modern secular thought. Sociologist Peter Berger asserts that this stream of thought has sought to invalidate the reality of any magico-religious view of the world, including that of Witches (Berger 1980, x). A scholar who takes belief seriously and acknowledges that the people studied *may* know something about the human condition that might be personally valid also for the anthropologist, runs the risk of going native, and thereby the risk of abandonment from the scientific community.

Leading anthropologists are now opposing this insider-outsider dualism and various rituals of scholarly detachment, arguing that their only function is to reinforce the dishonest illusion of objectivity (for example, Rosaldo 1980, Lewis 1980, Daniel 1984, Jackson 1989, and Csordas 1994). Instead they encourage their colleagues to empathetically "take belief seriously" in the actual research process and acknowledge the unavoidability of subjectivity, narrative, and emotion when studying "other" human fellows.[8] I will not object to these more or less postmodernist statements, but point out that we are, again, dealing with the general, with the a priori, which only has transformed the scope *of the general* 180 degrees. For the post-modernist argument is *not* raised primarily out of *empirical* concerns, from an urge to improve the research process, but rather on the philosophical and epistemological premises that scientific objectivity is a fallacy.

Coming from a field where the presumption is that all scholars are also "natives," which is the case with theology, it was never a question *if* I should take the Witches' beliefs seriously or not in a cognitive, personal sense. It was taken for granted that I would, just as it was expected that I would close my inquiry with some kind of evaluation of their contribution or noncontribution to modern, constructive theology. In the discipline of constructive or systematic theology it is not regarded as a fundamental methodological problem to move between "outside" and "inside" positions, or to gain personal insights from the phenomenon studied. Nor is engagement regarded as something that might blur the objectivity of the descriptions. The situation is rather the opposite: Firsthand experience *may* open the possibility to deep insight and the best description possible. Questioning the positivist and conflictual ideology of observer-observed or insider-outsider is an inherent part of this theological tradition. In fact, the father of modern constructive theology, Friedrich Schleiermacher (1768–1834), has formulated the experiential nature of theology thus: "Anyone who has not experienced will not understand" (cf. Gerrish 1993, 32). Hence, the art or craft of competent constructive theology is to evolve and deepen religious (and theological) experience, compassion, and understanding in the student, at the same time that she learns the skills of critical analysis and acquires the ability to deconstruct or revise the very same phenomenon that triggers her interest. Thus, if the beliefs and practices of feminist Witchcraft had not triggered any personal interest in me, I would never have chosen them as subjects for my studies. From a theological perspective such a choice would have been a waste of time—unless I wanted to become a religious studies scholar instead and change my scope and field, which always is a possibility.

So, when I decided to change my methods from textual to ethnographic studies, and redefine my angle of approach from deductive to inductive, my motivation was not metatheoretical or postmodernist, meaning that I *too* wanted to persuade the academic community of the epistemological errors of the insider-outsider conflict. No, the methodological calling came from my data, not from my soul or theoretical positioning. I approached anthropology precisely because I had experienced the inadequacies of my earlier methods: they didn't do justice to the material. As a theologian I had taken Witchcraft beliefs seriously in a cognitive sense all along, but not yet in an emotional or experiential sense. It was in order to do so that I embarked upon anthropology and the methods implied by "participant observation" and "fieldwork." As it turned out, however, in order to *really* gain access to feminist Witchcraft as a lived religion, I also needed to revise the anthropological methods available to me.

A Method of Compassion

Reclaiming Witches identify as modern mystics. Mysticism can be approached textually, but according to Witches, this is not enough. In order to truly grasp their beliefs, they insist that the scholar engage in ritual,

magic, and trance work as well. The problem is that the notion "participant observation" in anthropology does not specify accurately the kind of
participation required. The "genuinely social interaction" (Ellen 1984, 17)
of this method is often conditioned and its requested "direct observations
of relevant events" may easily resemble pretension. Such an attitude obviously belongs to the *outsider*, to one who enters in order to gather data, but
whose first article of belief is a commitment to not "going native."

Yet, the main reason it is not enough to conduct fieldwork from such
a normatively chosen "outside" position is that, in Witches' rituals, covens,
and classes, there is no outside where an observer can literally put herself.
In the practice of modern mystery religions, you are either in, or you are
not there at all. In my doctoral studies of feminist Witches, I therefore had
to establish a research position for myself in which I became a coparticipant and an apprentice, taking my own experiences seriously, observing
the development of my own possible new insights, presumably determined by my willingness to put myself under the discipline of magical
training and by my abilities for religious imagination, theologizing, and
engagement in general. Along with, and parallel to my redefined studies
of Reclaiming Witches, I also became my own informant.[9]

The obvious demands for involvement and subjective experience required from a student of Witchcraft have led to my deliberate choice of
the label "method of compassion" to designate this approach. "Compassion" in this context does not refer to a wholesale positive embrace, nor to
passionate criticisms and arguing, but to something in between: to hon-
esty. It designates an attitude in which belief is taken seriously, both cognitively and emotionally. This means leaving behind the anthropological
"method of pretension," which is mainly used in order to gain access, be it
to rituals, secret knowledge, or initiations, and instead taking on the attitude that "the subjects of one's research might actually know something
. . . that is personally valid for the anthropologist," as suggested by anthropologist Katherine P. Ewing (1994, 571).

On the other hand, when something is taken seriously in a cognitive
sense, it may also turn out that the informants do *not* know something that
can be personally valid. A method of compassion is necessarily critical in
the sense of being reflexive, since it cannot be effective without continual
assessments and evaluations (cf. Grimes 1990, 137). It also means respect
for the integrity of the people studied and for oneself as well. Anthropologists may, for example, be eager to gain access to esoteric traditions and
learn the knowledge of the initiates. But if religious initiation is accepted
entirely against one's own beliefs or solely in order to publish secret

knowledge, the act is incompatible with the ethics embedded in a method of compassion.

The benefits and challenges of becoming my own informant, of simultaneously exercising engagement (vivid participation) and holding a general view (distant observation) apply in particular to the study of ritual. In terms of magical rituals, engagement is important to *understand* while distance is important to observe, remember, and *record* details.[10] Since one of the goals of ritual is to alter the consciousness of *all* the participants through trance work, engagement and distance are counterproductive. To the extent that I have managed to be involved all through the ritual, I will also come out with an altered consciousness. Engagement is more than participation, and something other than pretending. To allow oneself to become engaged is to take the intent of ritual seriously. It is to be willing to let the trance induction take you into trance, to be willing to be emotionally moved, as is intended by certain ritual elements, and to go with what then happens. Distance, on the other hand, means observation, remembering the lyrics and symbols used in trance induction, remembering the ritual proceedings step by step, seeing what happens to the other participants, and noticing the social interaction, the symbolism, the artifacts, and the movements.

A scholar who wants to be her own informant must be a master of both positions. In practice, this can be attained through repeated participation in the same type of ritual. Through repetition, the skills and competence to participate and be distant at one and the same time are acquired. Ritologist Ronald L. Grimes even argues that it is crucial for *any* serious student of ritual, not only for students of modern mystery religions, to learn this method. However, this very subjective element marks a limit as to how deeply into a religion of this kind one can go. There is also the uncertainty about where a scholarly project like this will lead, because an innate part of becoming a "visiting member" of a mystery religion is to make a contract with yourself to change.

Unexpected Consequences of Being My Own Informant

Yet, my studies of Reclaiming are *not about me* in any postmodernist sense (cf. Clifford and Marcus 1986). I have become my own informant for methodological reasons only, in order to understand "the other" deeply and from the inside. This was also the reason why I (eventually) wanted to experience the full range of Witches' rituals, including the initiation process and its ultimate, secret rite. But, when I finally decided to become initiated into the Reclaiming tradition, which I have been, it was after six years of careful consideration and discussion with myself, my informants, and my theological and anthropological supervisors (at the University of Oslo). I met Reclaiming in 1984, I asked for initiation in 1991, and it finally happened in 1994. I could not do it only for curiosity or for empirical insight, which, of course, was tempting all the time; the act had to be consistent with a minimum of my own beliefs and values, not violating my integrity as a theologian (which I still am).[11]

When I first met Reclaiming, I had little knowledge about what an initiation actually was. I was, nevertheless, sincerely against it, regarding any form of initiation ritual as undemocratic, hierarchical, patriarchal, and exclusive, emphasizing human "deeds" instead of divine "grace." To ask for initiation at that point was out of the question, even though it would have been helpful to my studies. Ten years later I had changed my mind, partly from being a close observer and witness to another person's initiation process, partly from realizing that the absence of working initiation rituals and their embedded notion of the unfinished state of the human person in modern society probably represents as much loss as progress.

Thus, to be the subject of an initiation process would perhaps give me a unique opportunity to experience the practical consequences of very different notions of "grace" and the "human person" than those that have gained momentum in Protestant churches in the wake of the reforming fathers. In the controversy between Luther and Erasmus over the freedom of the will, Luther conceptualized "grace" as the promise of new life for a will that is so perverted it first must die, whereas "grace" for Erasmus meant help for the weak. For this humanist and mystic, "grace meant help to move persons beyond their present abilities; in Erasmus' own metaphor, grace is the parental boost that helps the child to its feet and enables it to walk" (Gerrish 1993, 21). Although "grace" is not a notion in Witchcraft, the analogy to Erasmus's theology is still valid, for the initiation process is interpreted as an opening of "the envelope" (the body) for the crafting work of the spirit, visualized as the Goddess of rebirth, growth, and regeneration.[12]

Since I have been initiated into Reclaiming Witchcraft primarily for hermeneutical and experiential reasons, I am not entitled to initiate anybody else into this tradition. The apprenticeship is over, and although I have learned a lot, I do not intend to bring about any further magical currents from having been initiated except reflective and reliable textual representations of this Craft tradition (including this article) and their various receptions in the reader; for my suggested "method of compassion" demands that we never forget that we are scholars. By this I mean two things. First, we must abandon the luxury of engaging in only those aspects of the religion that are immediately attractive or intelligible to us. We must dive as deeply into the religion as possible and relinquish the desire to choose from its well only what may suit our own biases. Second, we as scholars are indeed permitted spiritual and personal development from our work, but we may not end up as scholarly converts and proselytizers. Proselytizing and sound academic analysis are two different genres.

The necessity of studying mysticism from an experiential position "within" is not only part of feminist theological rhetoric. It was, for example, argued by religionist Frits Staal in his book *Exploring Mysticism* (1975). Considering the superficial knowledge one gets from studying Hindu yoga practices when not entering the experience of actually learning yoga, Staal suggests that the academic student of yoga learn it from a guru, but without "going native." The way to keep the awareness of a scholar throughout the period of learning is, according to Staal, to remember that we have entered the path of yoga to leave it when our learning is completed. We cannot enter it to stay. After leaving the path, Staal designs one of the scholar's tasks to be the development of a language to describe mystical yoga.

I agree that we, as scholars, must enter the path of mysticism in order to develop a descriptive terminology. Nevertheless, Staal's scientific belief in the possibilities of learning to be a mystic by the same will and mental equipment one uses to learn to cook seems to be put forward by somebody who has been some kind of an "outsider" throughout the process. He does not consider what compassion and the contract to be willing to change—which are both required conditions to actually be able to learn from a mystical path—will actually do to him and his study. Nor does he contemplate how the entrance onto the path of mysticism challenges the ideology of observer-observed and highlights the ethical dilemmas and coresponsibilities of any researcher in regard to actual happenings and processes among the people being studied. And finally, he does not seem to be willing to reflect hermeneutically on the way in which he partakes in the development, twisting, and diffusion of the tradition solely by writing a new text. How, for example, do Witches learn about yoga, or manage to incorporate yoga practices into their modernist mixture of meditative techniques? Maybe they have learned from a guru, maybe from having read Staal and his colleagues.

A majority of Witches are educated at Western universities and well read in the basic humanistic disciplines, including religious studies and classical anthropology. In the process of reconstructing their own religious alternative, they appropriate ethnographic and religious literature with the intention of turning what they learn into normative vehicles for cultural reforms, not in some exotic country, but in their own community. Academic texts (including mine) are therefore never merely descriptions or representations of "other" forms of life but participate in cultural changes in Western societies as well, totally independent of the scholar's perhaps "purely descriptive" intentions.

Furthermore, my own experience when studying the mystery religion of feminist Witchcraft cannot report on the problems proposed by Frits Staal, namely the supposed dilemma of moving back and forth between inside and outside and the temptation to "go native." To move back and forth between compassion and analysis is not at all the difficult part. But *to stay in*, in touch with "the native's" affirmative compassion, is indeed difficult. To accept those symbols as sacred that to my taste were vulgar, to play with pagan names as if they were "real names" for divine reality, to let go of criticism and be open to the ecstasy of ritual, to meditate on certain symbols "until they revealed their esoteric knowledge," and to grant exception to the belief that this really was *im*possible—when taken altogether, these are what have been difficult, challenging, and rewarding.

Conclusion

No academic discipline has yet developed an adequate methodology for the study of modern mystery religions because such a task probably requires a thoroughly interdisciplinary approach. In my case, anthropology has contributed the basic qualitative tools: the tradition of doing fieldwork, participant observation, and the skills of active listening to "the other"—including that which we do not like to hear. Theology has contributed the training of being in two mindsets simultaneously, which means being able to engage in the phenomenon studied as well as being critical and analytic.

As merely a sociologist or anthropologist I would never have been admitted to Reclaiming's inner circles. But as a theologian and feminist I was regarded as a religious being with a personally motivated interest in the subject of my study and, therefore, as possessing the necessary qualifications both to understand and to learn (about) Witchcraft. Without being a coparticipant guided by empathy and compassion I would not have been able to conduct my doctoral studies as intended. It is, therefore, my opinion that both theology and anthropology are being challenged by new religious phenomena to radically develop, each in its own terms, as inter-disciplinary disciplines.

Notes

1. A shorter version of this article was originally delivered as a paper for a roundtable discussion at the 97th annual meeting of the American Anthropolog-ical Association in Philadelphia, in December 1998 and a version was printed in *The Pomegranate. A Journal of Neopagan Thought* (8/1999).

2. For informative and well-founded research of Witchcraft and Neopagan-ism in the United States, see for example Berger 1999 and Pike 2000.

3. For an insider's account of Reclaiming Witchcraft, see Starhawk [1979] 1989.

4. This argument can be read in full in my MA thesis (Salomonsen 1986).

5. For a full discussion of Reclaiming people's attempts to create a female symbolic order and their returning limps into essentialist notions of gender, see Salomonsen 2002, 214–47.

6. The results of my long-term studies of the Reclaiming Witchcraft Tradi-tion can be read in Salomonsen 1996 and 2002.

7. The suggested methodological movement text-theory-text does not imply that I dismiss the insights of the "hermeneutical circle": I do not believe that I am "without theory" when confronting a new text or a new ethnographic field. But, I do *not* believe that our cultural, semiotic predispositions are total, or that we can only learn what we already know. For further discussions on this topic, see Iris Marion Young (1997).

8. I am, of course, not the only one who has responded positively to this en-couragement and will, for example, find many associates among other students of magical communities (cf. Foltz and Griffin 1996, Ramsey 1998).

9. My choice of method is to a certain extent informed by Brown's influen-tial work (1991). Favret-Saada (1980) also ended as her own informant when studying malignant witchcraft in contemporary rural France. But this happened against her own will, out of fear of the spells people presumably made against each other. She became her own informant to the extent that she observed her own fear and realized that without her own emotional reactions she would not have discovered this magical, but hidden, discourse.

10. During Reclaiming's rituals, tape recording is not *comme il faut*. Continu-ous note taking is impolite and would also spoil the subjective experience of rit-ual. In later reconstructions, the informants are seldom of any help. My questions about ritual proceedings and meanings are experienced as intruding on their own personal experience in ritual, desacralizing it, and the answers are mostly, "I don't remember very well."

11. This theological "minimum" is as follows: I can relate to Reclaiming Witches' efforts to establish female symbolism to represent "the face of God/dess," and to their dedication to create new patterns for ritualizing in Western culture, although I do not necessarily agree with all its contents. I cannot relate to their non-Christological consensus as a final goal in theology, and I am deeply critical of their self-identification as "Witches," including their uncritical embrace of an occult lineage and its very problematic and mythological historiography. But I am not morally offended by how they reconstruct a new religion by misreading the historical past or misrepresenting Judaism and Christianity, or other institutions in Western civilization. I believe that the invocation of simple, critical, and imaginative approaches to social (and religious) reality by so-called ordinary people (nonexperts) has always contributed to, and been a necessary part of, ongoing cultural changes in the Western Hemisphere: They hold the key to powerful, rebellious visions and actions.

12. I started to change my mind after having been invited to and then undergone a ten-day "Vision Quest" in the Inyo Desert in California in April 1989. This meditative quest was built on a model imitating the Lakota tradition, with four days in solitude on a mountaintop, fasting from food and shelter. For further reflections on this experience, which was meant to clarify a personal calling and induce growth in the participants (which it probably also did), cf. Salomonsen 1991 and 1999.

References

Berger, Helen A.
  1999 *A Community of Witches. Contemporary Neopaganism and Witchcraft in the United States.* Columbia: University of South Carolina Press.

Berger, Peter L.
  1970 *A Rumor of Angels.* New York: Doubleday.

———.
  1980 *The Heretical Imperative.* New York: Anchor Books.

Brown, Karen McCarthy
  1991 *Mama Lola: A Vodou Priestess in Brooklyn.* Berkeley: University of California Press.

Clifford, James, and George E. Marcus, eds.
  1986 *Writing Culture.* Berkeley: University of California Press.

Csordas, T. J.
  1994 *Embodiment and Experience: The Existential Ground of Culture and Self.* Cambridge: Cambridge University Press.

Daniel, E. Valiente
  1984 *Fluid Signs: Being a Person the Tamil Way.* Berkeley: University of California Press.

Ellen, R. F., ed.
1984 *Ethnographic Research. A Guide to General Conduct.* London: Academic Press.

Ewing, Katherine P.
1994 Dreams from a Saint: Anthropological Atheism and the Temptation to Believe. *American Anthropologist* 96(3): 571–83.

Foltz, Tanice G., and Wendy Griffin
1996 "She Changes Everything She Touches": Ethnographic Journeys of Self-Discovery. In *Composing Ethnography. Alternative Forms of Qualitative Writing,* edited by Carolyn Ellis and Arthur P. Bochner. Walnut Creek, Calif.: AltaMira.

Favret-Saada, J.
1980 *Deadly Words. Witchcraft in the Bocage.* Cambridge: Cambridge University Press.

Gerrish, B. A.
1993 *Continuing the Reformation. Essays on Modern Religious Thought.* Chicago: University of Chicago Press.

Grimes, Ronald L.
1990 *Ritual Criticism: Case Studies in Its Practice, Essays on Its Theory.* Columbia: University of South Carolina Press.

Jackson, Michael
1989 *Paths toward a Clearing.* Bloomington: Indiana University Press.

Lewis, Gilbert
1980 *Day of Shining Red.* Cambridge: Cambridge University Press.

Pike, Sara M.
2000 *Earthly Bodies, Magical Selves.* Berkeley: California University Press.

Ramsey, Nancy
1998 Remembering Who You Are and Whom You Represent: Researching Wicca as a Scholar and a Witch. *Circle Network News* 68 (Summer).

Rosaldo, Michelle Z.
1980 *Knowledge and Passion.* Cambridge: Cambridge University Press.

Salomonsen, Jone
1986 "The Poetry of Witchcraft as a Theology of Liberation. An Analysis of Esoteric Teachings and Ritual Symbolism." Unpublished MA thesis, University of Oslo.

———.
1991 *Når gud blir kvinne. Blant hekser, villmenn og sjamaner i USA.* Oslo: Pax Forlag.

———.

1996 "I Am a Witch—A Healer and a Bender." An Expression of Women's Religiosity in Contemporary USA." Unpublished Ph.D. thesis, University of Oslo.

———.

1999 *Riter. Religiøse overgangsritualer i vår tid.* Oslo: Pax Forlag.

———.

2002 *Enchanted Feminism. Ritual, Gender and Divinity among the Reclaiming Witches of San Francisco.* London: Routledge.

Staal, Frits
1975 *Exploring Mysticism.* Berkeley: University of California Press.

Starhawk
[1979] 1989 *The Spiral Dance. A Rebirth of the Ancient Religion of the Great Goddess.* San Francisco: Harper and Row.

Young, Iris Marion
1997 *Intersecting Voices. Dilemmas of Gender, Political Philosophy, and Policy.* Princeton, N.J.: Princeton University Press.

CHAPTER THREE

THE DEOSIL DANCE
Wendy Griffin

On Becoming Objective

I was in my second year of graduate school when my daughter was killed. I came home from a date to find a note on my front door saying there had been an accident. It was every single mother's worst nightmare, a crippling combination of fear and grief and guilt. Another grad student took over my teaching responsibilities so I could be with her the two weeks she lay in a coma, and then another two weeks after she died. On reflection, I know I went back to school too soon, but I couldn't stay home alone any longer. However, returning posed unique problems for me.

I had entered graduate school wanting to do research on single parents, suspecting that self-concepts, especially those of gender, would change significantly during the single-parenting experience. Mine certainly had during the decade I had been a single parent. I took two quarters off from this kind of research after the accident, passing time taking classes and learning to do oral histories. When I finally went back to my own research, I ran into trouble. I know now it was naïve of me to think I could return and do "objective research," as though subjectivity could be left hanging at the door like a raincoat wet with experience.

When the first single mother I interviewed in my pretesting began to cry, I found myself sobbing, caught up in the pain of her struggle as well as my own. Later I had to deal with the knowledge that my crying during the interview had changed its nature; it had "polluted" the data. It had been my intention to personally interview single mothers for my doctoral dissertation, but it was clear I would have to take a different approach. Fortunately, this realization coincided with my university's strong endorsement of quantitative methods. I spent the next several years learning survey methods, going through files of legal divorce proceedings in the basement of the local courthouse, generating a random sample of male and female custodial single parents, and learning the statistical techniques to analyze the hundreds of surveys that were mailed out and returned. I convinced myself that quantitative research was more scientific than qualitative, more scholarly. I was only dimly aware at the time that I also took this approach to protect myself.

I didn't like my doctoral dissertation much. Oh, I was proud of it in a way because the scholarship was solid, but after having published two novels before graduate school, my "objective" writing felt stiff and even boring. Three years after receiving my Ph.D., I found myself teaching five classes and classified as a part-time instructor at a state university. I knew that I needed a new research project and publications if I were to ever get a tenure-track position. But I was no longer interested in single parents and nothing seemed to inspire me.

Changing Methodologies

And then in the late 1980s, a student stood up in one of my classes and announced she was a Dianic Witch and invited the whole class to come to her coven's feminist ritual in celebration of the Spring Equinox. The students weren't particularly interested, but I mentioned it to another part-time instructor with whom I shared an office. Tanice Foltz and I didn't know each other well, but I felt comfortable going to the ritual with her. She had done her doctoral work on a healing group led by a well-known Kahuna, and thus she was more open to alternate forms of spirituality than I was. In addition to her fieldwork experience and company, Tanice offered me a buffer zone. The student who had issued the invitation was a lesbian and appeared at times to be flirting with me. I believed Tanice's presence would avert any misunderstandings.

We went to the ritual and had different reactions.[1] Tanice thought the group offered an excellent research opportunity; I initially thought the whole thing was a little weird. I was one of those feminists who dismissed spirituality and religion as irrelevant to my life and who was reluctant to engage in any pursuit that might reflect poorly on the women's movement. In my "objective" view, how could feminist Witches do anything else?

However, during the summer when school was out, I came to agree with Tanice. This was largely due to pragmatics. I *needed* a research project, and I was a little curious about how Witchcraft could be considered a religion. It certainly wasn't like the Episcopalian Church I had left decades before! Tanice offered to teach me what she knew about qualitative methods and suggested some books to read. I threw myself into learning all I could about fieldwork and wrote the coven a formal letter requesting permission to do research. I was invited to dinner and an interview. The coven members wanted to get to know me better and ask some questions about research before making a decision.

Tanice was out of town, so I went alone. Dinner was a barbecue in the backyard of a rented home in a working-class neighborhood where two of the coven members lived. Unused to the concept of "Pagan time," I arrived at the appointed hour, and was the first to do so. I was told we would just socialize and enjoy ourselves until everyone arrived. As we waited, one of the Witches brought out colored lights and candles and placed them around the yard. Two of them began to subtly dance deosil around the perimeter of the yard to the rhythm of African rattles they held as one sang a wordless tune.[2] My field notes from that day indicate that there was a lot of laughter and storytelling, but that there was also what I later learned to call "energy work" going on at the same time. The dancing and candles were creating both a mood and a space for assessing me and my intentions. Finally, all the coven members had arrived and the dancer brought out a marijuana cigarette. She lit it, took a hit, and passed it around. Everyone shared the joint and then it was passed to me.

I had been married to a musician in the 1960s, and had done my share of experimenting with the milder drugs. It wasn't that I was morally opposed to smoking; it just didn't seem like a very smart or appropriate thing for me to do. In addition, I wanted to stay completely alert and remember all the details of the evening for my field notes. Then I realized that all the coven members were looking at me. One woman who was watching me extremely closely said that things done within the coven were done "in perfect love and perfect trust." Suddenly I was absolutely convinced that if I didn't smoke, I would never be permitted to do research with the coven. They would never trust me. So I took the joint (and, yes, I did inhale). Later on, during intensive questioning of me, it was clear that two members had some reservations. The woman who watched me so closely all evening ended up arguing strongly in my favor. The group and I talked for several hours about what Tanice and I wanted to do in terms of research, what control the coven members might or might not have over what we wrote, and about our mutual responsibilities if we were given permission to go forward with the project. When I left that evening, I was unsure what the group's decision would be, but I knew I had done everything I could to gain access to the research setting.

This was a onetime event. Within a few months, one of the members' adult sons was killed in what appeared to be a drug deal gone bad, and the group never used illegal drugs as a group in my presence again. In fact, most of them became very opposed to drugs in general. Although I wrote this experience up in my fieldnotes, I never incorporated it into a paper. Part of me was concerned I had broken some kind of unwritten "Ethical Code of Good Research Methods"; sharing in illegal behavior certainly had never been discussed in graduate school, but then I had focused on quantitative methods. However, I eventually learned that other researchers have faced similar dilemmas and decided as I did. I wish I had known that on the night of the Witches' barbecue.

After terminating our year of research with the coven, I continued to do research in the general area with other groups, never personally affiliating with any of them. I used to say that the topic of feminist Witchcraft and Goddess spirituality chose me; I needed a topic and it presented itself. But the truth is more complex, especially as I stayed with the field. A researcher doesn't stay with something that is totally unrewarding. There were things in Goddess spirituality that resonated with me, with my childhood.[3] I wasn't studying the mating habits of clams; I was examining how some women find a spiritual family and meaning for their lives. I was not a disinterested scholar.

The Rhythm Method

Having finished our study of the coven we called Red Wood Moon,[4] access to other women's spiritual groups was not immediately available. It takes time to build the trust necessary for this kind of field research. But in 1989, I was introduced to women's drumming. A friend from work was part of a group of anywhere from ten to thirty women who met at her house to drum. Although I didn't know it at the time, my friend was one of the founders of a local women's spirituality group. The women who gathered at her house were involved in various manifestations of Wicca and women's spirituality, and called themselves The Hags from Hel.[5] The first time I went, I borrowed a conga and was captivated. Within a week I bought a conga of my own and began playing with them regularly.

The drumming done with the Hags was never very good, but it was great fun. Because of my friend's role in the local women's spirituality group, we began to play after the large public rituals while people feasted and danced. Then we were asked to play at the semiannual Solstice Fairs the group organized. Personalities and other commitments caused the group to disband, but those of us who loved drumming stayed to become The Furies. Now there were only seven of us, and we were asked to play *during* rituals instead of afterwards. We noticed that some ritual leaders and priestesses were able to work with the energy raised by the drumming and use it to set moods and facilitate altered states. Others seemed overpowered by the drums, or perhaps they simply felt there was too much competition or noise. When they began to make less use of The Furies, interest lagged and the drum group disbanded.

But shortly before that happened, we had begun to play the frame drum.[6] Although I had initially been captivated by the conga, the frame drum stole my heart. Noted frame drummer and author Layne Redmond came to Southern California, and I arranged for her to do a local performance and teach a workshop in my home. Her performance included a series of slides of ancient representations of women frame drummers that she later incorporated into a book that became extremely popular in women's spirituality and drumming communities.[7] In 1996, I was putting together a series of performance pieces for a conference on my campus and decided I wanted frame drummers in one. I called upon four other women who had attended the workshop, one of whom had been in The Furies. The reception to the drumming was so enthusiastic that we decided to continue working and performing together, and took the name of Lipushau, granddaughter of King Sargon, High Priestess in the Temple of the Moon in ancient Ur, and, according to Redmond's book, the first named drummer in history. We became fairly accomplished, playing in places as varied as local churches and universities, coffee shops, bookstores, weddings, festivals, cable television, the Radisson Wilshire Plaza Hotel, and the Beverly Hills Women's Club.

But our real specialty was playing for Goddess rituals, where we intentionally tried to evoke what we saw as archetypal images of female power. After one event, a young woman wrote to us that "What transpired was metamorphic. I was extremely inspired by these women. They played so beautifully together. I couldn't help but wonder what it would have been like 3,000 years ago to listen to women play the frame drum. A comment that was made [by another person] that the music gave her goose bumps. I thought it was only me. . . ."

Drumming gave me unique access to a wide variety of Pagan groups. People who didn't know me personally knew I was part of Lipushau. Event organizers who asked us to play knew I was an academic and doing research on Goddess Spirituality, but the drum seemed to signal that I could be trusted in a way that my presence alone would not have. I also found that the drum gave me a way to be engaging without having to fully engage. By that I mean that, besides providing entrée, it also gave me a sense of safety. At a workshop where women learned to dance with live pythons, for example, I was able to withdraw to my drum until my terror of snakes abated. Outside a sweat lodge where the stories grew so long and boring and, frankly, downright silly, I was able to grab a drum and deal effectively with my frustration without seeming critical of what was going on. One night at a ritual that focused on ecstatic dance, I physically retreated behind my drum as a couple became *very* ecstatic not three feet away from me on the floor. Whenever I felt that I was outside my comfort zone or being drawn in too far into emotions or self-revelation, the drum provided safety.

At the same time, I must admit that sometimes it facilitated a semi-trance state, so that the ritual was perhaps more meaningful to me than it would have been otherwise. These moments, however, were very rare. Although I am fairly successful in visualizing something during a guided meditation, it is extremely difficult for me to achieve an altered state. During ritual, even when I am not doing research, part of my brain is always assessing and critiquing what is going on. There is a riddle that begins by asking, What is the first thing a feminist sociologist does when she walks into a room of crying women? The answer, of course, is that she counts how many women are in the room.

It would be nice if I could turn off the sociologist in my head at will, so that I could feel what others are feeling, and later go think, assess, and write down my field notes. It would give me insights into Goddess Spirituality that otherwise I struggle to obtain. The drum sometimes lets me silence the sociologist, but then I am a drummer/participant in the ritual, and that is not the same as being a full participant. In a strange way, performance is still a way to remain safe.

I have never written up for publication a ritual in which my drumming group performed. The problem is that, when the drumming is successful, it changes the experience for those who are there. Whether it facilitates an altered state, makes the experience deeper or more intense, or simply inspires people to dance, the nature of the ritual has changed because of something I did. I help to shape the experience, and that pollutes the data. I have not been able to resolve that dilemma; however, after several women in the group moved away, Lipushau dissolved.

Dancing Deosil

After so many years in the Pagan community, access is no longer an issue for me. Nevertheless, the research in which I am presently engaged is quantitative again. I needed a larger sample than my local contacts could provide, and found myself in a position where I needed to gather data quickly. Thus, it was expediency that determined the methodology for this research, not safety for myself or the data. I designed a questionnaire, posted it online, and sent out an e-mail to 50 women I knew who were involved in Goddess Spirituality, asking them to pass the URL along to a few friends. The response to this snowball method of sampling was gratifying. As of this writing, 331 women from nine different countries had filled out the survey.

But I didn't just get answers to the survey questions. The last page of the online survey provided space for comments, offered the option for receiving the results of the study, and provided my e-mail address. I received thank you notes, photos of women's gardens, and over fifty e-mails from participants requesting the results of the survey.

"Thank you for your work in this area! It's so very important."(Survey 42)
"Thank you for taking the time to ask these questions" (Survey 325)
"Bless you for your studies" (Survey 196).

These were typical of the thanks I received.

But there were also unsolicited messages that forced me to re-examine and confront, not only my research methods, but problems in methodology in general.

"Thank you for that . . . you've made me think again—always a good thing *grin*" (Survey 266)
"This has been a lovely experience. Because I don't have a defined practice, I just try to live my spirituality, answering your questions made me slow down and consider my thoughts more carefully. Thank you for holding the mirror while I gazed at myself" (Survey 216)[8]
"Thank you for asking these questions. They re-iterate to me the importance that Nature has in my spiritual path" (Survey 079)

"Thank you for doing this survey—it made me aware of how much more I want to incorporate nature into my personal rituals & spirituality" (Survey 121).

Simply by asking the questions I asked, I made some respondents more aware of the role of nature in their own spirituality than they had been before filling out my survey. I had started out exploring *if* something existed, and I ended up reifying it. Using some of the most "objective" methodology available, I had polluted the data.

What I have learned from more than twenty years of research is that we do not, cannot leave ourselves behind when examining human experience, whether we are scholars in Pagan studies or gerontology. And in studying contemporary Goddess Spirituality and other traditions within Paganism that are still evolving, this inability may be particularly significant. Who we are, where we have been, and how we go about our research all contribute to shaping both our understanding of the spiritual practice and the practice itself. Knowing this, I cannot help but wonder what Paganism will look like tomorrow and if the next generation of researchers in Pagan studies will be looking at the results of *our* deosil dance.

Notes

1. For details on our reactions, our ultimate decision to study the coven, and how doing that research affected us, see Foltz and Griffin 1996.

2. Deosil—the sunwise circular direction. Goddess ritual usually begins by moving deosil to "cast" a circle and create a boundary around the area where magic is expected to occur. According to Starhawk (1979), deosil is also the direction of increase, of giving shape.

3. See Foltz and Griffin 1996.

4. See Lozano and Foltz 1990, 301–30.

5. According to Walker (1983), Hel is associated both with death and with the cauldron-womb of purification and rebirth.

6. The frame drum is any drum that is wider in diameter than in depth. The style I learned to play is where the drum is held much like a plate on edge and struck with the fingers.

7. In *When the Drummers Were Women* (1997), Redmond claims that women frame drummers were the primary drummers in the Middle East for over 3000 years. They performed both sacred and secular roles and were held in high regard. This style of drumming spread quickly across Northern Egypt, Greece, and the Roman Empire until it was banned by the Roman Church in a series of edicts from 375 to 576 C.E., when it was forbidden to teach women music.

8. A frequent act in Goddess ritual is to hold up a mirror for another woman to look into and say, "Thou art Goddess." When she sees the Goddess within her, she takes the mirror and holds it for the woman next to her, repeating the phrase/invocation.

References

Foltz, Tanice G., and Wendy Griffin
  1996 She Changes Everything She Touches: Ethnographic Journeys of Self Discovery. In *Composing Ethnographies*, edited by Carolyn Ellis and Arthur Bochner. Walnut Creek, Calif.: AltaMira.

Lozano, Wendy Griffin, and Tanice G. Foltz
  1990 Into the Darkness: An Ethnographic Study of Witchcraft and Death. *Qualitative Sociology* 13: 3 (Fall): 211–34.

Redmond, Layne
  1997 *When the Drummers Were Women*. New York: Three Rivers Press.

Starhawk
  1979 *The Spiral Dance*. San Francisco: Harper and Row.

Walker, Barbara
  1983 *The Woman's Encyclopedia of Myths and Secrets*. New York: Harper and Row.

Part Two

CHALLENGING OBJECTIVITY, THEORIZING SUBJECTIVITY

CHAPTER FOUR

PSYCHOLOGY OF RELIGION AND THE STUDY OF PAGANISM

Melissa Harrington

Academic studies of Paganism have not as yet tapped the potential offered by psychology of religion. Many of the present studies in this field are sociologically or anthropologically based. This chapter introduces psychology, and the contribution psychologists have made to our understanding of religion and religiosity. It discusses ways in which the foregoing work of psychologists could be drawn upon in the study of Paganism, and illustrates some of the dangers and benefits of using such an approach. Some of the methodological problems existing within the current paradigm for studying Paganism are discussed, along with suggestions as to how a psychological approach might benefit future research.

Psychology is the scientific study of the human mind and behavior. It has its roots in the philosophy of Socrates, Plato, and Aristotle, which sought to understand the nature of the human psyche, and in the physiology of Hippocrates, which connected the body and mind. It is an academic discipline that has developed over the last century, to such an extent that its discourse has become inextricably intertwined with the ideologies and language of late modern Western society.

Psychology approaches the phenomena of human behavior from five broadly banded perspectives: behavioral, biological, psychoanalytical, phenomenological, and cognitive. These include many subdivisions, each of which is an academic discipline in its own right. Professional psychologists work in numerous specialized areas of psychology, including biological, clinical, cognitive, developmental, educational, engineering, experimental, health, occupational, social, and sports. Although the humanistic schools of psychoanalytic and phenomenological psychology can be aligned more closely to the humanities than to hard science, the essential research mode of psychology is scientific. It uses a variety of experimental methods and designs that are aimed to ensure that research is as unbiased, objective, and as replicable as possible.

The psychology of religion includes the diverse strands of theology, philosophy, sociobiology, neurophysiology, psychological principles, behavioral and comparative theories, psychodynamics, the analytic tradition, and the humanistic synthesis. It uses methods of empirical and statistical analysis, trained observation, correlation studies, and laboratory experiments. It has generated such a vast body of literature that by 1930 it was deemed impossible to achieve "genuine mastery" over the field (Greuhn 1930).

This literature includes William James' early theoretical classic, *The Varieties of Religious Experience* (1960), and more recently Persinger's laboratory experiments in the 1980s that seemed to prove that God could be experienced via stimulating the temporal lobe of the brain (Persinger 1983, Persinger and Makarec 1987). The biological foundations of religion have been explored, behavioral and comparative theories of religion have evolved, and understanding of religious conversion has grown from the early "crisis-based" theory to those of conversion motifs and gradual and unconscious conversion. Psychologists of religion have explored perceptions of deity, and how the practice of religion affects adherents' daily lives. They have investigated religiosity in its different forms and uncovered developmental factors and processes of conformity, authoritarianism, and prejudice, as well as nonconformity, vision, and naturalist faith. Psychologists of religion are also interested in issues of mental health and religion, its positive or negative effects on a person's life, and its use in times of stress. They discuss religion as a coping mechanism, a source of self-esteem, and a factor in motivation, along with many more aspects of an individual's sense of self and their interaction with the social world. The psychology of religion has supplied other disciplines with the roots of religious theory, in the work of Freud, Jung, Eriksen, Maslow, and many more.

Contemporary work is regularly put into the public domain. *The Journal for the Scientific Study of Religion*, first published in 1961, publishes a plethora of articles by eminent scholars on all aspects of religion, many of which follow the classic form of a psychological experiment, complete with multivariate analysis. The newer but equally high-caliber *Journal of Mental Health, Culture and Religion* encourages work from a wide range of disciplines, but aims to provide a reference point and forum for academics and professionals working in mental health and religion. It has consistently published fascinating material pertaining to all aspects of mental health and religion.

One might expect more of this vast resource to be included within the study of Paganism. However, Pagan studies have been typified by an integrative approach that overwhelmingly favors anthropological, or sociological, theory and methodology. This is not surprising, since scholars of Paganism have been chiefly involved in demarcating a new field, locating Paganism within the contemporary sociological landscape, and developing the theoretical foundations for further study. Much of the academic literature generated so far has been of a descriptive nature, and the majority of Ph.D. theses on Paganism have been ethnographies or monographs. This is not to the detriment of Pagan studies; in fact it has been a very important stage of its development. It has been necessary to provide an overview of Pagan religion, to define it as much as possible, and to provide a firm basis for the next wave of scholastic study of Paganism.

Whether the study of Paganism will diverge from the current anthropological/sociological paradigm remains to be seen. That depends very much on who will be undertaking these studies, and to which institution they are affiliated. There are only so many institutions that are willing to provide supervisors for studies of Paganism, only so many academics supervisors who feel they have the necessary knowledge or interest to guide postgraduate work in this area, and only so much funding available for what is essentially a tiny subsection within the academy. The bulk of postgraduate work in this area has been undertaken within the remit of religious studies, with supervisors who usually teach religious studies, anthropology, sociology, and history.

It is clear that the use of psychology could significantly add to the study of Paganism. The wealth of knowledge that has already been generated by psychologists could be drawn upon at a much deeper level than it has been so far. Theories and studies from psychology could be referred to more often, including those of consciousness and altered states, motivation and emotion, personality and individuality, stress and coping, social beliefs and attitudes, and social interaction and influence. Psychodynamic and analytic perspectives could be applied, comparative models could be used, developmental perspectives could inform the study of spirituality, and cognitive-behavioral theory could be drawn upon. Psychological scales and tests, including those that have already been used in the study of religion, could be a useful starting place when designing fieldwork. All this could be achieved, and used in single studies of Paganism, or on a comparative basis alongside other faiths.

Social psychology is the discipline that most easily interfaces with the current paradigm in Pagan studies, which is to be expected since it merges to some extent with sociology. Social psychologists look at an individual's involvement in the social world, and the influence that that world has upon the individual. Areas of social psychology that might be fruitfully applied to studies of Paganism include attribution theory, attitude change, communication, affiliation, attraction, relationships, interpersonal behavior, group dynamics and interaction, leadership, communication networks, social influence in small groups, decision making, the influence of authority, intergroup relations, and group membership and social identification.

Certainly one area where studies of Paganism might draw upon psychology is that of research methods and measurements. Since psychology has always been taught as a science it has developed a weighty body of methodology in its search to empirically study the human mind. Psychology is the cradle of hypothesis testing and falsifying and the hypothetical deductive method. It seeks to attain reliability, standardized procedure, and ecological validity. Samples and groups are selected with great care, with an awareness of sampling bias, the need for representative samples, careful selection of random samples, and stratification and manipulation of subject groups via placebo and control groups. A wide variety of experimental methods are used, from the laboratory to ex post facto research, within a vast range of experimental designs stretching from participant observation to single-subject studies. Psychology teaches interview and survey technique and the use of questionnaires, scales, and tests, and ensures that its students are aware of the kinds of investigations that can be used, from student populations to cross-cultural or longitudinal studies. The measurement of data is a discipline in itself, with a body of literature devoted to statistical analysis. Ethical issues are also taken into serious consideration, and regulated by the British Psychological Society and the American Psychological Association.

However, much as psychology could add considerable depth to the study of Paganism, it should be used with care, and with an adequate knowledge of the area of psychology upon which a study is drawn. If a researcher strays too far from the academic discipline with which they are most familiar, and starts to apply theories from other areas of which they have a fleeting or superficial knowledge, they are in danger of making superficial or inaccurate assumptions. If those assumptions are shored up by neutral descriptive material and theory from their more familiar area of expertise, it becomes difficult for people reading their work to assess its validity, unless the reader has a good knowledge of all the disciplines that the writer is drawing upon.

This is exactly what happened in the case of Tanya Luhrmann, whose 1989 book *Persuasions of the Witch's Craft* has been widely criticized by other scholars of Paganism (Orion 1995, Pike 1996, Harvey 1999, Greenwood 2000, Pearson 2002). Luhrmann was trained in anthropology and undertook an anthropological study of esoteric groups in London for her Ph.D. This was very much an ethnography, detailing her personal spiritual journey alongside the magical rituals she attended. However, she called her work a "psychological anthropology" and tried to draw upon cognitive psychology, philosophy, cognitive dissonance theory, psychoanalysis, and psychotherapy (Luhrmann 1989, 13–15). Each of these areas is huge in its own right within the field of psychology and most psychologists specialize in one area alone; however, Luhrmann went on to use her very limited knowledge of psychology to form the basis of her theory of "interpretive drift," for which she claimed the basis was "cognitive science."

The resulting thesis presents a rich ethnography, replete with original anthropological material, but with a weak conclusion that has been refuted by practitioners and academics alike. Luhrmann's work does not adhere to the anthropological norm that an ethnography should be recognizable to the believers it claims to represent. A recognizable ethnography is not one that bows to believer pressure, or one in which the ethnographer has to be sympathetic to the believer, but it should be a clear portrait of the group studied. "Interpretive drift" neatly sums up not Witchcraft, not cognitive nor anthropological theory, but Tanya Lurhmann's own interpretation of her own journey into the esoteric community in London.

The academic critique of Luhrmann's work includes criticism that it was reductionist, and that although her methodology toward the occult was atheistic, she never once questioned the orthodoxy of her own belief. Harvey describes her theory of interpretive drift as being "less about the experience of magicians or Pagans and more about assertions of academic 'objectivity'" (Harvey 1999, 239). Ewing discussed anthropological atheism and used Luhrmann as an example of its failings, pointing out that Luhrmann did not question her own rationality and produced a theory "embedded within the atheistic hegemonic discourse in which anthropology participates," and that she insulted the people she worked with: "her denial is to make her claims of respect for the people she worked with sound somewhat hollow" (Ewing 1994, 573).

Tanya Luhrmann has been ruthlessly criticized for her thesis; but she should be given credit as a pioneer in her field, and some leeway as a post-graduate who was restricted in her research by having to maintain her status as an agnostic outsider, and as a young academic attempting to use an interesting integrative approach. Her failure to provide the clear cognitive model that she was striving for is proof that the integration of psychology into so-cioanthropological research must be undertaken with care, and with the help of a supervisor or colleagues who are sufficiently well-versed in the discipline to help to make sense of the data. Also, while Luhrmann's study of the London occult fraternity in the early 1980s does not successfully create a psychological model that explains belief in magic, it does provide a detailed ethnography. This faithfully records what she observed during her fieldwork, giving some leeway for the reader to draw their own conclusions about the underlying dynamics of the esoteric milieu of which she became a part.

When considering psychology and its application to the study of Paganism it is a useful and salutary exercise to contrast Luhrmann's careful anthropology with Faber's critique of modern Pagan Witchcraft (Faber 1993). Faber is a Freudian analyst who used Freudian theory to analyze Witchcraft. He concluded that it is a regressive, escapist, narcissistic fantasy that exhibits oedipal tendencies and represents the unfulfilled infantile urge to return to the womb of the mother. Of course Freud saw religion as an illusion, an infantile regressive desire that would be overcome by rationale and reason (Freud 1961); thus the Freudian view of religion is fundamentally a negative one, so it is not surprising that a Freudian should draw these conclusions. Nevertheless Faber's analysis implies a certain extra weak-mindedness in adherents of Witchcraft. It is interesting to contrast his purely theoretical essay with the work of Lilliston and Shepherd (1999), who performed a review of empirical work on New Religious Movements (NRMs) and found that contrary to the popular image of members being mentally weak, or brainwashed, there was little evidence of poor mental health in adherents of NRMs. They found members of NRMs to have better stress-defence and coping methods than the general populace and suggest that strong social support combined with use of techniques such as chanting, prayer, meditation, and positive imagery were important buffers in terms of mental health.

Freudian analysis is a very particular dish, even among psychologists, and the other giant of psychodynamics, Jung, is far more often invoked when considering the psychology of religion. One author who has very successfully used Jungian psychology to examine Pagan religion is Vivianne

Crowley. A Wiccan High Priestess of long standing, she is also a chartered psychologist, lecturer in psychology of religion, and transpersonal therapist. She has published a plethora of books on Paganism and Wicca, of which the consistently selling *Wicca: The Old Religion in the New Age* (1989) describes and analyzes Wicca in the light of Jungian psychology.

Her work on Wicca and Paganism is scholarly but not formally academic, being aimed at practitioners rather than academic peer review, and containing some prose and poetry; however, in one volume she explains far more about Wiccan practice and belief than many series of books by other authors, even when those books contain vast tracts of Wiccan ritual. Such has been the success of this particular book that it has become an unofficial textbook for many new members of the Wiccan community.

In preceding paragraphs I have outlined many areas where the study of Paganism could fruitfully draw on psychological theory and practice. However, the current research paradigm remains the most appropriate and useful one for contemporary Pagan research. It is broad enough to encompass any area of expertise a researcher might wish to include in their work, be it psychological, historical, neurological, philosophical, and so on, while the socioanthropological emphasis continues to locate Paganism within the contemporary spiritual and sociological landscape. My own academic work to date illustrates these points. I have conducted similar studies using both a pure form of experimental methodology and a socioanthropological research paradigm, and found the latter to be more appropriate, more informative, and richer in the data and information it supplied. That is, my undergraduate experimental design in a psychology B.Sc. was a study of conversion to Wicca. Published as Harrington 2000, this illustrates the limits of such an approach. I continued with this topic in my Ph.D. research, using a predominantly sociological research model. Work in progress was published as Harrington 2002, and it demonstrates that a more ethnographic approach can yield a far richer picture of the religious group that has participated in the study.

So, given the complexities of drawing upon this fascinating field, how may we best take advantage of psychology when studying the Pagan religion? What would be the most salient characteristic of the discipline that might be applied safely and productively to Pagan research? Psychological principles could be usefully integrated into the study of Paganism forthwith if researchers designing studies take into account the basic psychological premise that anybody, including a researcher, is the sum of their personal experience. Everybody is born with individual differences, guided by their own unconscious, formed by developmental patterns, subject to social and group forces, and at the mercy of their own cognitive-behavioral schemata. Individual differences occur in the context of an individual researcher's personal history, relationships they maintain, the social world they inhabit, the ideologies and institutions they adhere to, and the economic forces they contend with.

It is noteworthy that the recognizable methodologies employed in studies of Paganism so far are distinctly less divergent than the conclusions that have been drawn. While it is clear that each study has offered its own unique insight into Pagan belief and practice, I would argue that this illustrates how the methodology chosen for any study is not as crucial to its outcome as the cognitions and belief systems held by the researcher.

If we are to develop the study of Paganism it would perhaps be of value to became more reflexive in our work. Rather than trying to eradicate the personality of the researcher, and to pretend that they do not have bias or personal interests, by adopting a pseudoscientific approach in a nonscientific field, we could instead aim for further reflexivity. When creating or reviewing theories it might be preferable to have some insight into what has attracted the researcher to undertake the study and to choose particular theories as a foundation for their own research. It may be desirable for a researcher to question why they found those theories and that piece of research attractive, and how they and their own belief systems influence the data collection and analysis.

The search for objectivity in socioanthropological work has led to the notion that fieldwork should be undertaken by an outsider, who becomes involved with a community as a participant observer, then writes a detailed description of that community complete with an analysis informed by academic theory. This itself has led to a biased research model. A good proportion of studies of Paganism have been undertaken by younger researchers who get involved with various esoteric groups during the course of their Ph.D. They are more likely than parents, or more established academics, to be able to afford the time and the lack of remuneration involved in such studies. On a personal level the nature of such postgraduate work is attractive since it means that on leaving university they can spend time on a quest for meaning, knowledge, and spiritual satisfaction, and simultaneously achieve further academic qualifications.

Postgraduate researchers on a personal spiritual quest seeking entry to an esoteric group that they would like to be part of are least likely to be critical of that group. When designing fieldwork they are less likely to ask questions that an older person would ask. Thus we see that the study published in 1999 by tenured professor Helen Berger was the first one in the field to look at the place of children, and a second generation, in modern Pagan Witchcraft.

The nonnative outsider research model also leads to a certain naïveté in the literature produced by participant observation. Since these studies are done by people who are beginners in the esoteric world, they are informed by perceptions that reflect the limited length of time they have been involved, and their limited understanding of what they have been involved in.

An alternative to consider would be that more, rather than less, work should be done by "native researchers," particularly those who have been involved for longer periods of time. Not only would they not encounter the distrust generated by a "newbie," but they would not have to justify themselves if they are already a well-known member of the community. If they are known to the respondents they will be able to conduct interviews on sensitive or very personal areas of people's experiences with respondents who are relaxed, and in their "ecological" setting. Long-term "native researchers" are well versed in the Pagan religion, and bring to their work the depth that a theologian or priest might being to a Ph.D. on Christianity, as opposed to a recent convert conducting the same study.

The reflexive approach does not have to be a sort of "I" diary, far from it; it simply could be used to obtain a clearer picture of how a piece of research might be driven, and to allow pointers as to where its uncharted strengths and weaknesses may lie. If we apply a reflexive approach to this chapter then it is worth considering that the position of "native researcher" is the position from which my own research is undertaken. This information gives the reader an instant picture of why I see the role of the native researcher as a valid one, and where my research may have strengths or weaknesses that could be critically addressed. One can also see where my first degree in psychology has influenced my analysis of data drawn from fieldwork in my Ph.D., which was predominantly a socioanthropological study.

I was a member of the Wiccan community for thirteen years before I began to write up my thesis, which examines conversion to Wicca, with particular reference to male converts. I found that it was very enjoyable to research a subject population who shared my own beliefs, and that it was easy to generate original and interesting material when my respondents felt a deep-seated trust of me and my motives. However, I took care to use my background in psychology to try to make my fieldwork as unbiased, objective, and replicable as possible, while drawing upon my knowledge of

Wiccan theory and practice to try to ask questions, and use concepts, that had not been asked or used before. I found that my conclusions where diametrically opposed to Tanya Luhrmann's, and that far from accepting magic via a form of "interpretive drift," Wiccans sought a religion that fitted with their preexisting religious beliefs, of which magic was but a part. I called the model that evolved during the research the Schematic Integration Model, based upon stage theory and cognitive-behavioral schema theory (Harrington 2003).

Schemas (or schemata) are cognitive structures first developed in childhood to organize the constant stream of information that children are receiving. They are idiosyncratic for each individual and "provide the instructions to guide the focus, direction, and qualities of daily life and special contingencies" (Beck et al. 1990, 4). The contents of cognitive schemas are core beliefs that represent a person's understanding of their world, themselves, and others. These influence how information is processed and reactions to that information. Young notes that schemas can be "extremely stable and enduring themes that develop during childhood and are elaborated upon throughout an individual's lifetime" (Young 1990, 9).

The Schematic Integration Model for conversion to Wicca proposes a series of stages of development of schemas that are linked to a person's individual stages of mental and psychic development in conjunction with cultural, psychological, social, and developmental factors. Initiation into Wicca brings a sense of homecoming when the long-held mental templates (schemas) are finally fulfilled by a religious match of best fit. As such it is extremely powerful on an emotional level, since it confirms and validates the religious querant's own belief system, and thereby validates the initiate him- or herself.

This model offers an explanation for the feelings of recognition and coming home that are so often spoken of by people who seek out Pagan religions in general, and Wicca in particular. It could equally be applied to conversion processes for any religion, with an individual model emerging for each religion depending on what early schemas were laid down for converts, and what psychosocial variables influenced their schemas through the development of their belief and ethics systems. I am interested to see if my model will stand the test of time.

In summary, if the current research paradigm is widened to include more academic disciplines, it is likely that the tiny school that is "Pagan studies" will grow and develop. If scholars in other areas find the work that is produced pertaining to Paganism to be understandable in the light of, or even applicable to, their own work, then this field might emerge from the small and rather specialized academic milieu in which it is currently located.

The wide-ranging field of psychology has much that it can offer researchers in terms of theory, methodology, and a wealth of previous literature. Social psychology is one area that could very easily be integrated into the study of Paganism. However, psychology is a complex discipline in its own right, and care needs to be taken when attempting to integrate it directly into any socioanthropological study. Where psychology could immediately be drawn from would be in beginning to work with concepts of unconscious drives, motivations, emotions, personality, and individual differences, to try to achieve a more reflexive approach in contemporary fieldwork, rather than attempting to adhere to a false sense of scientific objectivity. If psychodynamic forces within a researcher's own psyche are acknowledged, and possible influences upon that researcher declared from the start of a study, then it is possible that a much richer understanding could be developed about the interactions with, and conclusions drawn from, any researched community.

References

Allport, G. W., and J. M. Ross
  1967 Personal Religious Orientation and Prejudice. *Journal of Personality and Social Psychology* 5: 432–33.

Altemeyer, B.
  1988 *Enemies of Freedom; Understanding Right Wing Authoritarianism.* San Francisco: Jossey-Bass.

Arweck, E.
  2002 The Insider/Outsider Problem in the Study of New Religious Movements. In *Theorizing Faith; The Insider/Outsider Problem in the Study of Ritual,* edited by E. Arweck and M. D. Stringer. Birmingham, UK: University of Birmingham Press.

Arweck, E., and M. D. Stringer, eds.
  2002 *Theorizing Faith; The Insider/Outsider Problem in the Study of Ritual.* Birmingham, UK: University of Birmingham Press.

Batson, C. D.
  1976 Latent Aspects of "From Jerusalem to Jericho." In *The Research Experience,* edited by M. P. Golden. Itasca, Ill.: F. E. Peacock.

Batson, C. D., and W. L. Ventis
1982 *The Religious Experience: A Social-Psychological Perspective*. New York: Oxford University Press.

Bear, D, and P. Fedio
1977 Quantitative Analysis of Interictal Behaviour in Temporal Lobe Epilepsy. *Archives of Neurology* 34: 454–67.

Beck, A. T., A. Freeman, and Associates
1990 *Cognitive Therapy of Personality Disorder*. New York: International Universities Press.

Berger, H.
1999 *A Community of Witches, Contemporary Neo-Paganism and Witchcraft in the United States*. Columbia: University of South Carolina Press.

Brown, L. B.
1987 *The Psychology of Religious Belief*. London: Academic Press.

Clark, E. T.
1929 *The Psychology of Religious Awakening*. New York: Macmillan.

Crowley, V.
1989 *Wicca, The Old Religion in the New Age*. London: Aquarian. Reprinted in 1996 as *Wicca, The Old Religion in the New Millennium*. London: Thorsons.

Ewing, K. P.
1994 Dreams from a Saint: Anthropological Atheism and the Temptation to Believe. *American Anthropologist* 96(3): 571–83.

Faber, M. D.
1993 *Modern Witchcraft and Psychoanalysis*. London: Associated University Presses.

Freud, S.
[1927] 1961 The Future of an Illusion. In *Standard Edition*, 21: 1–56.

Greenwood, S.
2000 *Magic, Witchcraft and the Otherworld: An Anthropology*. Oxford: Berg.

Greuhn, W.
1930 Forschungsmethoden und Ergebinisse der extakten empirischen Religionspychologie seit 1921. In *Der seelische Aufbau des religiosen Erlebens*, by K. Girgensohn, 2nd ed., 703–898.

Harrington, M.
2000 Conversion to Wicca? *DISKUS* http: //www.uni.marburg.de/ religionswissenschaft/journal/diskus/harrington.html.

Harrington, M. J.
2002 The Long Journey Home: A Study of the Conversion Profiles of 35 Wiccan Men. *REVER* http://www.pucsp.br/rever/rv2_2002/t-harring.html.

———.
2003 *A Study of Conversion Processes in Wicca, with Specific Reference to Male Converts.* Ph.D. thesis. Kings College, London University.

Harvey, G.
1999 Coming Home and Coming out Pagan (but not Converting). In *Religious Conversion, Contemporary Practices and Controversies*, edited by C. Lamb and M. D. Bryant. London: Cassell.

James, W.
[1902] 1960 *The Varieties of Religious Experience: A Study in Human Nature.* London: Collins.

Journal for the Scientific Study of Religion
Society for the Scientific Study of Religion.

Lilliston, L., and G. Shepherd
1999 New Religious Movements and Mental Health. In *New Religious Movements: Challenge and Response*, edited by B. R. Wilson and J. Cresswell. London: Routledge.

Lofland, J., and N. Skonovd
1981 Conversion Motifs. *Journal for the Scientific Study of Religion* 20(4): 373–85.

Lowenthal, K. M.
1995 *Mental Health and Religion.* London: Chapman Hall.

Luhrmann, T. M.
1989 *Persuasions of the Witches Craft: Ritual Magic in Contemporary England.* Oxford: Blackwell.

Marty, M. E., and R. S. Appleby, eds.
1995 *Fundamentalisms Comprehended.* Chicago: Chicago University Press.

Maslow, A. H.
1970 *Motivation and Personality.* London: Harper and Row.

Orion, L.
1995 *Never Again the Burning Times: Paganism Revisited.* Prospect Heights, Ill.: Waveland Press.

Pearson, J. E.
2002 "Going Native in Reverse"; The Insider as Researcher in British Wicca. In *Theorizing Faith; The Insider/Outsider Problem in the Study of Ritual*, edited by

E. Arwech and M. D. Stringer. Birmingham, UK: University of Birmingham Press.

Persinger, M. A.
1983 Religious and Mystical Experiences as Artefacts of Temporal Lobes Function: A General Hypothesis. *Perception and Motor Skills* 57: 1255–62.

Persinger, M. A., and K. Makarec
1987 *Neuropysychological Bases of God Beliefs.* New York: Praeger.

Pike, S. M.
1996 Rationalizing the Margins: A Review of Legitimation and Ethnographic Practice in the Scholarly Research on Neo-Paganism. In *Magical Religion and Modern Witchcraft,* edited by J. R. Lewis. New York: State University of New York Press.

Wulff, D. M.
1991 *Psychology of Religion, Classic and Contemporary views.* New York: Wiley.

Young, J. E.
1990 *Schema-Focused Cognitive Therapy for Personality Disorders: A Schema-Focused Approach.* Sarasota, Fla.: Professional Resource Exchange.

CHAPTER FIVE

DRUGS, BOOKS, AND WITCHES
Chas S. Clifton

Ⴈ

In his book *Alternative Altars: Unconventional and Eastern Spirituality in America*, the historian of religion Robert S. Ellwood Jr. uses the term *excursus religion* to describe the practices of those who turn away from the dominant religious ideologies of an era. He included among the recurrent markers of American excursus religion "such symbols as meditation, monism, feminine spiritual meditation, and orientation towards a distant and exotic culture," at least three (and in some cases all four) of which apply to contemporary American Pagan traditions. For the individual, Ellwood observed,

> If emergent religions are the alternative to which those who turn away from established religion of the temple have recourse, their journeys are individual excursions. If the emergent religious tradition has certain unifying themes, and a hidden history which shows continuities among its many manifestations past and present, for each voyager the journey is unique and solitary because it enacts a personal subjective quest. However much both goal and pilgrim path may pre-exist or conform to well-trodden patterns, the experience ordinarily comes to a person conditioned by normative cultural religion as an excursus away from the familiar and toward that which draws just because it is strange, yet in its very strangeness seems to offer a promise of new kinds of self discovery.[1]

Ellwood's book was published in 1979, and I encountered it as a graduate student in religious studies in the mid-1980s. The term *excursus* resonated with me, because it could easily define a constellation of my own interests. An essay, too, is a sort of *excursus*, a moving outward to try out some idea, and in this essay I want to show how that idea connects for me two areas of scholarship as well as a religious path, from which I must in turn move out. First, I had entered on the Pagan path in the early 1970s as a solitary pilgrim, not even knowing for certain if there were others like me. Second, as a budding academic, my interest lay not in the established religious traditions with their textual accretions, but in the new religious movements and the ways in which they manipulated symbols, histories, and rhetoric to establish themselves as legitimate—a process further complicated in Wicca's case by its practitioners' ambivalence toward the word "witchcraft," which in turn would produce various strategies (such as the promulgation of alternative etymologies) to simultaneously tame its connotations and exploit its ancient glamour. And third, I had come of age during the Psychedelic Era of the 1960s and 1970s. While too young to have sat at the feet of Timothy Leary, the apostle of LSD (let alone his more urbane forerunners such as Aldous Huxley or Richard Schultes), I had grown up in the shadow of Leary's own exhortation to *excursus*: "Turn on, tune in, drop out." By age twenty I was well familiar with the "turn on" part, having sampled most of the "psychedelics" available. Whether I was "tuned in" or not is debatable, but I had "dropped out" at intervals, even living briefly in a religious commune.[2] More importantly, my psychedelic experiences had contributed to my rejection of the "religion of the temple," although that process had begun well before the first tablet of LSD crossed my tongue. It was and is possible to "drop out" while still going to work every day.

In fact, my personal "psychedelic era" had ended when my Witchcraft practice began in the mid-1970s. I was even a little astonished to learn that certain friends, such as the late Craft musician Gwydion Pendderwen, had never drawn the same line of separation but had cheerfully continued, at times, to carry out magical ritual under the influence of what I later came to call "entheogens." In fact, as the national Pagan festival scene blossomed around 1980, not long before his death, he traveled to several and led what he called "the Faerie shaman" ritual, an ingestion of LSD (which he sold) combined with invocations and meditations to establish the participants' mindset before they went their individual ways. Nevertheless, my earlier experience with entheogens would have two lasting effects. In a practical sense, when I returned to the hands-on examination of some of the plants associated with traditional witchcraft, I had those experiences to draw on, rather than being a completely uninstructed neophyte. Secondly, my earlier experiences, particularly with LSD, had done much to break down such distinctions as "sacred" and "secular," "nature" and "culture." I could never go meekly into "the temple" again.

Then, after about a decade in the Craft, I made the decision to switch professions from journalism to academia, and the new perspectives and intellectual habits gained from that experience would in turn both set me at odds with some of my coreligionists (as happens so often in other faiths as well!) and place me in another liminal position, on the border between the world of scholarship and the world of witchcraft. Finally, I would learn that my interest in exploring the connections between entheogens, shamanism, and witchcraft also would not be universally welcomed by other Pagans, particularly some of those involved in interfaith councils and others having a vested interest in presenting outsiders with a conventional and nonthreatening version of our religion.

My initial separation of the two realms of the Craft and Psychedelia (a position that I have since abandoned) and Gwydion Pendderwen's integration of them might exemplify two attitudes toward the interplay of magical religion and entheogens. The first is the position often found in the works of such writers as Aldous Huxley and Huston Smith, who argued that certain kinds of mystical experience, with or without the aid of entheogens, were phenomenologically identical. Given a person's description of his or her mystical experience, an outsider could not tell the difference. Smith, in fact, put that assertion to the test (as did the psychologist Lawrence LeShan. During a period of the 1960s when Smith was teaching at the Massachusetts Institute of Technology (where Huxley was briefly a visiting professor, Smith "took accounts of classical mystical experiences and intermingled them with descriptions that [Timothy] Leary's subjects [in LSD and psilocybin experiments at Harvard] provided and asked knowledgeable judges to separate them into their original piles. They were unable to do so."[3] But the corollary of that identity was summed up by Smith in the phrase, "altered traits, not altered states," which he borrowed from psychologist Robert Ornstein; in other words, there was much more to a person's life than peak experiences. "Experience comes and go, whereas it is life's sustained quality that counts."[4]

In his book *Cleansing the Doors of Perception*, which collects his writings on entheogens from the 1960s through 2000, Smith adopted the term "entheogens" where before he had used "psychedelic drugs." The term "entheogen" was birthed by a group of researchers including Jonathan Ott, R. Gordon Wasson, and Carl A. P. Ruck. Ott commented,

As we know from personal experience that shamanic inebriants do not provoke "hallucinations" or "psychosis," and feel it incongruous to refer to traditional shamanic use of *psychedelic* plants (that word, pejorative for

many, referring invariably to sixties' western drug use), we coined this
new term in 1979. . . . The term is not meant to specify a pharmacolog-
ical class of drugs . . . rather, it designates drugs which provoke ecstasy
and have traditionally been used as shamanic or religious inebriants, as
well as their active principles and artificial congeners.[5]

In other words, the term "entheogen" is a definition based on context
rather than on chemistry.

This first attitude toward entheogens, then, is that they are a foretaste
of paradise, an opening of the door of mysticism, which must, however, be
kept open by other forms of spiritual practice. In *The Doors of Perception*,
which summarized his thinking in the early 1950s, Huxley reflects,

> I am not so foolish as to equate what happens under the influence of
> mescalin or of any other drug, prepared or in the future preparable, with
> the realization of the end and ultimate purpose of human life: Enlight-
> enment, the Beatific Vision. All I am suggesting is that the mescalin ex-
> perience is what Catholic theologians call "a gratuitous grace," not
> necessary to salvation but potentially helpful and to be accepted thank-
> fully, if made available. To be shaken out of the ruts of ordinary percep-
> tion, to be shown for a few timeless hours the outer and the inner world,
> not as they appear to an animal obsessed with survival or to a human be-
> ing obsessed with words and notions, but as they are apprehended, di-
> rectly and unconditionally, by Mind at Large—this is an experience of
> inestimable value to everyone and especially to the intellectual.[6]

Thus the title of Huxley's book, from *The Marriage of Heaven and Hell* by
William Blake: "If the doors of perception were cleansed every thing
would appear to man as it is, infinite."

Huston Smith and many of my colleagues in religious studies would
probably be comfortable with this approach to entheogens, the "gratuitous
grace" approach. It enables them to categorize the entheogenic experience.
Having encountered *The Doors of Perception* as an undergraduate, it was
the way that I too rationalized my use of entheogens in my early twenties
and whatever aspirations toward enlightenment that I entertained. The
drugs were just showers of the way, reminders of larger realities, but not
ends in themselves. They were instruments, not allies.

*The clouds on the western horizon hint at rain, but in this dry spring, when
the phrase "100-year drought" keeps popping up in the newspapers, I walk
through the pines to where I have planted two species of datura and one of*

henbane. The witch's garden, blooming at night and attracting hawk moths seemingly out of nowhere.

Carlos Castaneda has been treated as a guru and as a hoaxer: did his books accurately recount his experiences, were they fictionalized versions, or were they concocted in his university library? But *The Teachings of Don Juan* and his other works gave us the term "ally" for plants such as *Amanita muscaria*, the *Daturas*, and many others. "Ally" is a useful word. Its connotations of friendship and relationship match another approach to entheogenic plants: they are allies in a mysterious journey of exploration. We could also call this the gnostic approach: it is not for everyone, it is socially rebellious, even antinomian; and, once experienced, it marks a person forever.

I think there is a difference between a plant and a pill in this regard, for it is difficult to think of a pill as an "ally" in quite the same way. "Mother's little helper" was the last generation's slang for the "minor tranquilizers" so frequently prescribed for unhappy women. Someone manufactures a pill and hands it to you, and it really does not matter whether the process took place in a clandestine laboratory or a major drug firm's pharmaceutical factory where thousands of identical capsules rumble down chutes past white-coated inspectors. Compare that to the traditional, if sometimes overelaborated, rituals of gathering plants according to their season, the phase of the Moon, and various seasonal holy days. "It is preferable to employ these plants fresh, having been ritually gathered according to the Tabu of their genii," as one occultist puts it.[7]

Contemporary Witches and other Pagans, however, are hopelessly divided on the issue of entheogens. For all their self-definition as an excursus religion, much of their discussion simply rehashes the rhetorical clichés of the so-called War on Drugs versus those of cognitive liberty. Missing from the discussion is the very sense of inspiration by ancient Paganisms and by "nature" that are so often invoked at other times. In many cases, the anti-entheogen response is based on fear, an argument that goes like this: "Society says that witches are bad. Society says that drugs are bad. It is tough enough to call ourselves 'witches' and to try to reclaim that word without being labeled 'drug-users' as well." Other contemporary Pagans strike the rhetorical position of school crossing guards. For instance, after the late Evan John Jones published an article on the ritual use of nightshade wine in the British Craft magazine *The Cauldron*, reader P. Hampton reacted, "Should material of this type be put out to the public, or rather should it remain safely within the secret, initiated circle of the

Craft? . . . I would be very interested to know what possessed Mr Jones to break cover and go public on this matter."[8]

One also encounters the argument of "Who needs a crutch to meet the gods?" which is, if nothing else, historically inaccurate.[9] From the cannabis seeds in Neolithic burial mounds to the opium poppies depicted with the goddess Demeter and the *Datura* flowers shown in some Egyptian sacred art, to the strong possibility that the Eleusinian mysteries involved an entheogenic substance, to the debates over whether the *soma* of the Vedas was *Amanita muscaria* or *Peganum harmala*, entheogens have been intertwined with pre-Christian Indo-European religions for millennia. And that is to speak only of the Old World—we should also consider the enormous part played by entheogens in much New World tribal religion, shamanism, and newer movements such as the Native American Church, Santo Daime, UDV, and the like.

In the 1990s I began a project of seeking out people who were still making use of the traditional "witch's garden," which from a botanical standpoint means a heavy reliance on the *Solanaceae*: the daturas, mandrake, henbane, belladonna, and their relatives, plus other traditional Eurasian entheogens such as Syrian rue (*Peganum harmala*) and *Amanita* mushrooms. (From the viewpoint of America's drug wars, none of these are currently illegal.) As the German ethnobotanist Christian Rätsch points out, *Cannabis* could also be included in this group, based on archaeological and folk traditions. *Cannabis*, of course, is one of the group whose users, depending on locality, face legal penalties, which is ironic in that, unlike henbane, for example, it cannot produce a fatal overdose. Rätsch describes how he himself progressed from treating *Cannabis* as an exotic recreational drug to realizing that its use in Germany (not to mention ancient Greece and Rome) had ancient precedents: "To me it was a revelation to understand that this plant belongs to my ancestors and belongs to my cultural roots, and therefore I have to worship it and to use it and to continue the tradition of the place." He continues:

> If you look at the [previous] literature on ancient Greece, you never find any hint of the use of psychoactive plants by these people. The nineteenth-century humanistic perception of Classical antiquity really pictures the ancient Greeks like very noble men who were certainly not "into drugs," but it's not true. The Greeks had a whole pharmacopoeia of psychoactive materials. You can find a lot of reference in all the Classical textbooks. For example in Pliny you find statements of twenty to thirty psychoactive plants. . . . The literature is full of that, but it has never been fully received. The same is true of Greek authors such as Dioscorides.[10]

As a practitioner and researcher, I must of course realize that there is an element of advocacy in my writing and teaching. By presenting and then publishing a paper on, for example, the use of Solanaceous plants by contemporary Pagans,[11] I am in effect saying to my coreligionists, "Here is a part of your tradition which too many of you are neglecting, because you are swayed by the official propaganda of the War on (Some) Drugs. Think like a true witch, shaman, polytheist, rebel, and you might find some value in these plant allies." Furthermore, as practitioner and researcher, I must maintain my authorial credibility, if only for myself, by learning something firsthand about these sacred plants—conducting "bioassays," as the contributors to *The Entheogen Review* are fond of saying. If my local environment permits, I should grow them and learn all of the plants' life cycles. And that word "bioassay" reminds me that "essay" and "assay" are etymologically twins. Both are attempts to test an idea or a perception, journeys of the mind and psyche, not recapitulations of received doctrine or someone's "party line."

To write on entheogens, then, is consonant with one of my longtime concerns, that those of us who say we practice an "earth religion" or "nature religion" truly walk the walk as well as talk the talk. As an academic, I have long pondered how new religious movements articulate themselves and "position" themselves in the advertiser's sense (I will confess to having been briefly a copywriter in an ad agency), while my second major concern is the constantly fluid relationship between "culture" and "nature" in the American psyche, a relationship exploited by the use of the term "nature religion" by American Pagans.

In addition, seeing entheogens as "allies" produces a more shamanic view of the universe, one of interpenetrating realities and multiple powers. In his book *Psychedelic Shamanism*, Jim DeKorne, the first editor of *The Entheogen Review*, suggests that the entheogenic experience wakes up people so that they can no longer approach Deity as "passive and obedient" children.[12] DeKorne seems torn between suggesting that entheogens serve as catalysts for "entities" in our own unconscious and a self-consciously gnostic interpretation in which there are indeed Powers—Archons—in the universe that only wish to exploit humankind. Comparing the speech of the famous Mazatec Indian shaman María Sabina, entheogen writer Terence McKenna, and some of the Nag Hammadi gnostic gospels, DeKorne notes,

The consistently overblown language broadcast through these [human] channels suggests the existence of incorporeal forces infesting human awareness which are primarily concerned with impressing us with their importance. . . . The gnostic Archons, then, are intelligences existing in the imaginal realm in "bodies" consisting of thought and feeling. . . . They feed off of our allocation of energy to their dimension and compete with other Archons on other levels in the overall hierarchy for their nourishment.[13]

While this resonates with much of the Classical Gnostic literature, De-Korne and I do not share the Gnostics' methods. He does not seek to purify himself and bypass the archonic checkpoints on his way to The Light. Rather, his method is shamanic: "It is also the essence of shamanism to acquire helpers (allies, teachers) who instruct one how to manipulate the artifacts of non-ordinary reality. In traditional cultures these entities are often seen as the resident spirits of the hallucinogenic plants."[14]

Studying new religious movements, being a witch, and advocating the use of entheogenic plant "allies" together comprise a set of minority positions. The last, in fact, is a minority position even within contemporary Paganism, as I described in my 2001 paper on the use of the Solanaceae in today's witchcraft. Within the discipline of religious studies, new religious movements remain problematic, unsteeped as they are in tradition and as short as they usually are on ancient scriptures with reams of commentary. As a discipline, religious studies is the stepdaughter of theology and still most comfortable with textual studies. Thus all three positions are each an *excursus*, a going out, a reconnaissance, a scout trip.

Members of minority religious communities are open to the criticism made by Sam Gill of the University of Colorado in the *Journal of the American Academy of Religion* that we privilege our own status as participants, insisting in an essentialist way that only we are uniquely qualified to conduct, in our case, Pagan studies. "[W]hat has thrived [too often in the academic study of religion] is the *religious study of religion*, that is studies in which the scholar is studying his or her own religion . . . primarily for the purpose or purposes stipulated by the religion studied rather than the purpose or purposes stipulated by the academy."[15] To do so, Gill strongly hints, is a recipe for being marginalized. There is some truth to Professor Gill's remarks: I have seen members of minority communities at times show two faces among their colleagues in religious studies, one reserved and laconic—and another more lively when in the safer spaces and communties of "their people." Gill's essay describes the entire field of "the academic study of religion" as underdeveloped because too many of its members are pursuing instead "the religious study of religion." Within that larger category, "Pagan studies" is but an infant; the term itself was only introduced in the second half of the 1990s when a group of Pagan scholars—and scholars of Paganism—began meeting on their own during the American Academy of Religion's annual meeting. (I believe that the first British academic conferences on Pagan studies were held at about the same time.) Much of our energy has gone into "discourse about the shape and nature of [our] field," to quote Gill again—a necessary developmental step—but the remainder of his sentence should caution us: "[I]t is a sure sign of the tenuousness and irrelevance of the field when this talk about the field becomes the principal topic of discussion, the main product of the field."

From the "insiders'" perspective the relationship between scholarship and cotemporary, revived Paganism has been close but contentious. Thinkers whom the contemporary academy regards as exhibits in the museum of ideas, such as the anthropologists Frazer and Bachofen, or Margaret Murray as historian of witchcraft, still loom large in contemporary Pagan writing, despite the critiques of academic Pagans. For example, the scanty bibliography of a rather vapid new work entitled *Philosophy of Wicca* lists Frazer's *Golden Bough*, Robert Graves' *White Goddess*, and of course Margaret Murray, but not Ronald Hutton, Carlo Ginzberg, or any other deeply rooted contemporary historian.[16] This author is not unique, unfortunately, and it is easy to conclude that an attitude of "don't confuse me with new ideas" is at work.

As a Pagan scholar, I feel this tension acutely, for I have also written for a popular market, including editorship of the four-volume *Witchcraft Today* series published in the early 1990s by Llewellyn Publications, the largest publisher of Pagan books in the United States. Earlier, I had edited a short-lived journal called *Iron Mountain: A Journal of Magical Religion* from 1986 to 1988, which was in turn absorbed by a larger publication, *Gnosis: A Journal of Western Inner Traditions*. With the Llewellyn work, I knew that the audience was not particular about historical underpinnings, wishing at most to know that underpinnings existed. I forbade use of such phrases as "legend has it . . . " and "it is said that . . .," insisting that contributors provide some reasonable documentation of what, for instance, the "ancient Celts" did; but I could not in that venue examine such tricky questions as just who was a "Celt" and whether they themselves proclaimed any sort of "Celtic" identity. *Gnosis*, while not the journal of a learned society, had higher standards of documentation to begin with, although contributors were expected to write for that other useful fiction, the interested but general reader. In all cases, I wanted to show that one could write for people for whom new Pagan traditions were vital without sacrificing academic rigor in favor of copying older books and writing voluminous how-to-be-a-witch passages that were ungrounded in personal experience.

Pagans outside academia do tend to regard those of us inside it as being in the proverbial ivory tower; yet, ironically, lately I have begun to find the writing of Pagan academics more provocative, more "edgy," and more grounded in experience than much of what is produced by Llewellyn, ECW Press, and the other publishers catering to the Pagan market. These tend to produce countless blandly assured self-help manuals that, increasingly, appear to reflect a desire for religious respectability while surrendering those aspects of Paganism—Witchcraft in particular—that might raise eyebrows at the interfaith council luncheon.

Excursus might well define my roles as scholar and practitioner in the world of "drugs, books, and witches." Scholars such as Huston Smith and Robert Fuller have made theoretical arguments for the roles of entheogens in religion: as Fuller writes, they are part of a "quest for greater subjective richness, a more intense mode of experiencing life."[17] That quest is what brought me to the Craft, as it has many others. In a way, "a more intense mode of experiencing life" was also a product of returning to graduate school at age thirty-two after a decade in the marketplace: certainly a "greater subjective richness" results from the immersion in the academic study of religion. To follow a minority religious path is an excursus; to leave the certainties of that (Pagan) world for academia is another. To enter the world of entheogenic plants is, of course, a going out; and to enter the new academic field of Pagan studies is still another excursus from the temple. The result of all these excursuses is a new web of connections. At a recent Pagan festival in my home state of Colorado, I presented a lecture and discussion on the issue of "flying ointments" in the witch-trial period, illustrated with sample plants from the witch's garden. (A fascinating monograph remains to be written on this aspect of the trials in light of more recent historical studies of the period.[18]) The audience was engaged, interested, and in some cases quite knowledgeable. At the end, I had no trouble finding homes for my tray of henbane and datura seedlings.

Notes

1. Robert S. Ellwood Jr., *Alternative Altars: Unconventional and Eastern Spirituality in America* (Chicago: University of Chicago Press, 1979), 20–21.

2. This communal household in Loveland, Colorado, was actually the project of a group of Baha'is, a religion that does not normally practice communal living. But communes were part of the cultural landscape that year, 1969. See Timothy Miller, *The 60s Communes: Hippies and Beyond* (Syracuse, N.Y.: Syracuse University Press, 1999).

3. Huston Smith, *Cleansing the Doors of Perception: The Religious Significance of Entheogenic Plants and Chemicals* (New York: Tarcher/Putnam, 2000), 152.

4. Smith, *Cleansing the Doors of Perception,* 153.

5. Jonathan Ott, *Pharmacotheon: Entheogenic Drugs, Their Plant Sources and History,* 2nd ed. (Kennewick, Wash.: Natural Products, 1996), 15.

6. Aldous Huxley, *The Doors of Perception* (New York: Harper and Row, 1954, 1970), 73.

7. Daniel A. Schulke, "The Garden of Oneiros," *The Cauldron* 102 (November 2001): 32. The noted research chemist Alexander Shulgin, discoverer of dozens of psychoactive compounds, however, vociferously disagreed with this "vitalist" approach. See his autobiographical work *Pihkal* (Berkeley, Calif.: Transform Press, 1991).

8. P. Hampton, letter to the editor, *The Cauldron* 109 (August 2003): 39.

9. Daniel Webster Christiansen, "Who Needs a Crutch to Meet the Gods?" *PanGaia* 22 (Winter 1999–2000): 31–32.

10. Christian Rätsch, "Sacred Plants of Ancient Europe," lecture presented at the conference Entheobotany (San Francisco, October 18–20, 1996).

11. Chas S. Clifton, "If Witches No Longer Fly," *The Pomegranate* 16 (May 2001): 17–23.

12. Jim DeKorne, *Psychedelic Shamanism: The Cultivation, Preparation, and Shamanic Use of Psychotropic Plants* (Port Townsend, Wash.: Loompanics Unlimited, 1994), 47.

13. DeKorne, *Psychedelic Shamanism,* 47–48.

14. DeKorne, *Psychedelic Shamanism,* 58.

15. Sam Gill, "The Academic Study of Religion," *Journal of the American Academy of Religion* 62 (1994): 964–75. Emphasis added.

16. Amber Laine Fisher, *Philosophy of Wicca* (Toronto: ECW Press, 2002).

17. Robert C. Fuller, *Stairways to Heaven: Drugs in American Religious History* (Boulder, Colo.: Westview, 2000), 190.

18. The anthropologist Michael Harner presents some interesting speculation in his edited book *Hallucinogens and Shamanism* (London: Oxford University Press, 1973), but they need to be revisited in the light of subsequent historical study.

References

Christiansen, Daniel Webster
    1999–2000 Who Needs a Crutch to Meet the Gods? *PanGaia* 22 (Winter): 31–32.

Clifton, Chas S.
    2001 If Witches No Longer Fly. *The Pomegranate* 16 (May): 17–23.

DeKorne, Jim
1994 *Psychedelic Shamanism: The Cultivation, Preparation, and Shamanic Use of Psychotropic Plants.* Port Townsend, Wash.: Loompanics Unlimited.

Ellwood, Robert S. Jr.
1979 *Alternative Altars: Unconventional and Eastern Spirituality in America.* Chicago: University of Chicago Press.

Fisher, Amber Laine
2002 *Philosophy of Wicca.* Toronto: ECW Press.

Fuller, Robert C.
2000 *Stairways to Heaven: Drugs in American Religious History.* Boulder, Colo.: Westview.

Gill, Sam
1994 The Academic Study of Religion. *Journal of the American Academy of Religion* 62: 964–75.

Hampton, P.
2003 Letter to the Editor. *The Cauldron* 109 (August): 39.

Harner, Michael
1973 *Hallucinogens and Shamanism.* London: Oxford University Press.

Huxley, Aldous
[1954] 1970 *The Doors of Perception.* New York: Harper and Row.

Miller, Timothy
1999 *The 60s Communes: Hippies and Beyond.* Syracuse, N.Y.: Syracuse University Press.

Ott, Johnathan
1996 *Pharmacotheon: Entheogenic Drugs, Their Plant Sources and History.* 2nd ed. Kennewick, Wash.: Natural Products, 1996.

Rätsch, Christian
1996 Sacred Plants of Ancient Europe. Lecture presented at the conference Entheobotany (San Francisco, October 18–20).

Schulke, Daniel A.
2001 The Garden of Oneiros. *The Cauldron* 102 (November): 32.

Shulgin, Alexander.
1991 *Pihkal.* Berkeley, Calif.: Transform Press.

Smith, Huston
2000 *Cleansing the Doors of Perception: The Religious Significance of Entheogenic Plants and Chemicals.* New York: Tarcher/Putnam.

CHAPTER SIX

GLEANINGS FROM THE FIELD: LEFTOVER TALES OF GRIEF AND DESIRE
Sarah M. Pike

A gnes Varda's film "The Gleaners," which she calls a "wandering-road-documentary," tells the story of people who gather up the leftovers from fields that have been harvested and urban super-market trash. It is a film "woven from various strands," including the emotions she felt "when confronted with precariousness."[1] The most powerful experiences and the ones that most affected my understanding of neo-Paganism were the leftovers after my book manuscript was done (*Earthly Bodies, Magical Selves*, 2001).[2] Once my field notes and drafts had been harvested for the academic fruit they could yield—first a dissertation and later a book—what remained were not just the leftovers of a harvest but the very soil that nourished what I had produced, the life-changing experience of fieldwork. The fieldwork experiences that were most profound and affected my life in deep and subtle ways remained in my field notes and early drafts of my dissertation. Yet they haunted the text, shaping the ways I recalled certain rituals and described particular events and people, coloring my understandings of the autobiographical narratives I collected. The text I wrote for publication only brushed the surface of how I experienced festivals through body and movement, grief and desire. In her introductory essay for *The Vulnerable Observer: Anthropology that Breaks Your Heart* (1996), Ruth Behar advocates writing about one's own vulnerability in the research process. She urges ethnographers to take seriously, then push beyond, anthropologist Clifford Geertz's observations about the effects of immersing oneself in another culture. According to Geertz, "You don't exactly penetrate another culture, as the masculinist image would have it. You put yourself in its way and it bodies forth and enmeshes you."[3] This enmeshment is what I want to talk about, and especially how I became enmeshed in neo-Paganism through three aspects of human experience: sacred space, eroticism, and grief. It was through participant observation that I learned about the importance of sacred space, how it shapes and is shaped by our emotions and our bodies.

Every summer I make a pilgrimage with my children from northern California to southern Indiana and other places east of the Mississippi to visit friends and family. As part of my annual journey I usually return to the woods of "Lothlorien," a neo-Pagan nature sanctuary where I once attended several festivals a year, spent hours listening to the stories of people's lives shared around campfires, danced myself into a trance to late night drumming, helped construct ritual spaces, cleared trails, and left offerings for the dead at shrines nestled in the woods. Whenever I return to Lothlorien I think of how place penetrates a person—its sounds and smells, the play of light through certain trees at different times of year, the joyful noises of children splashing in a limestone waterfall, and the unmistakable smell of sage smoke clouding the air at the beginning of ritual. In my book on neo-Pagan festivals, I described how my body felt different every time I drove through the gates of Lothlorien, got out of my car, and heard the drums, as if it knew that we had entered a different kind of place. Right away, I moved differently and felt differently, and I came to see that for many others, especially for the drummers and dancers who did their ritual work all through the night, the shift of movement into a different register was a central part of their experience. Local neo-Pagans told me that Lothlorien was enchanted, and over the years I came to experience it that way, and every time I step foot upon the land I recall drums beating through the night, the smell of rain in the lush green trees, and the faces of people who became important to me there. In the circles created in those woods—Heartwood, Thunder Shrine, Ancestors Shrine, Avalon—I watched festivalgoers fall in love and marry, bless their babies, and mourn their dead. I return to the woods to revisit past history, enjoy the thick groves of trees circling ritual spaces, and reminisce about those who left the community to move on with their lives elsewhere, as well as those who have died.

Lothlorien was the site at which bodily experience, grief, and desire converged in my fieldwork and it became the touchstone for my entry into neo-Pagan culture. At a large festival I attended at Lothlorien during my first summer of festival going, I was adopted by Laughing Starheart, a gay tattoo artist who told me he worked as a window dresser for an upscale department store in Detroit. He invited me to camp next to him because of mutual friends whom I knew from the university and whom he had met at festivals. Because he was a friendly and outgoing merchant and tattoo artist selling his wares along "Merchants Row," many people stopped by to visit his camp, and thus I made many neo-Pagan friends because of Starheart. He was very supportive of my research and eager to help me make my way into the community. For all the inscrutable reasons why ethnographers connect with particular people, I connected with him.

At that first festival I learned through him something about ritual space at festivals, and especially the late night fire rituals that so many neo-Pagans described to me as being particularly transformative. As in many other instances during my research, a phenomenon I had heard about from other people was brought home to me only after I experienced it. It was late at night after all the scheduled workshops and rituals were over and people had gathered at "Thunderdome," a sandy ritual circle with a firepit in the center that was created for community rituals and late night drumming and dancing. Participants gathered at the fire carrying their djembe drums and clothed in ritual finery. Starheart dressed up for the occasion in rainbow-colored pants and a long black velvet cloak to keep out the cold. We danced around the fire for a long time, breathing in the sage someone had put on the fiery logs and thrilling to the drums. Starheart was an agile and expressive dancer, casting off his cloak and baring his chest, his colorful pants flowing around his ankles as he glided by observers along the edge of the fire. He was the kind of outgoing and creative person who was always performing or on display. After a while I noticed that he was no longer among the few of us still dancing around the fire, so I stepped out of the dance and looked for him along the shadowy outskirts of the ritual space. When I found him, he was once again enveloped in his velvet cloak and he was weeping. I reached out for his hand and asked him what was wrong, but he could not speak. The fire, the drums, and the dance had released in him a deep and unspeakable grief. I held him and stroked his head. We were soaked with sweat, his mascara was running, and my skin was smeared with ash from the fire. There was something primal and unbounded about being in that space as we were—physically spent and full of emotion. Even though I scarcely knew Starheart then, I wept with him for all of my own unnamed sadness. We stayed there by the fire for quite a while, in a ritual space that I knew was special to him. I realized when we bonded in Thunder Shrine, in a way strangers often bond in neo-Pagan rituals, that these rituals stir up deep feelings and that this is part of their purpose and one of the reasons for their efficacy.

I suspected then that the community and its members would pull at my heart, that the journey I had embarked on was not to be one of research kept at a safe distance, that fieldwork would draw me in, that these people would become my friends, and that I would leave the field marked for life. But that night I also chose an engaged role as participant observer. I could have found one of Starheart's other friends to care for him, or I could have gone to sleep early like other festivalgoers who wanted to avoid the heavy eroticism and raw emotions of the late night fire. At the time, I was not aware of making a choice, but I had given myself over to the experience and a new model for my research emerged that night. In my years of research, people like Starheart and their lives became inextricably associated with place in my memory and these associations shaped my understanding of neo-Paganism.

The stories that people told me at festivals became very much connected to the places in which they were told, the rocks we sat on, the trees we sat under, the ritual space around us, the shrine in the woods next to us. I came to love this place because it was both itself and the expression of a community with all its problems and infighting, power struggles, romance and divorce, death and birth. Because the places of Lothlorien and the people in the community came alive for me, I began to understand them in the context of sacred space. Lothlorien was special because it had done its work on me, transformed me over those years of research and life when I was writing about neo-Pagan festivals. Whenever I left the busy festival field to walk in the woods and sit and write field notes, as I did at least once every day during my festival research, the woods had their way with me; they shaped my feelings and thus my words and interpretations. Whether we "make" places powerful or they have some intrinsic value no longer seems to me to be the pressing question. Did I experience Lothlorien as powerful because of the emotions people invested in it with their shrines, altars, statues, stone circles, flowers, and herbs? Was power something intrinsic to the land? Or was it sacred because of the powerful emotions I experienced and the friendships that were cemented there? Sacred space became real to me as I lived in it over time and as I returned to it year after year, just as the many neo-Pagans who described to me their attachment to festival sites return to Lothlorien and to other places they love—Circle Sanctuary in Wisconsin, Harbin Hot Springs in northern California, Brushwood Folklore Center in western New York, Wisteria Nature Sanctuary in southeastern Ohio, and many other such places. I began to understand how some places become special and powerful in themselves, as well as to the people who move through them and make them home, even if only for a long weekend.

My training in the discipline of religious studies gave me little guidance in understanding my responses to place and the role of emotions and the body in research. I read the work of feminist theologians Sallie

McFague and Rosemary Ruether, who discuss the body of God and how embodiment might shape one's understanding of deity, but no one talked about what I was experiencing: the researcher's vulnerability, intimate friendships with my "sources" that developed over the years, how my consciousness changed through dance and movement, the ways in which ritual experience moved me and marked my being, and how grief and desire were prompted by some rituals and not others.

Thanks to the guidance of anthropologist Michael Jackson's graduate classes and to conversations about fieldwork with my graduate student colleagues, especially Africanist John McCall, whose book *Dancing Histories: Heuristic Ethnography with the Ohafia Igbo* (2000) calls for "an open exchange of ideas between the researcher and the people studied . . . because practical knowledges are often embodied in and realized through lived experience rather than formalized discourse,"[4] I found other ways to understand what was happening to me. The postmodern turn in anthropology in the past twenty years, or what George Marcus and Michael Fisher in 1986 dubbed the "experimental moment," has resulted in attention to how the anthropologist is shaped by his or her experience in the field and how he or she in turn shapes the written "results" of research that are disseminated into the academy and beyond. What George Marcus calls the "crises of representation" in his introduction to *Critical Anthropology Now: Unexpected Contexts, Shifting Contingencies, Changing Agendas* (1999) necessitated a number of changes in ethnographic methods, including an awareness of the ethnographer's complex and multifaceted position and the need to "shift personal positions in relation to one's subjects and other active discourses in the field that overlap with one's own."[5] Michael Jackson's work on intersubjective understanding (*Minima Ethnographica: Intersubjectivity and the Anthropological Project*, 1998), radical empiricism (*Paths Toward a Clearing: Radical Empiricism and Ethnographic Inquiry*, 1989), and phenomenological anthropology (*Things As They Are: New Directions in Phenomenological Anthropology*, 1996) and his questions to me about my field work—in what ways did I connect with the lives and experiences of my informants? what was my bodily experience of ritual like?—made me rethink the approach of objectivity and distance that religious studies, in its defensive move away from research driven by faith commitments, asked me to take. According to Jackson, "ethnographic fieldwork brings us into direct dialogue with others, affording us opportunities to explore knowledge not as something that grasps inherent and hidden truths but as an intersubjective process of sharing experience, comparing notes, exchanging ideas, and finding common ground."[6] This sounded nothing like the objective observer

I thought I was supposed to be; it sounded ambiguous and a little scary. For Jackson, the search for common ground belies the inscrutability of other cultures. Like ethnographers, other people around the world give birth, feel joy, grieve, desire, and die. The problem lies in our attempt to stand apart as researchers from the people we study and write about, and the assumption that knowledge either lies within "us" or "them" rather than in the interstices of our relationships. Because this is the case, Jackson believes that, "the task for anthropology is to recover the sense in which experience is situated within relationships and between persons."[7] I have taken this to mean that anyone involved with fieldwork should be aware of the ways in which knowledge arises intersubjectively, how emotions and bodily experience in the field do not occur in a vacuum but always in relation to others and should become sources of research data in much the same way as ritual observations and informants' narratives.

To focus on intersubjectivity is to try to make the relationship between researcher and informants one of equals. In *Writing Women's Worlds: Bedouin Stories* (1993), Lila Abu-Lughod quotes Edward Said's critique of the ways in which otherness and difference acquired "talismanic qualities" in anthropological writing, a practice she tries to avoid in her ethnography on Bedouin women. She takes the challenges of Said and others to heart:

> Whether its goal is to engage in cultural self-critique or to assert enlightened tolerance through relativism, anthropology needs others that are different from the self. Yet a difference between self and other will always be hierarchical because the self is sensed as primary, self-formed, active, and complex, if not positive. At the very least the self is always the interpreter and the other the interpreted. Anyone interested in working against this hierarchizing must seek ways to undermine the essentialized notion of "cultures" different from ours and people separate from us.[8]

As I shared a love of wooded spaces with neo-Pagans, ate meals with them, discussed books and mythology, and made close friends at festivals just as they did, I came to see their lives as very much like my own. But my task, like Abu-Lughod's, was further complicated by the fact that neo-Paganism, like Islam, is often misrepresented and demonized by outsiders. My informants worried about religious persecution in custody disputes and at their jobs, while I did not. I did not share their position at the religious margins of American society, yet our vulnerability was similar because my project researching them was also seen as marginal by some of the professors in my department. With all this in mind I approached my fieldwork with some trepidation.

As I began the process of researching my local neo-Pagan community I simply "put myself in its way," as Geertz suggested. I went to gatherings and gave myself over to the process of becoming part of the community. In this process, intersubjective knowledge emerged through my physical and emotional experiences (as in the fire circle with Starheart) as much as through observation and interviews. I had questions in mind, and began with some formal interviews, but it very quickly became clear to me that I would learn the most about neo-Pagan lifeworlds by becoming "enmeshed" in them, or to invoke Ruth Behar's term again, becoming "vulnerable" to them. The first time I put myself in the way of neo-Pagan culture occurred when one of the other graduate students in an anthropology class came up to me after the first class during which we had introduced ourselves. He told me that his wife Rose was a neo-Pagan priestess and invited me to meet her. Shortly thereafter I traveled to their house and for the first time met a woman who embodied the notion of priestess that I had been reading about in Starhawk's *Dreaming the Dark: A Rebirth of the Religion of the Great Goddess* (1979) and Margot Adler's *Drawing Down the Moon: Witches, Druids, Goddess-Worshippers, and Other Pagans in America Today* (1979).[9] Rose was pregnant at the time, and her swollen belly was wrapped in a gown of African fabric and a scarf was wound around her wispy reddish blonde hair. She told me that she had been initiated into the Faerie (or "Feri") tradition, a form of witchcraft that is based on the visions of its founder, Victor Anderson (1917–2001). It is a tradition that has influenced many other branches of neo-Paganism, especially through the writings, rituals and activist work of Starhawk, who was trained by Anderson.

That my introduction to neo-Pagan ritual at the hands of a Fairie priestess was highly erotic and emotionally charged is no surprise given the religion's origins in Anderson's own erotic initiation. In *Drawing Down the Moon*, her groundbreaking study of neo-Paganism, journalist Margot Adler wrote of her encounter with Victor Anderson that "his was the only story I heard that was clearly from the land of faery." Anderson told Adler that when he was around nine he met an old woman who told him that he was a Witch. As a child he had become almost completely blind, but nevertheless he witnessed a ritual involving a god and goddess. He came across the old woman sitting in the middle of a circle in the woods and he took off his clothes and experienced a "sexual initiation." Then he recalled that "We seemed to be floating in space. . . . I heard a voice, a very distant voice saying 'Tana, Tana.' It became louder and louder. It was a very female voice but it was as powerful as thunder and as hard as a diamond and yet very soft. Then it came on very loud. It said 'I am Tana.' Then, suddenly, I could see there was a great sky overhead like a tropical sky, full of stars, glittering brilliant stars, and I could see perfectly in this vision, despite my blindness. The moon was there, but it was green." He saw that they were on the edge of a jungle and that out of the jungle a male figure was approaching them: "A beautiful man. There was something effeminate about him, and yet very powerful. His phallus was quite erect. He had horns and a blue flame came out of his head. He came walking toward me, and so did she. I realized without being told that this was the mighty Horned God. But he was not her lord and master or any-thing like that, but her lover and consort. She contained within herself all the principles and potencies of nature." Soon after the appearance of the god and goddess, the darkness vanished and Anderson was back in the cir-cle with the old woman, who showed him how to use herbs in ritual and bathed him. Then he put his clothes on, went back to his house and slept.

The first neo-Pagan ritual I ever participated in was designed by Rose for my thirtieth birthday. I was nervous as I drove to her home because I was simultaneously drawn to and intimidated by her. She had a charis-matic presence that I was not used to, that was quite different from the in-tellectual power and charisma possessed by my favorite teachers at the university. Later I came to see this kind of power as an embodiment of di-vinity, the living and breathing presence of what neo-Pagans call the God-dess, a way of being that Rose had perfected through many hours of ritual work and self-examination.

On the evening of my birthday, I arrived at her door where she wel-comed me and led me inside. The lights were low and the room smelled of scented candles and incense. She told me that before the ritual we should bathe and she then drew a steaming bath of herbs and lavender oil. We undressed and slowly lowered ourselves into the tub. I felt as though I had left my other self outside the door of her home and had entered an enchanted and unknown world. She bathed me with the care and nurtur-ing of a mother, but touched me with the slow intensity of a lover. She led me into a temple that was draped in African fabric and lined with mirrors, where she explained that the tall candle at the back of her altar was for the Star Goddess (a Faerie version of the Great Goddess) and that two other candles represented the God and Goddess. Dried flowers and herbs were scattered around them, as were several crystals of different sizes, a belt of bells, and a chalice engraved with a design. On one end of the room a dark cloth was draped over a mirror and next to the mirror Rose's black cloak was hanging. She asked me to sit on the floor in front of the center altar where she lit the candles and then cast a circle by dancing and singing around the room. She called to many goddesses, some of whom I had never heard of, and requested the presence of the elements air, earth, fire, and water, singing the verses of invocation for each one in her melodious voice. As she went through this process, I knew I was watching a woman manifest what the books I had read about contemporary Paganism described as "goddess energy." Her body and voice expanded to fill the room. She went to the altar and lit the incense and candles for the deities. Holding up one of the candles with both hands, she recited the names of many goddesses. After repeating the litany of names several times she put down the goddess candle and lit the God candle, reciting his many names several times as well. She anointed me with oil and I anointed her in turn, from head to chest and from belly to the base of the spine. We applied the oil to each other's bodies with slow and deliberately gentle strokes. At each point, meant to correspond to the Hindu notion of chakras, we described what qualities we saw in the other. She suggested that I imagine a looking glass between us that we could move through to become one with the other. I imagined that we were one being—initiate, priestess, goddess—that the bounds of our bodies had disappeared. When we moved over to the large mirror, the distinction between self and other returned and she asked me to look into the mirror, right through myself, and to choose a magical name, which I did. That evening I learned that neo-Pagan ritual is emotional, sensual, erotic, and embodied in deep and subtle ways I would never have understood by simply observing and asking questions.

Rose's ritual gave me a completely new understanding of how a priestess or priest can engage participants and what it means to belong to a religion in which sexuality is sacred and the erotic is a power to be tapped into and used to explore the self and make changes in the world. The erotic energy of Rose's ritual allowed me to be open and vulnerable and thus able to look at myself differently in the mirror, to see parts of myself that I had never before noticed. I had become immersed in a neo-Pagan world that was unlike any religion I had previously encountered. Many rituals since then have brought me back to the scent of the bath, the lavender oil with which Rose anointed me, the grace of her movements around her altar, and the presence of something divine in the room with us. Rose and I did not make love that night, but the ritual was in every other way a seduction, an opening between self and other, between worshipper and goddess, between researcher and informant. I had learned firsthand that the sensual and aesthetic aspects of neo-Pagan ritual are key components in their ability to provide participants with powerful experiences. When I wrote about my encounter with Rose in my field notes, I described in detail the appearance of her temple and the events that occurred, as well as my own physical and emotional responses to the ritual. I was impressed repeatedly over the years of my research by the ways that ritual space and ritualists have texture; there are layers of meaning in their altars, their velvet cloaks, scented skin, and shadowy, candlelit rooms. I tried to create a densely layered description that would come as close as possible to what I experienced at the time. My understanding of neo-Pagan ritual that began late at night in a sweet-smelling bedroom transformed into a divine temple by Rose acquired more layers during the two years I participated in a weekly ritual group in another candlelit temple. Ritual meaning and experience became denser and more complicated for me through dozens of festival rituals facilitated by other priests and priestesses from different traditions—layers of lives and stories of close observation that come from living and working together. What was it about my ritual experiences that led me to a deeper understanding of theirs? I witnessed a woman become transformed in the role of priest or priestess and discovered how that transformation affected me as a participant.

My intersubjective understandings of neo-Paganism came about in different ways: in friendships that spanned the years, by collapsing the space between myself and others in ritual, through the emotionally charged field of festivals, and in the presence of priests and priestesses embodying spiritual power. New meanings of neo-Pagan religious life emerged for me through the embodied practices of festival and ritual. During the many hours I spent dancing next to others around sacred fires and maypoles I was perhaps most aware of how self dissolves into other like the blurring of boundaries between lovers and lifelong friends, or the process of a priestess drawing down the goddess into her body. As my fieldwork progressed, I made note of the parallels as well as the divergences between neo-Pagan experiences and my own. I discovered, for instance, that the movement between priestess and goddess was somewhat like the movement between my two personas of participant and observer. At one moment I was a ritual participant dancing ecstatically around a bonfire, and at another, a scholar escaping deep in the woods away from everyone else, writing in her notebook. Understanding and meaning came about in the movement between phases, between selves, intersubjective meanings that can never be completely captured in words, meanings that flit like a dancer's shadow, moving with the drumming but never the same as it, or like the priestess who is goddess, but also remains herself.

Like other self-reflexive ethnographers shaped by the lessons of ethnographic critique over the past twenty years, I believe that it is important to look at how my own identity was situated in relationship to the people I researched and wrote about. I am not the kind of person who, like Rose and many of the other neo-Pagans I have met during my research, has visions, out-of-body experiences, or hears the voices of gods. I was raised a liberal Episcopalian and my Anglican-style rationalism led me to proclaim myself an atheist at the age of twelve. But I never stopped being curious about other people's strange and powerful experiences, even if I did not share their experiences before the night of my birthday ritual with Rose. I had never been completely immersed in a ritual, certainly not in the churches of my childhood and not even later during college when I visited Pentecostal and Black Baptist services that were much more full of spirit and movement than the Episcopal services I attended as a child. For many years religion had been for me an intellectual engagement with ideas, not with God, and certainly not with Goddess, sacred space, or eroticism. My ideas of religion had to do with the social consciousness of my liberal church leaders and my parents, and were influenced by the small communities that gathered at our house once in a while for "house church," an experiment by my parents' church in creating alternative religious spaces. Social action and community-building activity seemed reasonable to me, but not particularly attractive, and I did not participate in any full sense. I certainly had no glimmer of what Paganism might be and did not conceive of the natural world (embodied for me now by Lothlorien) as being part of "religion" or the presence of bodies together in sacred space as being an important aspect of ritual.

Why are researchers attracted to particular topics? Why did a not particularly religious child end up in a religious studies graduate program researching contemporary Witches and Druids? I entered the field like a sojourner stepping into a world both strange and familiar, as if I had "crossed the tracks" to find a neighborhood that had always been off limits, but was right next door to where I had always lived. Although my religious upbringing did not incline me either positively toward neo-Pagan rituals, as some former Catholics report, or negatively, like former conservative Protestants, I shared a similar childhood background with many of the people I studied. A convergence of interests and events led me along my path of study. For instance, my recently acquired feminist consciousness made me curious about how Goddess-based religions might differ from the religious traditions I was most familiar with. But mostly I wanted to see how people who were very much like me (and some who were not at all) in their love of the fantasy fiction of J. R. R. Tolkien, C. S. Lewis, and Lloyd Alexander, had taken such a different religious path, had chosen to re-create a world of magic and lore in their religious lives. Exploring the worlds of neo-Pagans was often a rediscovery of childhood for me, at the same time that it was a journey into something new.

Like most of the neo-Pagans I spoke to and shared rituals with, I used my involvement with this community to work on my own issues, such as problems with relationships and work. My grandfather died the spring before my first full summer of fieldwork, my marriage was falling apart, and I had to meet the needs of two young children who were caught in the middle of it all. I had a tenuous foothold in a fledgling doctoral program that had rejected me once for a project that some thought was a questionable use of my time and theirs. It was a vulnerable period of my life, and for this reason, it was also a time that allowed me to connect with the lives of the many I met who were troubled or working through problems in their personal lives. I was not an established scholar or an expert of any kind. I was a struggling graduate student, mother, and wife trying to find a place in the world. Like them, I was a seeker, but I was seeking an intellectual identity while they were seeking a spiritual one. Even the successful and well-known priests and priestesses I met were vulnerable people trying to live up to their ideals, experimenting with alternative lifestyles, open marriages, gay marriages, celibacy, intensely demanding spiritual paths, life-threatening illness, and wounds from the past.

Because of my ambiguous role as participant observer and my critical stance toward narrative, I was self-conscious about the writing process. I kept two separate notebooks during my fieldwork years: a personal journal as well as a field notebook. I tried to follow the suggestions of my thesis adviser, Robert Orsi, who cautioned me to take an ironic view, to stay slightly off balance and on edge, to be aware of how my own therapeutic process and friendships with my informants shaped my interpretations. Still, my notes kept transgressing the boundaries I tried to draw. I experimented with making myself a character in my field notes, a technique I found to be useful in keeping an ironic stance toward my own experiences, while at the same time being able to learn from them. And so I walked an uncomfortable line between my roles, at moments slipping into the community and forgetting my professional self, and at other times becoming aware of my outsiderness, my research agenda, stepping aside to analyze what was happening to myself and others. But neo-Pagans undergo a similar kind of self-reflexive process, analyzing the effects of a particular ritual and describing their spiritual struggles and personal journeys through Jungian archetypes or mythological categories.

When I described neo-Pagans' stories about their experiences in narrative form, I was constructing stories using the same narrative frames I ascribed to others. Both of us generalized through the lens of our own experience. They universalized childhood visions and gifts, their discovery of neo-Paganism, the feeling of invoking deities and going into trance, the symbolic meaning of ritual tools, just as I generalized from my experiences about what neo-Pagans felt about sacred spaces or erotic dancing. One neo-Pagan use of narrative became clear to me during my birthday ritual with Rose, who asked me to tell stories about what I saw in the mirror, to put into words what I was feeling, to make vivid with words what at first seemed vague images. I learned that neo-Pagan rituals are not just about experience, but also about making meaning of experience through narrative, that the data from my senses, the feeling of dancing to the drums for hours, moving through a birth canal of hands, weaving a web of community, serving patrons at a medieval feast, volunteering in a community kitchen first thing in the morning or in a first aid station in the middle of the night, clearing brush from ritual sites, tending communal fires, entertaining children, all fit into a story about my personal and spiritual progress through the neo-Pagan world. The life-transforming stories I recorded in reference to other people were also reflected in my own transformation through fieldwork. Just as they were initiated on their spiritual paths, so was I on an intellectual journey towards my identity as a scholar. Like the people I wrote about, I too made meaning by telling stories. They shared their stories in postritual discussions and festival workshops, published them in neo-Pagan newsletters, or shared them by e-mail. My ethnography, like their writing, attempted to put the ineffable into words, as we both struggled to find meaningful metaphors to describe bodily and emotional experiences.

When I was working on the conclusion to my dissertation, I had in mind a tragic story I had heard during one of my summer visits to Lothlorien. It was a story that in some ways undermined the hopefulness that many participants feel about festivals and their sense of festivals as utopian spaces apart from the rest of society, but I wanted to include it. However, I did not want to eclipse the sense of wonder and enchantment, the visual beauty, the life-changing ritual experiences, and the pleasure of festivals. Perhaps my more critical readings of festival experience came out of the need to distance myself from that world and from the changes the festivals wrought in me. Finishing up the project meant coming to terms with my involvement with festival communities and my relationships with the many neo-Pagans I became close to during my fieldwork. I wanted to leave open the possibility for neo-Pagan self-transformation, but I also want to identify the limits of making and re-making the self. There were two stories in my dissertation's conclusion. The first explored the ambiguity of fire-dancing, which I saw as at one and the same time an erotic display and an expression of self-empowerment. The second story and the note on which I ended the dissertation, according to one of my dissertation readers, went over like a "ton of bricks," and so I edited it out of the book I later wrote based on my dissertation (*Earthly Bodies, Magical Selves*). But that story came back to me whenever I opened the book, breaking the silence I had imposed, and so I revisit it now as a way of showing that the gleanings of fieldwork offer other stories, other truths, that are often left out of published accounts of fieldwork.

I returned to Lothlorien in the summer of 1997 after moving away to take a job in California. I had not been to a Lothlorien festival for two years and had lost touch with many of my festival friends. When I entered the gate to Lothlorien, I stopped at one of the permanent residences, where two Lothlorien landowners and ELF elders, Tindome and Arafel, were living. They invited me into the nearly completed solar home that they had been working on for several years. Arafel then led me on a tour through the new ELF "long hall," a large two-story building for indoor meetings and festival workshops. I recalled funds being raised for its construction many years before, and in it lay the labor of many people, the mistakes of well-intentioned amateurs engaged in a communal effort, long years of fund-raising and lots of recycled colored glass bottles.

As we were walking down the main road through Lothlorien, a road I had been down many times when festivals were in full swing, I asked Arafel about the most recent ELFest. She said it was a sad year because there had been several unexpected deaths in the community. Arafel also told me that Laughing Starheart, who had been my closest festival companion and informant—at Starwood, ELF festivals, and Pagan Spirit Gathering—had been "kicked out" of ELFest this year. She explained that Starheart, after many years of being HIV positive, had developed full-blown AIDS, that dementia had set in, and that he was completely unable to take care of himself at the festival. Most regular festival participants had known about his condition, even though his youthful beauty belied the presence of the disease. He had also claimed for the past couple of years that the many spiritual healing techniques he had tried were working, and that he was disease-free. He had even quit his mundane job to work full time at festivals and crafts fairs selling the shirts he designed and giving tattoos.[10] Starheart was the most organized and best-prepared festival camper I had encountered during my years of festivalgoing. He seemed to have endless quantities of food to share, teddy bears to give out to children, costumes for every occasion, and a gift for gathering groups of people together for chanting sessions or small rituals. He lived in the festival world more fully than most festivalgoers, which was why I sought out his company and why he appears so frequently in the pages of my book. It was easy to believe that the disease could not harm such a playful and delightful creature, who paraded around the festival grounds swinging his rainbow parasol, showing off the colorful tattoos on his smooth, bare chest, dancing around the fire as gracefully as any of the women, and leading chant workshops with a voice honed from years of singing in a Presbyterian church choir. I believe that these images of Starheart are true in some sense, just as I believe that he created an illusion of health and vitality for himself and for us, his festival "family," as the disease waited in his body. The self that he performed was "real," as was his sense of being healed, but the disease that exiled him from the festival world forever made painfully visible the limits of the land of "faerie."

Now when I return to the land of Lothlorien, Starheart's absence is part of my experience, as is the sensual pleasure of being there with my memories. It is as if my physical and emotional attachment to festivals and my sense of them as sacred and special has been put to rest and I have a good excuse to move on, to return to an intellectual life with fewer remaining bonds to festival communities. At times during my fieldwork, I "went native" and felt like I was truly a Pagan too, but I always returned to my intellectual roots and my desire as a scholar to tell others' stories. In some sense I was a Pagan and still am, because there is no going back to who I was before my research began; the people, places, and experiences of fieldwork have all shaped my sense of self. Still, this has been a troubled movement at times when I have felt wholly Pagan and related to others as such, but then left behind the neo-Pagan world to return to my own.

These reflections on my experiences are intended to suggest the complexity of fieldwork and the importance of paying attention to the researcher's position in the field and during the writing process. I held out the hope that I could recreate my feelings and impressions about sacred space and ritual in order to convey most fully what it was like for myself and others to be there. Just as I observed other festivalgoers create new selves or experiment with new forms of self-expression, so I came into being as a researcher during my first festival. According to Michael Jackson, "selfhood emerges and is negotiated in a field of interpersonal relations, as a mode of being in the world."[11] The ethnographer's self may also emerge this way, by undergoing an ordeal or initiatory process that transforms the self into someone else, which is what these rituals did for me. Fieldwork, as many ethnographers have noted, is itself a transformative rite of passage. The researcher who entered the field as a neophyte leaves it more or less as an initiated member of a community of ethnographers. I left festivals behind and moved on to other projects with the sorrow and loss one feels about precious times in one's past, or moving away from a place that was a beloved home to live in a different part of the country. For me this meant leaving for a time, at least, the world of neo-Pagan festivals for the world of scholarship.

Notes

1. http://www.zeitgeistfilms.com/current/gleaners/gleaners.filming.html (accessed 11/03).
2. Sarah M. Pike, *Earthly Bodies, Magical Selves: Contemporary Pagans and the Search for Community* (Berkeley: University of California Press, 2001).
3. Ruth Behar, *The Vulnerable Observer: Anthropology that Breaks Your Heart* (Boston: Beacon Press, 1996), 5.
4. John McCall, *Dancing Histories: Heuristic Ethnography with the Ohafia Igbo* (Ann Arbor: University of Michigan Press, 2000), 19.
5. George Marcus, ed., *Critical Anthropology Now: Unexpected Contexts, Shifting Contingencies, Changing Agendas* (Santa Fe, N.Mex.: SAR Press, 1999), 17.
6. Michael Jackson, ed., *Things As They Are: New Directions in Phenomenological Anthropology* (Bloomington: Indiana University Press, 1996), 8.
7. Jackson, *Things As They Are*, 26.
8. Lila Abu-Lughod, *Writing Women's Worlds: Bedouin Stories* (Berkeley: University of California Press, 1993), 13.
9. Starhawk, *The Spiral Dance: A Rebirth of the Ancient Religion of the Great Goddess* (New York: Harper and Row, 1979); Margot Adler, *Drawing Down the Moon: Witches, Druids, Goddess-Worshippers, and Other Pagans in America Today* (Boston: Beacon Press, 1979).
10. I should clarify here that Starheart always informed his tattoo clients that he was HIV positive, and from what I could see, his hygienic practices were impeccable.
11. Michael Jackson, *Minima Ethnographica: Intersubjectivity and the Anthropological Project* (Chicago: University of Chicago Press, 1998), 28.

CHAPTER SEVEN

RELIGIOUS ETHNOGRAPHY: PRACTICING THE WITCH'S CRAFT
Douglas Ezzy

This chapter begins by recounting my own discussions about spirituality with, on the one hand, a professor of sociology, and on the other, a Quaker mystic. I demonstrate that sociological and anthropological studies of spiritual experience draw on a postenlightenment rationalism that is methodologically atheist. Most ethnographers of religious experience assume that religious belief is absurd, and needs to be explained away. In contrast, I argue that spiritual experiences are both socially constructed and "real." Drawing on recent ethnographies of contemporary Witchcraft, I problematize attempts to explain away the beliefs of Witches by some ethnographers and highlight the academic pressure to privilege a secular modernist scientific worldview faced by participant ethnographers of new religious movements. These ethnographies are utilized to illustrate a more general contemporary debate about ethnographic method. Influenced by postmodernist thought and cultural studies, contemporary ethnographers have problematized traditional images of researchers as objective observers. Specifically, advocates of innovation have called on researchers to be explicit about their own subjective positioning vis-à-vis the people they are studying, to locate their research in more general political and cultural processes, and to experiment with innovative forms of presentation of findings such as poetry and stories. Drawing on the hermeneutics of Ricoeur, I argue that these innovations provide a theoretically sophisticated response to some of the challenges to ethnographic method raised by postmodernists. In particular, I demonstrate how the spiritual experiences of Witches can be understood as both real and socially constructed. I conclude with some reflections on my own ethnographic study of contemporary Witchcraft.

Prior to my honors year studying sociology at the University of Tasmania, Australia, I had been a conservative Christian for a few of my teenage years, having been brought up within an occult and spiritualist milieu by my mother. During that honors year my encounter with Professor Rodney Crook profoundly transformed my fundamentalist faith. Certainly there were other events in my life that precipitated my deconversion, but the intellectual exploits of that year were central to the process. I recall explaining to Professor Crook the need to believe in God because without the certainty He provided there was no truth, no meaning in life. Professor Crook replied with something along the lines of: "I understand your argument, but I don't reach the same conclusion." This was a profound moment for me. It put the final nail in my deconversion. It undid my modernist rationalist defence of my faith, although I did not at the time understand things quite that way. Faith, it seemed, was not rationally justifiable within the sociological worldview, if at all.

My honors research involved constructing a 3 by 3 table in which the three phases of conversion to Pentecostalism (separation, transition, integration) were mapped across the three facets of the self (beliefs, emotional attachments, and patterns of interaction) (Ezzy 1989). Incidentally, I could analyze my own deconversion as a reverse 3 by 3 table. Unbelieving is just as much socially generated as believing—but I'll come to that later.

At the same time I regularly visited my great-aunt Ruth Sansom. She was an erudite woman and leader of the Quaker community in Australia. She could recite long segments from many of the classical poets and published books of poetry and children's stories. I spent many Sunday afternoons with her. She meditated, went into trance, and entered another spiritual world, where she spoke with Jesus and her dead husband and sang with celestial choirs of angels. She was an inspiring and joyful woman.

In many ways this chapter is a product of the dialogue between these two people who will never meet in this life (Aunty Ruth passed away in 1995), but who converse constantly in my inner dialogues, my soliloquies. The argument of this chapter, simply put, is that much of the sociology of religion lacks humility. Buber (1995, 43) wrote, "He is truly humble who feels the other as himself and himself as the other." Alternatively, as Collins (2002, 93) elegantly puts it, ethnographers have too often tended to create, "in Martin Buber's terms, an I-It relationship with those in the field, when they should be actively seeking the I-Thou."

More concretely, Comte was at one stage placed on the Vatican banned list of books and sociologists have returned the compliment. The secularizing assumptions of American sociology, as represented in the editorial decisions of its main journals, was one of the reasons that *Social Analysis* (now titled *Sociology of Religion*) was published by the American Catholic Sociological Society. They wanted to maintain the legitimacy of a religious sociology that the American Sociological Association refused to accept as objective scientific study of religion (White n.d.).

The broader "grand narrative" that these specific details fit into is that of the early sociological belief that science would take over the functions of religion. In the mythology of early modern sociology it was assumed that modern societies were better societies. Studies expressed an imperialist colonial attitude toward non-European societies. Modernization, so the mythology argued, would lead to a more democratic, egalitarian, and rational society. Further, modernization would lead to secularization, because religious belief was, after all, completely irrational.

Early sociological and anthropological theories of religion stem from postenlightenment rationalism that cannot explain spiritual experience on its own terms. These theories are methodologically atheistic in their assumptions, not methodologically agnostic as they so often claim. Cunningham (1999) provides an excellent summary of the main approaches to the social scientific study of religion, including: the intellectualists such as Spencer, Tylor, and Frazer who argued that religion and magical beliefs were a product of intellectual errors of logic; the emotionalists such as Malinowski and Freud who argued that religion and magic serve emotional functions such as the alleviation of stress; structural functionalists such as Durkheim who saw the significance of religion in its social effects, such as providing moral integration to a community; the interpretative approach such as that of Weber and Geertz, who saw religion as a symbolic system that orders existence, providing an interpretative framework within which to make sense of reality.

All these approaches deny the reality of spiritual experiences. Religious beliefs are understood to be a product of incomplete knowledge and errors of logic, or a product of a "primitive mind" that does not comprehend the importance of the indirect sources and effects of religious belief in social experiences. Evans Pritchard summarizes the intent of these approaches succinctly:

> They sought, and found, in primitive religious a weapon which could, they thought, be used with deadly effect against Christianity. If primitive religion could be explained away as an intellectual aberration, as a mirage induced by emotional stress, or by its social function, it was implied that the higher religions could be discredited and disposed of in the same way. . . . *Religious belief was to these anthropologists absurd.* (quoted in Stark and Finke 2000, 8, emphasis added)

Traditional sociological and anthropological approaches to the study of religion have had a more or less explicit agenda that assumes that spiritual beliefs are ridiculous. Spiritual experiences are assumed to be *prima facie* false or delusional. This is methodological atheism, and it is this assumption that I challenge in this chapter. Methodological atheism needs to be challenged because it is not good science. The assumption does not derive from careful observation or reasoned argument. It is simply assumed.

Let me underline that I am not arguing that religious rituals and spiritual experiences are not shaped by the sorts of social processes described in existing social scientific studies of religion. I think they are shaped by these social processes and I will discuss this below. However, I do argue that it is bad social science to assume *prima facie* that spiritual experiences are not genuine or real. Stark and Finke conclude their review of these issues saying:

> It now is impossible to do credible work in the social scientific study of religion based on the assumption that religiousness is a sign of stupidity, neurosis, poverty, ignorance, or false consciousness, or represents a flight from modernity. Unfortunately, social scientists not involved in the study of religion have been very slow to get the word, and most still accept the old impieties. (2000, 18)

The next section of the chapter examines this issue through a detailed review of two academic studies of contemporary Witchcraft.

Ethnographies of Contemporary Witchcraft

Contemporary Witchcraft (or Wicca) is a modern spirituality not typically organized as a formal religious institution, although there are a number of organizational loci of the modern Witchcraft movement. There are a growing number of people who claim to be witches and a growing number of published ethnographies of Witchcraft by academic participant observers (Luhrmann 1989; York 1995; Hume 1997; Berger 1999; Hutton 1999; Griffin 2000; Greenwood 2000).

The modern witchcraft movement began in the 1950s in England, largely as a consequence of the work of Gerald Gardner. Gardner (1954) wrote *Witchcraft Today*, in which he claimed that he had been initiated into an old witch's coven. Gardner then began initiating people into his own covens and so began the modern movement of Witchcraft or Wicca. Wiccans mostly meet in small groups of around a dozen people. Their religious system revolves around the seasons of the moon and the sun. They meet on full moons, and they celebrate the solstices and equinoxes (Harvey 1997).

Although the distinction is blurred, Witchcraft can be differentiated into two main types. Popularized Witchcraft is driven primarily by consumerist marketing and is represented by movies, television shows, commercial magazines, and consumer goods like spell books and bottles of lotion. I have provided an extensive analysis of this elsewhere (Ezzy 2001, 2003a). Popularized Witchcraft bears many similarities to the casual part-time New Age participants described by Heelas (1996). In contrast traditional or coven-based Wiccans are typically similar to "fully engaged" New Age practitioners. This section of the paper focuses on this form of traditional Witchcraft. I use the term "traditional Witchcraft" to refer to the whole range of the more established forms of Witchcraft including hedgewitches, Alexandrians and Gardnerians, eclectic Witches, Starhawk and the Reclaiming collective, and the myriad of other traditions.

Wicca is a mystery religion in the sense that the aim of the rituals and practices is for practitioners to experience the otherworld. For example, drawing down the moon is an important Witchcraft ritual, although one not celebrated in all Witchcraft traditions. First the circle is cast and gods and goddesses invoked to guard the circle, and various other ritual events occur as usual in the setting up of a Witchcraft circle (see Hume 1997 for a detailed description of these types of rituals). The ritual of drawing down the moon occurs when the high priest kneels before the high priestess and invokes, or calls down, the Goddess of the Moon into the High Priestess. The High Priestess becomes the Goddess. She is not just her representative, or her container, but becomes the Goddess. The High Priestess will often recite a set of verses known as the Charge of the Goddess, sometimes as part of a trancelike experience. There is a wide variation in the reported experience of drawing down the moon (see Greenwood 2000, 96). However, as an illustration, Orion describes her experience this way:

> As I have come to understand it, the drawing down ceremony bridges the gap between form (human) and idea (divinity); it is an invitation for inspiration. The witches assume the role of Demiurge in their rituals. . . . Like artists seeking inspiration from the "muses," witches "draw down" divine inspiration from their gods, and like artists offer their bodies as vehicles of expression for these sacred influences. In other words, the witch as creator attempts to transcend the individual ego in order to express a sacred or more universal force. (Orion 1995, 35)

The exact content of the experience is less important than that it is typically understood as an "otherworldly" encounter. What is a sociologist to do with these experiences? They are often profound and life-transforming for the people involved. The argument of this chapter is that they need to be taken at face value.

The remainder of this section examines how two Ph.D. ethnographies of Witchcraft and ritual magic in England have interpreted these sorts of experiences. First, I review Tanya Luhrmann's (1989) *Persuasions of the Witch's Craft*—originally a Ph.D. completed through Christ College at Cambridge University. Second, I review Susan Greenwood's (2000) *Magic Witchcraft and the Otherworld*, originally a Ph.D. completed through Goldsmith's College at the University of London.

Luhrmann's study of Witchcraft has already been heavily criticized in the academic literature. For example, Pearson's (2002) critique of Luhrmann focuses on Luhrmann's betrayal of trust. According to Pearson, Luhrmann pretended to be an insider to Wiccans but wrote as an outsider. However, while Luhrmann's betrayal of trust is problematic, it is the methodological atheism that I find most disturbing in her work.

Luhrmann's thesis is fascinating for the questions she poses. Chapter one's title is: "What makes magic reasonable?" Earlier she says: "The goal of this book is to describe the process by which this [belief in magic] happens, and the particular experiences, linguistic transformations, analytic mutations, and intellectual strategies which seem central to the transformations" (Luhrmann 1989, 11). There is nothing particularly problematic about this. Luhrmann argues that religious belief is constructed socially, emotionally, and culturally, and she develops a theory of interpretive drift to explain this religious belief. However, what is problematic is the rider that goes with this explanation:

> The only reason I continued to think of myself as an anthropologist, rather than as a witch, was that I had a strong disincentive against asserting that rituals had an effect upon the material world. The anthropologist is meant to become involved, but not native. The very purpose of my involvement—to write an observer's text—would have been undermined by my assent to truth of magical ideas. . . . I stood to gain nothing by belief except power which I was told I could exercise unconsciously even if I made no explicit acceptance, but I stood to loose credibility and career by adherence. (Luhrmann 1989: 320–21)

Luhrmann argues that to believe would prevent her from understanding objectively. The social scientist, it seems, has to be an atheist. As indicated earlier, there is a long history of academic disciplinary boundary work that this argument derives from. However, she further argues that to believe is to lose academic credibility. She has a lot to lose, she says, if she believes. This is, of course, a sociological point. Notice the explicitly social sources of her self-understanding as a social scientist. Luhrmann rejects belief not because of her own experience or evidence, but because of the paradigms of acceptable practice among academics. The methodological atheism at the heart of Luhrmann's thesis does not derive from an attempt to sensitively understand the experiences of Witches, but from her enforced adherence, on pain of significant social sanction, to the atheistic tenets of academe.

This critique of endemic methodological atheism in academic studies of religion is not new. Stark and Finke (2000) make a similar argument with reference to studies of religion in the United States, Edith Turner (1994) has made this point in her ethnography of her encounter with a spirit in Zambia, and Jenny Blain's (2002) study of *seidr* shamanism provides an excellent example of an alternative ethnographic methodology that is not reductionist.

It is important to separate out two theoretical arguments in this critique of methodological atheism. First, I continue to argue that beliefs are socially constructed, and culturally and socially located. Along with Stark and Finke, and Turner, it is important to emphasize that an argument against methodological atheism is not an argument against the social construction of religious beliefs. I am quite happy to accept Luhrmann's argument that Witches come to accept and believe in magic through a socially generated process of interpretive drift.

Second, however, it is also often assumed that if beliefs are demonstrably socially and culturally constructed that they must be false. This is an error of logic. Feminists have been arguing for some time that gender differences are socially constructed, but that does not mean that gender differences are not real. If reality is socially constructed, and I think that it is, and spiritual experiences are also socially constructed, then they are also, surely, real. To demonstrate that the magical beliefs of Witches are a product of interpretive drift does not also demonstrate that these beliefs are false or unreasonable.

Ethnographers of religious experience systematically assume that religious beliefs are false or unreasonable as a product of an unexamined assumption of methodological atheism endemic within sociological and anthropological practice and writing. I will now turn to another contemporary study of Witchcraft that has challenged this methodological atheism.

Susan Greenwood (2000, 39) argues that in previous studies of magic, "European notions of rationality and the discourse of an often positivistic science have been used as a universal benchmark against which other cultures are judged." This is both a form of European imperialism and methodological atheism. That is to say, the interpretation of other cultures is not based on a genuine sociological practice of the inductive development of understanding but is shaped by preexisting unexamined assumptions about the nature of reality.

In contrast, Greenwood (2000, 3) accepts the claimed reality of otherworldly experiences, arguing that "Magicians' identities are formed from their relationship with the otherworld." Previous anthropological and sociological studies of magic typically ignore Witches' interactions with the otherworld. This stems from the endemic methodological atheism and a culturally narrow understanding of science that devalues magical beliefs. This has very important consequences for providing an adequate description of magical practices and beliefs: "By failing to attach sufficient importance to the otherworld, these analyses miss what pagans see as the essence of magic: otherworldly experience" (Greenwood, 2000, 3). Greenwood puts this most provocatively when she argues that:

> I suggest that magical identities are structured through a psycho-spiritual interaction with the otherworld, rather than constructed from social discourses of the ordinary world, as suggested by some recent works on identity formation in the social sciences. (2000, 118)

Let me underline the significance of this statement. This is from an academic book based on a contemporary Ph.D. thesis in Anthropology at the University of London. The statement above argues that magical identities do not have social sources. Rather, magical identities are formed through spiritual experiences! It is not through a social process of interpretive drift that Witches come to believe in magic, but through real otherworldly encounters. To translate this into a Christian context, a similar argument would be that if you become a Christian, this is not just a product of social processes, but a product of a real meeting with Jesus.

Greenwood goes on to examine how various magical rituals and encounters with the otherworld have effects on the practitioners or Witchcraft. She argues that: magical rituals provide healing, particularly psychotherapeutic healing; magical rituals lead to the acquisition of power, both this-worldly and otherworldly power; magical rituals facilitate the exploration of and experimentation with sex and sexuality; and magic influences personal morality.

The basic thesis of Greenwood's argument is compelling. Magical experiences in the otherworld have real consequences in this world. To explain away magical experiences is to misunderstand them. A similar argument could be developed out of the phenomenological tradition in sociology and anthropology. Thomas' (1928, 584) dictum, for example, states that "if people define situations as real, they are real in their consequences." Magical encounters are experienced as real and have real consequences. Notice that this way of interpreting magical experiences does not require belief by the researcher in the particular magical reality; it simply requires an acceptance by the researcher of the reality of the experience for the Witch.

However, Greenwood takes her analysis further. She argues that otherworldly experiences are also profoundly influenced by this-worldly processes. First, she examines how power is misused and abused for personal gain. Witches sometimes say that magical processes are beyond the social. In contrast, Greenwood shows how personal and social projects enter into magical rites and profoundly shape them. Second, Greenwood argues that of the three forms of Witchcraft she studied, High Magic and Wicca do not really challenge the dominant understandings of gender polarities, but simply reflect them. On the other hand, feminist Witchcraft provides a much more progressive understanding of gender roles. Third, she suggests that magic is sometimes a form of escapism and fantasy that allows people to avoid dealing with issues and problems in the everyday world. This parallels a critique made by political feminists of feminist Witches in the UK (Gallagher 2000).

In other words, her subsequent sociological analysis of magical practice complicates and nuances her first argument that magical identities are not shaped by social processes. Otherworldly encounters may certainly be real, but they are clearly also shaped by this-worldly social processes and cultural frameworks. The spiritual experiences may be real, or at least they are experienced as real in the same sort of way as any other social experience. To explain them away is to misunderstand what's going on here. However, these spiritual experiences are just as profoundly shaped by social forces as are any other social experiences. The next section turns to a more general discussion of recent debate focused around postmodernism to develop this point.

A Hermeneutics of Religious Experience

When my teenage faith in Christianity began to crumble, I would now argue that at the root of my difficulty was my desire for a modernist rational defence of belief in God. God was either really there, and this could be proven scientifically, or there was no God. I now argue that this is altogether too simplistic a view of both the social world and the otherworld. In some ways the argument about the nature of otherworldly experiences parallels the straw man argument between the postmodernist and realist ethnographies of some symbolic interactionists. Norman Denzin suggests that what puts the realist ethnographies of symbolic interactionists outside a postmodernist project is their insistence that "there is an empirical world out there that must be respected" (1992, 120). Denzin argues that symbolic interactionists need to take on the insights of postmodernism. However, Denzin's point is not that the empirical world does not exist. To "seriously question" the "ontological status" of the empirical world, as Denzin suggests, is not to deny it, but to problematize it. These are very different things. Some commentators seem to think problematizing empirical reality means denying its existence. The point is to examine the interpretative process through which empirical and subjective realities are created.

Farberman (1992, 375), an anti-postmodernist realist ethnographer, interprets Fee (1992), a pro-postmodernist, as arguing that according to postmodernism "there is no empirical world out there aside from what is created by ideologically suffused language." However, Fee's comments are more qualified, suggesting that postmodernism provides "sufficient reason to rethink many of our taken-for-granted assumptions about the empirical world *out there*" (1992, 368, original emphasis). The implication of arguing that language has nothing to do with empirical objects is quite different to that of suggesting rethinking our knowledge of empirical objects in the light of the complexity of the interpretative process.

In a similar way, methodologically atheist sociological and anthropological studies of religion appear to have argued that descriptions of spiritual experience have nothing to do with a spiritual reality. Spiritual experiences or otherworldly encounters are just the products of ideologically suffused language of one form or another. Further, in a similar way, I argue that this misunderstands the central role of language and interpretation in making spiritual experience real.

Skeptical analyses of the role of language set up a false dichotomy. Either language is transparent and reflects lived experience accurately, or it is a distorting screen that always projects experience out of its own categories. If language is viewed as unavoidably distorting understanding, and there are no criteria that can be used to judge an explanation's correctness, then all explanations of events are "equally legitimate and adequate" (Spence 1988, 68). This understanding typically rests on an argument for the underlying disorder of "reality" derived from Nietzsche. "Reality" is conceived to be indescribable and there is a radical disjunction between reality and narrative. In a similar way studies of spiritual experience have set up a false dichotomy. Either spiritual and otherworldly encounters are true and not influenced by social processes, or they are false, and simply a product of social and cultural processes. The dichotomy between real spiritual encounters and social processes is false in the same way that the dichotomy between objective uninterpreted experience and subjective interpretation is false. Whether the point is made by a positivist, interactionist, cultural theorist, sociologist of religion, or a believer, to dichotomize experience and interpretation demonstrates a misunderstanding of the hermeneutic point about the nature of reality. It is the result of a lingering positivism that attempts to deny the linguistically mediated nature of the events of lived experience (Bruner 1990, 111).

Action is always symbolically mediated, symbols acting as a quasi-text that allow conduct to be interpreted (Ricoeur 1984, 1985, 1988, 1992). Life is always already interpreted, and there is no getting out of this hermeneutic circle. Spiritual realities are not exempt from this process. Acknowledging their socially constructed nature does not make spiritual realities, or everyday realities, illusions.

Following Merleau-Ponty, Polkinghorne (1988, 26) suggests that language brings the real to human experience: "Languages may be the device that allows reality to show forth in experience. Rather than standing in the way of the experience of the real, language may be the lens whose flexibility makes reality appear in sharp focus before experience." Similarly, the social and cultural sources of this-worldly and otherworldly realities sustain these realities and facilitate our experience of them.

The otherworldly encounters described by Witches, and any other spiritual experience for that matter, need not be conceptualized as a different order of reality to other social realities. Spiritual experiences are shaped by linguistic processes and social forces, and have profound social consequences. Rather than trying to demonstrate that they are irrational, implausible, or false, ethnographic research would be better served by examining the symbolic and social processes that operate in the spiritual realm. How do people make sense and meaning of these experiences?

Positivist methodologies try to prevent or avoid the influence of subjective understandings and have tried to bracket out spiritual experience as too subjective. In so doing they seriously misunderstand the nature of spiritual experience. From this perspective the important issue is not whether Jesus, Buddha, the Goddess, or Pan really exist. Rather, it is enough to note that people believe they do exist. This belief is at the base of their struggles to tell stories truthfully about their experiences. That is to say, the focus of a hermeneutically and phenomenologically oriented ethnographic methodology is the way people tell their stories, rather than the accuracy or otherwise of the account. Neither the realities of spiritual experience, nor the integral role of social and cultural processes that shape interpretation are ignored. Rather, the focus is on the relationship between experience and interpretation, between symbolically constructed realities and their consequences.

In other words, do people really meet Jesus, or become the Goddess? I don't have any problem with saying that they do. The problem I have is with an unreconstructed understanding of truth or reality. Truth and reality are always and already socially and linguistically constructed. Both believers and atheists try to escape this hermeneutic circle in different ways. Some believers argue that spiritual experiences are uninfluenced by social processes. Alternatively, methodological atheism denies the social reality of spiritual experiences. I don't think either approach is particularly useful as a sophisticated way of understanding spirituality.

Put another way, I am not arguing that sociologists who study religion should be believers. I am simply arguing that they should be able to suspend disbelief, particularly when studying religious or spiritual experience. The problem with much of the sociology of religion, and particularly ethnographies of religious groups, is that the aim has been to explain away religious belief as either irrational or delusional. A more sophisticated approach to spiritual experiences needs to take believers' claims at face value, not presuming to be able to answer the question about whether God or the Gods or Goddess exist. The truth, or falsity, of spiritual realities is not a question ethnographers should presume to answer. Rather, ethnographers should treat spiritual encounters and realities as genuinely social experiences with social antecedents and social consequences. If reality is multiple, and I think it is, then may we have the humility to respect others' interpretations that differ from our own.

Concluding Reflections

> If it becomes respectable for anthropologists to admit to such experiences when they occur, it would become possible to speak from *within* a culture, rather than as an outsider. Ethnography could become an endeavour shared by natives and anthropologists. (Turner 1994, 86–87)

In many ways my reading of the hermeneutics of Paul Ricoeur reconverted me, though not to Christianity. Through Ricoeur I began to understand social life as both real and socially constructed, both my social life in this world and my social life in the otherworld. My own spirituality is probably better described as Pagan, though it remains unclear to me exactly of what variety. While I can argue theoretically for a sophisticated hermeneutic approach to the sociology of religion, this does not always resolve the politics of my academic practice. Perhaps commentators have been too hard on Luhrmann's act of bad faith, failing to remember that she was a pioneer on a number of fronts. In the 1980s Witchcraft was still a very obscure religious tradition and Luhrmann did indeed face a stark choice between belief and her academic career.

I have chosen differently. My "ethnography" of contemporary Witchcraft involved inviting sixteen Witches from around Australia to write about their own experience of being a Witch (Ezzy 2003b). Such an approach enabled me to partly avoid the problem of the omniscient author because the Witches wrote about themselves, although I did choose who was invited to write, and I shaped their contributions through commentary and corrections. It also provided royalties to the contributors—I was not the only beneficiary of my publication. Following the lead of Hutton (1999) and Hume (1997) I played with the ambiguity of my voice as an academic who may or may not be a participant, although it is reasonably obvious where my own beliefs lie to anyone who reads between the lines.

However, my book is, apparently, of questionable academic merit. It does not qualify as an academic monograph, nor even as an academic edited collection, because it was not peer reviewed. The politics of the academic status game continues to privilege texts that use modernist methodologies and writing practices. While Turner may be right to argue that ethnography can become a shared endeavor between "natives" and anthropologists, this is still only a possibility that is not readily understood by many academics.

The work of ethnographers such as Greenwood (2000) and Blain (2002) can be seen as part of a trend within sociology and anthropology toward a more sophisticated approach to spiritual experience. This reflects a more general trend within sociology toward ethnographies by insiders that explicitly work the insider/outsider tension. These include, for example, studies of clinical depression (Karp 1996), Goth subculture (Hodkinson 2002), and anorexia (Garrett 1998). It would be a mistake to argue that ethnographies can only ever be done by insiders in a perverse mirror image of the elitism of modernist ethnographic practice. Rather, I hope that ethnography will continue to support the dialogue between insider and outsider, making it, in Edith Turner's words, "an endeavor shared by natives and anthropologists" (1994, 87).

To return to the opening discussion between Rod Crook's methodological atheism and the experiential reality of Ruth Sansom's mysticism,
I now say: "I have understood Rod Crook's arguments, and I do not reach
the same conclusion."

References

Berger, Helen
1999 *A Community of Witches.* Columbia: University of South Carolina Press.

Blain, Jenny
2002 *Nine Worlds of Seid-Magic: Ecstasy and Neo-Shamanism in North European Paganism.* London: Routledge.

Bruner, Jerome
1990 *Acts of Meaning.* Cambridge, Mass.: Harvard University Press.

Buber, Martin
1995 *The Legend of the Baal-Shem.* Translated by M. Briedman. Princeton,
N.J.: Princeton University Press.

Collins, Peter
2002 Connecting Anthropology and Quakerism: Transcending the Insider/
Outsider Dichotomy. In *Theorizing Faith: The Insider/Outsider Problem in the
Study of Ritual,* edited by E. Arweck and M. Stringer. Birmingham, UK:
University of Birmingham Press.

Cunningham, Graham
1999 *Religion and Magic.* New York: New York University Press.

Denzin, Norman
1992 *Symbolic Interactionism and Cultural Studies.* Cambridge, Mass.: Blackwell.

Ezzy, D.
2001 The Commodification of Witchcraft. *Australian Religion Studies Review* 14(1): 31–44.

———.
2003a New Age Witchcraft? *Culture and Religion* 4(1): 47–65.

Ezzy, D., ed.
2003b *Practising the Witch's Craft.* Sydney: Allen and Unwin.

Ezzy, Douglas
1989 Pentecostal Conversion as Identity Transformation. Unpublished Ho-
nours Thesis, Sociology, University of Tasmania, Australia.

Farberman, Harvey
1992 The Grounds of Critique. *Symbolic Interaction* 15: 375–79.

Fee, D.

1992 Symbolic Interaction and Postmodern Possibilities. *Symbolic Interaction* 15: 367–73.

Gallagher, Ann-Marie

2000 Woven Apart and Weaving Together: Conflict and Mutuality in Feminist and Pagan Communities in Britain. In *Daughters of the Goddess*, edited by Wendy Griffin. Walnut Creek, Calif.: AltaMira.

Gardner, Gerald

1954 *Witchcraft Today*. London: Rider.

Garrett, Catherine

1998 *Beyond Anorexia: Narrative, Spirituality and Recovery*. Cambridge: Cambridge University Press.

Greenwood, Susan

2000 *Magic, Witchcraft and the Otherworld: An Anthropology*. Oxford: Berg.

Griffin, Wendy, ed.

2000 *Daughters of the Goddess*. Walnut Creek, Calif.: AltaMira.

Harvey, Graham

1997 *Listening People, Speaking Earth: Contemporary Paganism*. Adelaide, Australia: Wakefield Press.

Heelas, Paul

1996 *The New Age Movement*. Oxford: Blackwell.

Hodkinson, Paul

2002 *Goth: Identity, Style and Subculture*. Oxford: Berg.

Hume, Lynne

1997 *Witchcraft and Paganism in Australia*. Melbourne: Melbourne University Press.

Hutton, Ronald

1999 *Triumph of the Moon*. Oxford: Oxford University Press.

Karp, David

1996 *Speaking of Sadness: Depression, Disconnection, and the Meanings of Illness*. New York: Oxford University Press.

Luhrmann, Tanya

1989 *Persuasions of the Witch's Craft*. Oxford: Blackwell.

Orion, Loretta

1995 *Never Again the Burning Times*. Prospect Heights, Ill.: Waveland Press.

Pearson, Jo

2002 "Going Native in Reverse": The Insider as Researcher in British Wicca. In *Theorizing Faith: The Insider/Outsider Problem in the Study of Ritual*, edited by E. Arweck and M. Stringer. Birmingham, UK: University of Birmingham Press.

Polkinghorne, Donald
1988 *Narrative Knowing and the Human Sciences*. New York: State University of New York Press.

Ricoeur, Paul
1984 *Time and Narrative*, vol. 1. Translated by K. McLaughlin and D. Pellauer. Chicago: University of Chicago Press.

———.
1985 *Time and Narrative*, vol. 2. Translated by K. McLaughlin and D. Pellauer. Chicago: University of Chicago Press.

———.
1988 *Time and Narrative*, vol. 3. Translated by K. Blamey and D. Pellauer. Chicago: University of Chicago Press.

———.
1992 *Oneself as Another*. Translated by K. Blamey. Chicago: University of Chicago Press.

Spence, D.
1988 Thought and Tender-Minded Hermeneutics. In *Hermeneutics and Psychological Theory*, edited by S. Messer, L. Saas, and R. Woolfolk. New Brunswick, N.J.: Rutgers University Press.

Stark, Rodney, and Roger Finke
2000 *Acts of Faith*. Berkeley: University of California Press.

Thomas, W.
1928 *The Child in America*. New York: Knopf.

Turner, Edith
1994 A Visible Spirit Form in Zambia. In *Being Changed: The Anthropology of Extraordinary Experience*, edited by D. Young and J. Goulet. New York: Broadview Press.

White, Robert
n.d. Hick, Micks and Sociologics: A Case Study in the Disciplinarity of Rural and Catholic Sociologies. Unpublished Paper, Sociology, University of Tasmania, Australia.

York, Michael
1995 *The Emerging Network*. Lanham, Md.: Rowman & Littlefield.

Part Three
EMBODYING RELATIONSHIPS, COMMUNITY, AND HISTORY

CHAPTER EIGHT

AT THE WATER'S EDGE: AN ECOLOGICALLY INSPIRED METHODOLOGY

Sylvie Shaw

It is midwinter in Melbourne, crisp, cold, clear, yet there's a touch of spring in the air. I get up early to enjoy the unseasonable warmth and go running along the beach. It's not far from the city center, but here seabirds like the giant pacific gull wander along the shore picking at seaweed and rummaging through the piles of shells and other rubbish washed up on the sand, while cormorants sit drying their wings on a sign which says: "Danger. No Diving." Lucky for them they can't read. As I run along the water's edge, watching the birds swoop and dive, I am thankful there are still small pockets of wild nature in the city that have the power to inspire. In this article I tell you about how this beach, particularly the intertidal zone, became the inspiration for my research methodology, where the movement of the tides reflects the shifting boundaries between researchers and the people we study. Later in the chapter I use this notion of shifting boundaries and flowing waters to illustrate one of the major themes that emerged from my study, the entwining of body and nature.

My research explores the role nature plays in the lives of people who care for the earth and the role they play in protecting it. These "nature carers" are activists, adventurers, artists, farmers, gardeners, and spiritual practitioners who are involved in myriad actions to restore and safeguard the earth. They see this as spiritual work. Nature carers are well-educated, highly independent, self-motivated, adventurous, altruistic, and fun-loving individuals, yet they are profoundly despairing about the future of the planet. Most are middle class from an "Anglo-Celtic" background and this reflects the demographics of people in the environment movement generally in Australia. They are inspired by the intricacies of the natural world and have a particular passion for wild places. They love the awesome beauty

131

of nature and share a deep respect for its awesome power. Most work either in the outdoors or in jobs related to the environment, and they have chosen these careers largely as a result of their childhood encounters with nature. All share a belief that the earth is in peril and something urgently needs to be done. Some prefer to get involved in what they see as constructive rather than confrontational activities and choose land restoration, reconciliation, and ritual rather than frontline action. Others take part in forest blockades, run community festivals, write music, organize dance parties, go surfing, encourage their children's curiosity about the natural world, or do some or all of these things. And whether they are involved in spiritual groups, religious organizations, or worship alone, all hold nature to be sacred.

Most define their religion as "pagan," seeing it as a religion that venerates nature, but only a small number are involved in formal spiritual groups or Wiccan covens, although most take part in seasonal rituals as well as perform ceremony for special places and enact daily prayers of thanksgiving. A few combine Paganism or earth-connected rituals with mainstream religions, while others retain the religion of their childhood and are seeking an affirmation of nature within that practice. Another group (around 20 percent) are atheist or agnostic but also claim a deep spiritual feeling for the land. This led one of the participants to remark that "what matters is not which path you choose but the action you take as a result of that."

As I run past joggers, and people meditating on the beach or walking their dogs, the outside world falls away and I tune into the movement along the water's edge, watching the swell of the tide and feeling the pull in my body. When Pagans chant *"We are the flow and we are the ebb; We are the weavers, we are the web,"* they are recognizing the pull of the moon, the flow of the tides, and the interconnection with all life. This framework of flow and interconnection is the foundation for an ecologically inspired research methodology.

The Research Process

One of the underlying themes surrounding the beliefs and practice of nature religion is the celebration of interconnectedness, so I wanted to design a research method that embodied this notion. To this end I was guided by methodologies that blend inner, subjective, experiential processes with more outward objective approaches, a fusion that recognizes the desire to be in the experience as well as comment on it. I drew inspiration from a number of self-reflexive ethnographic studies. These included such techniques as: heuristic self-reflexivity (Moustakas 1990); naturalistic inquiry (Lincoln and Guba 1985); feminist and ecofeminist research, particularly by Smith (1987), Fonow and Cook (1991), and Slicer (1998); subjectivity, defined as "research on lived experience" by Jackson (1989), and Ellis and Flaherty (1992); the "internal-external" process discussed by Ely et al. (1997); and the "inside-out/outside-in" approach of Hunt (1987). However, I found that while these offer ways to bridge theory with praxis, they lack an ecological dimension. They focus on social relationships but do not acknowledge the dynamic interrelationship between people and nature (Kearns 2002). I was seeking a methodology that embraces holism, spirit, people, and nature, a concept expressed beautifully by Susan Griffin:

> Human knowledge, if nothing else, is a testament to the connectedness and interdependence of life. There can be no subject apart from an object. This understanding should transform our epistemologies by embedding not only being but the capacity to know in an earth imbued with intrinsic significance. (1995, 86)

Still contemplating what to do about the research issue, I go running along the beach. As I dodge the waves at the water's edge, the solution suddenly becomes obvious. It lies right under my feet in the intertidal zone, a place described by pioneer environmentalist Rachel Carson (1998, 2) as an "enchanted place," a "magical zone," a place invested with hidden meaning.

The shoreline is a place of interconnecting waters, a boundary place or edge space that is sometimes land, sometimes sea: a place which is neither sea nor land, or perhaps both sea and land, where my feet sink into the soft wet sand, where crabs scuttle to hide under rocks, where I drift with the sound of waves washing along the shore. I have grounded my methodological approach in this terrain, within the tidal zone, where patterns of life intermingle and flourish. It is a metaphor for both the overall theme of my research—the interplay between earth-connected activism and spiritual practice, and the particular approach I have chosen—the interplay between theoretical discourse and personal experience, my own and that of the nature carers (e.g., Jackson 1989, Berg 1998, Reinharz 1992). This place engages all my senses, and with the wind whistling around me and the salt spray sticking to my skin, I fall into the subtle rhythms of moon and earth.

In the natural world, places where diverse ecosystems come together are known as "ecotones." According to Shulman (1995, 234), "an ecotone is an environmental edge where two systems meet. It is here at the edge that species stretch their limits and extend their range, creating entirely new forms." This is precisely my intention in creating an earth-based methodology. The ecotone is a zone of rich fecundity, where differences come together, where mutual interaction is inevitable, where space is fluid and boundaries seamless, where the incoming-outgoing movement of the water is linked to the movement of tides across the globe, to the pull of the moon, to the dance in the body, to the flow of thoughts, feelings, visions, and dreams (see also Krall 1994). It is not wilderness here, but even in the "tame" domesticated and constructed beach near my home, with the noisy peak hour traffic close by and the sight of brown haze spreading across the city, there are possibilities to shift realities and find new ways of seeing. In terms of my research methodology, these new insights are found in the intensely personal and self-reflective techniques that move beyond the limitations of the purely objective without discarding it like shells washed up along the shore.

My research approach then is one of relationship. Embracing interconnection and creating a dialogue between self and other (where other can be other people, other species or the natural world) transcends the dualisms inherent in Western thought that split mind from body, matter from spirit, people from nature, visible from invisible, and ideas from experience. Greenway maintains that

> so long as our fundamental mental processes remain dualistic we will not have the benefit of consciousness of the flow of the world around us. Our knowing will perhaps be acute, laced with accuracies gleaned laboriously from the efforts of science, but the full picture—the emotional, experiential, fully interactive sense of connectedness—will elude us. (1996, 186)

Maintaining this sense of connectedness is intrinsic to the research process. Each day as I run along the shoreline I feel that the intertidal zone is working with me, helping me clarify issues or opening up new avenues for exploration. The richly textured stories the nature carers shared with me also inspire new directions for inquiry. Sometimes it seems as if I am leading the research; sometimes it seems to be leading me. In their book *Composing Ethnography*, Ellis and Bochner (1996, 22) write that this type of approach aims "to allow another person's world of experience to inspire critical reflection of your own." This is certainly what occurred through the ongoing conversations I had with the local naturescape as well as with the nature carers.

As I talked with more and more people I found their stories began to overlap. Patterns emerged. Certain ways of knowing and ways of experiencing the world were common among many of the people regardless of age or background. I found a similar level of consciousness about the extent of environmental damage, a widespread feeling of grief and despair, and a common awareness that building community, sharing experiences, and performing ritual are essential elements of their spiritual activism. They also share an understanding that being in nature is a vital pathway for healing and regeneration—of themselves and the world.

Spending time in nature, particularly wild places, not only renews their commitment and nourishes their spirit; it is also something they really love. Wild places can be breathtaking, magical, beautiful, spiritual places that delight the senses and ignite the spark of imagination, adventure, playfulness, and creativity that sustains their activism (see also Stringer and McEvoy 1992, Roberts 1996, Fox 1999). And although the nature carers say their experiences are more profound in wild nature, they are also nurtured by nature through gardening or restoring remnants of bushland in their local neighborhoods. What is important, they say, is the process. It's not just a question of going out into nature and expecting immediate transformation. It is a process of creating relationship, getting to know nature, becoming familiar with the local terrain, meeting the neighbors (human and other-than-human), and spending time strengthening the relationship. Beginning the process in a conscious sense may increase one's awareness about what's going on in nature, the turning of the seasons, the phases of the moon, the migration of birds, and the impact of environmental degradation at home and further afield. Becoming more aware and reflecting deeply on these issues may lead to action. At least this is the experience of the nature carers.

These findings definitely put me on the side of the participants. This is a terrain that I feel passionate about and have considerable involvement in. I love the outdoors, especially seakayaking, hiking, and gardening. I have worked in the environment movement and have been involved in different facets of nature religion for more than a decade. Being partisan means that I am able to share certain knowledges, feelings, and experiences with them. This commonality helped build trust, respect, and profound interaction. The participants were comfortable with my questions and I was able to discuss some of my own feelings and experiences with them. They often mentioned how the conversations had encouraged them to think more deeply about issues that were close to their heart that they had either taken for granted or never analyzed before. The conversations also helped me reflect on my own engagement with nature, activism, and spiritual practice. It was an enlightening time for both of us.

Being Partisan

Working within the rich area of overlap between researcher and re-searched, subjective and objective, insider and outsider, there is a potential richness that makes for creative researching. But I am confronted by a lin-gering suspicion about the validity of this approach often dismissed by the academy in colonialist terms as "going native." I question this distinction between outsider (good) and insider (suspect) research. I suspect that these terms, which are supposed to distinguish the people we are from the people we study, represents another kind of dualism needing to be decon-structed. Can't we be both insider and outsider and compress the distinc-tions that set us apart from the communities we study? Rather than preferring one viewpoint or the other, perhaps there are layers or textures of involvement. Being partisan involves a sense of accountability to the participants, a duty of care to the views and values they hold (Plows 1998). Partisan research has been criticized for lacking a critical reflection of, and for being too close to, both topic and participants. But I would counter that by saying that all research strategies have built-in problems. It is my role as researcher to be aware of the criticisms and act accordingly. For in-stance, Smith (1988, 93; also see 1987) warns that working from direct personal experience may lead to solipsism or ethnocentrism, where the re-searcher assumes that all experiences are alike and uses her "privileged speaking to construct a sociological version which we then impose upon [the other] as their reality." Taking this into account I draw strength from those feminist research strategies that outline that explicitly identifying with the goals and views of the participants is one of the most effective ways of obtaining in-depth and accurate data (Mies 1991, Roseneil 1995).

Although I share several characteristics with the majority of nature car-ers in terms of class, education level, ethnicity, and concern for the environ-ment, I am not speaking for them. My role is to gather their stories and craft them in such a way so that a chorus of voices emerges echoing their deep attachment to this land. Writing about transformative experiences in nature might lead the reader to reflect on their own encounters with the natural world or reconsider their feelings about the ecological crisis. Using the par-ticipants' voices to tell the multitextured stories of nature connecting may, as Ronai (1992, 123) suggests, foster "the understanding that we are all processual, emergent, multivoiced entities living different situations yet sharing similar lived emotional experiences." She believes that reading the stories told by these different voices may lead to "a precognitive apprehending that is sublime, unstructured, and nonverbal in nature," but I would prefer something a little more visceral. In terms of this research, I hope it not only encourages the reader at least to reflect on the issues raised, but also to take off their shoes and dance barefoot on the earth.

The Body and Nature

Nature carers relish such jubilation in the outdoors. Theirs is an intimate relationship with the land that, for some, overflows into sensual-sexual encounters with the natural world. I call this relationship "the ecoerotic," where the animating life force present in all of nature overflows into the sexual, and where, according to Abram (1998, 13), "the bond between our bodies and the breathing Earth" is renewed. Perhaps too, the bond of mutual respect and interaction established with the participants helped unearth this rich terrain for deeper exploration. When I asked participants to talk about how their body feels in nature or to give me examples of their physical as well as emotional and spiritual connections with nature, most people spoke about their engagement with special places, the joys of gardening and getting their hands dirty, the feel of the wind, their tired muscles after a day's rugged hiking; these were the kinds of stories I expected. But when some of them revealed their sexual encounters with earthy elements, I felt we had stumbled onto something profound, a latent or forgotten dimension of the human-nature dynamic. They spoke about their heightened sensual awareness being enveloped in nature, lured by the intoxicating smell of the earth, the smoothness of boulders, the erotic touch of eucalypt bark, and the taste of luscious fruit. It was like an awakening. This was a direction I had not anticipated, and I delighted in the research adventure and the stories they shared. For instance, Lucy, a writer and deep ecology activist, told me she discovered her embodied nature connection by chance when she enrolled in a workshop about the ecology of her local area. Her experience during the workshop was the trigger for a growing fascination about the eroticism of the natural world.

> It was a warm afternoon and I decided to take a walk by myself. First I came across dozens of butterflies around a bush and as I watched them, I began to feel excited. My mind seemed to spring open to a sharp awareness of the subtle variations that make each living thing unique. A little

further on I came to an area of ferns. They were hay-scented ferns which we'd learned about that morning, so I knew them by name like they were friends. As I waded through the ferns I felt them softly stroking my legs. The sun warmed them and they seemed to release their sweet green earthy scent all around me. It was intoxicating. It surrounded me and I lay down amongst them and breathed, and breathed, and breathed with them until I felt almost one with them. I became that scent, that warm greenness. It was quite a new feeling for me. (Lucy, Writer and Activist)

Although Lucy was already a committed activist before she attended the workshop, she was unaware that the earth could awaken the senses in such an evocative way. She describes her experience as "an epiphany, a memorable encounter with nature where the boundaries between you disappear, where you are at one with all creation."

Several nature carers told me about similar experiences of self-transcendence in nature that acted as catalysts for their deeper involvement in spiritual activism. For Amy, an activist and musician who composes lyrical images inspired by the sounds and beauty of the land, the encounter with eros and nature was a rite of passage. On a weekend school excursion out camping in the magnificent Grampian Ranges in northeast Victoria, Amy says that she "became aware of the magical" for the very first time. Among the stunning sandstone bluffs, in a cave on a mountaintop, under the full moon, fifteen-year-old Amy was utterly transformed.

There was full moon and a few of us, girls and boys, decided to climb the mountain which looks down on the whole of the Grampian Range. We camped overnight in a cave on top of the mountain and when I woke up in the morning I was a different person. It was like an initiation into adolescence or something. I had grown up partly because a boy had kissed me there; it was my first kiss. It was also being in contact with the unknown—with boys and with that fear, that body fear. But there was something about that place and the experience of waking up at dawn to an incredible golden landscape on a hot summer's morning; it really changed me, utterly. From the moment I woke up I was different. Before that experience I was very shy and retiring and scared but afterwards I became outgoing. I found outlets for my newfound passion, not physical passion because I didn't kiss a boy again for another three years, but it was more the sense of destiny and calling and relationship to nature. It was very much about creating relationship with nature. (Amy, Activist and Musician)

This was a magical moment for Amy. The place, the full moon, the cave, the view from the mountaintop, the golden sunrise, the heat of the morning, and the first kiss all contributed to her initiation. It was an awakening of the senses where nature itself seemed to play a role in her seduction. The boundaries shifted and she was "different."

Sensuous landscapes arouse and captivate as Eric, an avid bushwalker, discovered while out walking in his beloved mountains. Now in his early 70s, Eric lives on the edge of Victoria's magnificent alpine region and is still involved in local environmental issues and bush regeneration. He had already retired from his profession as an engineer when he fell in love with Sara, the owner of a local plant nursery. Now he too works at the nursery, but the two of them manage to get away to the mountains as often as possible.

> Often when Sara and I are walking along we stop and give each other a hug or an expression of our love. We decided to stop and have lunch on a beautiful rock face, a gently sloping smooth rock. We didn't speak much at all during lunch, just enjoying the experience. Then after lunch I took off my clothes and lay down on the rock, on my stomach, spread-eagled, and I could feel the heartbeat. Now people say that is your own heartbeat and maybe they're right. But I felt the heartbeat of Mother Earth. Then Sara joined me and she did the same thing. It became a totally surrendering kind of experience, a very sensual experience and a connecting experience between me and the rock. It was like a kind of a sexual intercoursing with nature. It was so amazing. I totally surrendered and it took me a long time to come back to so-called reality. That was a beautiful wonderful experience and very sacred. (Eric, Bushwalker and Plantsman)

What is common among these examples is the feeling of sacredness, a sense of pleasure and freedom where the physical body's boundaries drop away and a new body-nature being emerges. Experiences such as breathing the ferns' heady aroma, being initiated on a mountaintop, merging with the heartbeat of the warm rocks, body boundaries dissolved, are reminiscent of the liminal space of the ecotone, where the interflow of tidal waters reflects the communion between human and living world. To illustrate this idea further, Eric told me of another special time in his beloved alps when he and Sara performed a ritual of deep intimacy.

> It was on top of the mountain. Sara and I had gone there to do ceremony. She was menstruating and we were both naked and she shared her blood with me on the soles of my feet and on my forehead and I became so emotionally involved with the feminine—not only with her femininity but with my own and of the Mother's. The experience just came out of the blue and I was totally overcome by it. I had no words. I could not speak. I didn't know where I was. I don't really know what happened. It

was done in a totally beautiful way—this is us together with the Mother, with nature, and we were consecrating our relationship. It was a real religious experience. It was not a sexual experience but something entirely sacred, honoring the feminine and the earth. We walked back to the car and not a word was said for ages. (Eric)

For Eric, the union of body, the sacred and the natural world is overwhelming. This is mirrored in the expressions he uses, such as "totally surrendering," "amazing," "had no words," "didn't know where I was," "totally overcome," "totally beautiful," as well in as his comment that it takes him "a long time to come back to so-called reality." He is lost in the movement of permeable boundaries and fluid identities, responsive to desire, spirit, and connecting.

In a similar vein, the psychologist Janni loses herself in the sexual moment of a world charged with eros.

I like to express my connection to nature by exploring and letting myself be free like playing in the mud and dirt, smearing my body with mud, or going outside without clothes and letting the wind flow over my body. It's such a pleasurable feeling. It's like a sexual satisfaction but it's not only sexual. It's a feeling of connection. In a sexual interaction, you feel totally connected to the other person; it's blissful and cosmic. That same feeling happens to me in nature. That's why I love it. It can be pure bliss where you feel like you are part of nature and nature is a part of you.

That's what happened to me on Australia Rock [a rocky outcrop shaped like the continent]. We were down at the ocean and I went to explore this rocky outcrop that had waves crashing into it. As I started to climb the huge rock, I felt like I was climbing up the phallus. I was very aware of the intellectual thought processes that were going on—I knew I was climbing up an image of a phallus but I was also quite wary thinking: "Do I really want to do this?" When I got to the top, I lay down sprawled out over the rock. I felt that my body was the rock and that the physical boundaries between us were blurred. That was really beautiful and I sang a song about it: "I touch the rock, I touch my body, I touch the rock, I feel my soul."

Then I climbed down to an area that had a lot of pigface [a succulent ground cover] growing around it and I straddled one of the sandy mounds. It was soft and I sat down purposefully in a kind of sexually promiscuous way. Then I looked at all this pigface that was hot in the sun and I picked off some red-looking leaves and began to munch. It was a really erotic experience. Eating the red sticky and gooey leaves was like eating cum and I got into enjoying eating this piece of sexual pigface in an erotic kind of way. Here was a total freedom to explore and do what I wanted without having to please or disappoint. I don't think I'm a very repressed person sexually, I just got into it and went—Wow, this is great. (Janni, Psychologist)

Janni also told me that as well as having this kind of erotic relationship with nature, she also likes tongue-kissing rocks and believes they kiss back. In search of any discussion about the ecoerotic I trawled through books on eroticism, pornography, and sexuality (e.g., Bataille 1990, Kroker and Kroker 1988, Abramson and Pinkerton 1995, Soble 1997, Featherstone 1999) but found that most focus on human-human relations. Most talk of fantasies and fetishes; others mention bestiality (e.g. Lingis 2000). But after hearing the stories of sacred erotic nature connecting, I do not see them as sexual perversions or deviant sexual behavior—ecoerotica perhaps. The main difference seems that with the nature carers' ecoerotic lovemaking, there is no sense of domination, exploitation, or denigration involved.

The sensual allurement of the natural world is however mentioned in the evocative nature writing of Terry Tempest Williams, Richard Nelson, and Scott Russell Sanders, and in the work of ecofeminists like Susan Griffin and Riane Eisler. It is embraced in Native American mythology (see Gunn Allen 1990), and even within my own English heritage there are rare mentions of the sacred relationship between body and nature, such as in Andrew Marvell's evocative poem "The Garden," written in the seventeenth century. Marvell writes of the garden's sensuous pleasures, its intoxicating kisses, seductive fruits and flowers, and sexual attractions.

> No white nor red was ever seen
> So am'rous as this lovely green.
>
> Here at the fountains sliding foot
> Or at some fruit trees mossy root,
> Casting the bodies vest aside,
> My soul into the boughs does glide.
>
> The luscious cluster of the vine
> Upon my mouth do crush their wine.
>
> Stumbling on melons as I pass
> Insnared with flowers I fall on grass.

For Marvell, the garden is a place for retreat and contemplation where the body is cast aside and the soul is free to merge with the surrounding nature. While his poem depicts the division between body and soul, it is one of the few instances I found that recognizes the profound relationship between the sensuality of nature and grace. It is as if we have forgotten what our ancestors once knew and practiced (Metzner 1995).

Perhaps the reason it is so rarely discussed is that people may not be involved intimately with nature or even be aware that such a thing is possible. In contrast, Canadian artist and environmental educator Lisa Lipset is direct about the importance of what Abram (1998) refers to as "sensuous modes of knowing."

> Without this erotic, creative energy I believe there is no sustainable relationship with nature. The sexual creative energy we feel is the same spark that germinates a seed, forces the early roots to penetrate the soil and the new leaves to burst forth to the sky. It is the life force. As long as we sentimentally romanticize it, compartmentalize it (in dark bedrooms) and distort it (as in pornography), we've missed out on an embodied earth centered relationship. (Personal communication)

When Lucy, the activist and writer, attended an ecology workshop she was excited by her unexpected discovery of the sensuousness of the natural world. But when she joined a protest to stop a grove of oaks from being logged, she was not prepared for the intensity of the feeling that arose. Lucy was arrested in the action and went to court, where she was granted permission to speak on behalf of the fallen trees. What happened after that was totally unexpected.

> Going for a walk to visit the trees is like going to meet a lover, very exciting, full of anticipation and desire. Gradually the excitement transformed into a desire to connect more deeply with them. I started touching them and when I did I felt as if waves of energy were flowing right into me from them. This sense of upward-flowing energy was very erotic and warmed me right through in a way that I clearly felt as sexual, like a deep sweet kiss. What is this energy flow, this pulsing that comes into my body as sexual excitement? (Lucy, Writer and Activist)

Lucy has interpreted these feelings as relating to the sap flowing in the trees and the fertility of nature. She wonders whether her feelings are a kind of projection, as if the "tree spirit" is actually an aspect of her psyche, but feels, due to the intensity and nature of the experience, that this is not the case. Still pondering the question, Lucy comments that "in some ways, it seems very strange to be making love with trees instead of people." But perhaps it is not so strange, as Starhawk (1988, 143) believes there is a direct connection between losing ourselves in the essence of trees and the desire to fight for their preservation.

> When we feel it deeply, perhaps with an oak, when we feel the tree's aura move into our bodies, feel our energy flow through the ground into its roots, let ourselves merge and feel at one with its tree-ness, we are sustained in the fight to keep the ax from its trunk, the radiation from its leaves.

What is common among all these stories is the sense of blurred boundaries, as the human-animal body communes with the body of the earth. There is an erotic power bound up in these stories that effervesces in spiritual activism. For the nature carers, it is palpable—an experience of sensuous nature seduction. It tells of wild love, lust, fertility, and commitment. Becoming ecoerotic is like falling in love with the land, relishing in its raw earthiness and our own. It is a two-way feeling that fuses sex, ecology, and the sacred with action, a combination that Harris defines as "sacred ecology." He explains that we are compelled to act "to protect the Earth because we know, in every cell of our bodies, that our lives, our communities and our land are sacred." (1996, 153)

Conclusion

Throughout my interviews with the nature carers and in the writing-up process, I have fluctuated between deep despair over environmental devastation and incredible optimism at the whole variety of imaginative actions and diverse projects they are engaged in. Their stories may involve sacrifice and suffering but they are not hampered by self-pity or powerlessness. Although they feel grief at the loss of wildness and pain at the alienation from nature, they draw on an inner strength that has been fashioned in childhood. From early childhood on they have built an intimate bond with the natural world. In creating this relationship they have trusted their senses. Through their sensory visceral connection and ecoerotic lovemaking, through their caretaking of the land, through their gardens and their rituals, they have renewed the bond between their bodies and the earth. They are nourished and in return they nourish the earth. It is a heartfelt practice. Now when I walk along the shoreline and contemplate the exquisite stories that were shared, I have begun to see the research process as a kind of ritual, a sacred process, inspired by, and in service of, the earth.

References

Abram, D.
1998 Trust Your Senses. *Resurgence* 187 (March–April): 13–15.

Abramson, P. R., and S. D. Pinkerton
1995 *With Pleasure: Thoughts on the Nature of Human Sexuality.* Oxford: Oxford University Press.

Bataille, G.
[1962] 1990 *Eroticism.* Translated by M. Dalwood. New York: Marion Boyars.

Berg, B. L.
[1989] 1998 *Qualitative Research Methods for the Social Sciences,* 3rd ed. Boston: Allyn and Bacon.

Carson, R.
[1965] 1998 *The Edge of the Sea.* Boston: Houghton Mifflin.

Ellis, C., and A. P. Bochner, eds.
1996 *Composing Ethnography: Alternative Forms of Qualitative Writing.* Walnut Creek, Calif.: AltaMira.

Ellis, C., and M. G. Flaherty, eds.
1992 *Investigating Subjectivity: Research on Lived Experience.* London: Sage.

Ely, M., et al.
1997 *On Writing Qualitative Research: Living by Words.* London: Falmer.

Featherstone, M., ed.
1999 *Love and Eroticism.* London: Sage.

Fonow, M. M., and J. A. Cook, eds.
1991 *Beyond Methodology: Feminist Scholarship as Lived Research.* Bloomington: Indiana University Press.

Fox, R.
1999 Enhancing Spiritual Experience in Adventure Programs. In *Adventure Programming,* edited by J. C. Miles and S. Priest. State College, Pa.: Venture.

Greenway, R.
1996 Healing by the Wilderness Experience. In *Wild Ideas,* edited by D. Rothenberg. Minneapolis: University of Minnesota Press.

Griffin, S.
1995 *The Eros of Everday Life: Essays on Ecology, Gender and Society.* New York: Doubleday.

Gunn Allen, P.
1990 *Spider Woman's Grandaughters: Traditional Tales and Contemporary Writing by Native American Women.* London: Women's Press.

Harris, A.
1996 Sacred Ecology. In *Paganism Today,* edited by G. Harvey and C. Hardman. London: Thorsons.

Hunt, D. E.
1987 *Beginning with Ourselves: In Practice, Theory, and Human Affairs.* Cambridge, Mass.: Brookline Books.

Jackson, M.
1989 *Paths toward a Clearing. Radical Empiricism and Ethnographic Inquiry.* Bloomington: Indiana University Press.

Kearns, L.
2002 Greening Ethnography and the Study of Religion. In *Personal Knowledge and Beyond,* edited by V. J. Spickard, J. S. Landres, and M. McGuire. New York: New York University Press.

Krall, F. R.
1994 *Ecotone: Wayfaring on the Margins.* Albany: State University of New York Press.

Kroker, A., and M. Kroker, eds.
1988 *Body Invaders: Sexuality and the Postmodern Condition.* Houndmills, UK: Macmillan Education.

Lincoln, Y. S., and E. G. Guba.
1985 *Naturalistic Inquiry.* Beverly Hills, Calif.: Sage.

Lingis, A.
2000 *Dangerous Emotions.* Berkeley: University of California Press.

Metzner, R.
1995 The Psychopathology of Human-Nature Relationship. In *Ecopsychology: Restoring the Earth, Healing the Mind,* edited by T. Roszak, M. E. Gomes, and A. D. Kanner. San Francisco: Sierra Club.

Mies, M.
1991 Women's Research or Feminist Research? The Debate Surrounding Feminist Science and Methodology. In *Beyond Methodology: Feminist Scholarship as Lived Research,* edited by M. M. Fonow and J. A. Cook. Bloomington: Indiana University Press.

Moustakas, C. E.
1990 *Heuristic Research: Design, Methodology and Applications.* Newbury Park, Calif.: Sage.

Plows, A.
1998 "In with the In Crowd": Examining the Methodological Implications of Practising Partisan, Reflexive, "Insider" Research. Unpublished MA thesis, University of Wales, Bangor.

Reinharz, S.
1992 *Feminist Methods in Social Research.* Oxford: Oxford University Press.

Roberts, E. J.
1996 Place and Spirit in Land Management. In *Nature and the Human Spirit: Toward an Expanded Land Management Ethic,* edited by B. L. Driver et al. State College, Pa.: Venture.

Ronai, C. R.
1992 The Reflective Self through Narrative. In *Investigating Subjectivity: Research on Lived Experience,* edited by C. Ellis and M. G. Flaherty. London: Sage.

Roseneil, S.
1995 *Disarming Patriarchy: Feminism and Political Action at Greenham.* Bristol, Pa.: Open University Press.

Shulman, A. K.
1995 *Drinking the Rain.* New York: Penguin.

Slicer, D.
1998 Towards an Ecofeminist Standpoint Theory: Bodies as Grounds. In *Ecofeminist Literary Criticism: Theory, Interpretation, Pedagogy,* edited by G. C. Gaard and P. D. Murphy. Chicago: University of Chicago Press.

Smith, D. E.
1987 Women's Perspective as a Radical Critique of Sociology. In *Feminism and Methodology: Social Science Issues,* edited by S. Harding. Bloomington: Indiana University Press; and Milton Keynes, UK: Open University Press.

Smith, D. E.
1988 *The Everyday World as Problematic: A Feminist Sociology.* Milton Keynes, UK: Open University Press.

Soble, A., ed.
1997 *The Philosophy of Sex: Contemporary Readings.* Lanham, Md.: Rowman & Littlefield.

Starhawk
[1982] 1988 *Dreaming the Dark: Magic, Sex and Politics.* London: Mandala Unwin Paperbacks.

Stringer, L. A., and L. H. McAvoy
1992 The Need for Something Different: Spirituality and Wilderness Adventure. *Journal of Experiential Education* 15(1): 13–20.

CHAPTER NINE

THEALOGIES IN PROCESS: RE-SEARCHING AND THEORIZING SPIRITUALITIES, SUBJECTIVITIES, AND GODDESS-TALK
Ruth Mantin

Introduction

The growth of studies into contemporary paganisms and indigenous religions has allowed further analysis and critique of the many ethnocentric and colonial assumptions underlying Western academic attempts to study and categorize faith communities. I wish to make a small contribution to this process. In my case, however, I am not examining an opportunity for ethnographic enquiry, nor are the collaborators in my research all Pagan. However, I want to claim that these reflections on the methodology employed to produce my doctoral thesis[1] raise issues, questions, and possibilities that connect to a wider movement in which the boundaries of what has been traditionally demarcated as the sacred are being challenged. Similarly, I want to suggest that my research also relates to the epistemological implications of this paradigm shift. These implications place the possibilities generated by such a change in mindset within a current movement characterized by terms such as "postmodern" and "poststructural." The focus of this chapter will, therefore, be on the exploration of such possibilities.

My research is placed within an examination of the contemporary Western feminist Goddess movement. The relationships between Paganism, Witchcraft, "Wicca," and feminism in the Goddess movement are complex ones and cannot properly be explored here.[2] The Goddess movement is, nevertheless, being recognized as a significant feature of contemporary religious expression. Similarly, thealogy, reflection on the nature of divinity within a female perspective, is beginning to be acknowledged as a distinctive discipline. The focus of early expressions of Goddess feminism was on the regenerative power of reclaimed language and symbolism. As this emphasis has been investigated, the nonrealist aspects of thealogy have been discussed and debated by participants in and commentators on the Goddess movement.[3] I, however, am arguing for further discussion of the possibilities for nonrealist thealogical discourse to transform the religious and cultural imaginary. In my research, I was proposing a radical, postrealist approach to "Goddess-talk," which offers the potential of refiguring expressions of spirituality and of the sacred in a postmetaphysical, postmodern context.

Most commentators on and within the Goddess movement refer to *the* Goddess, but the issue of whether this relates to one deity or many is an area of debate for thealogy. Many Goddess feminists understand the paradigm shift generated by Goddess-talk to challenge a monotheistic worldview in which one supreme deity replicates and sanctions a hierarchical power structure. For such thealogians therefore, monotheism is the antithesis of Goddess spirituality. When thealogians draw on a mythology provided by female images of the divine they have access to a multiplicity of Goddess names and images. For many this plurality is a vital feature of what Goddess-talk offers and some Goddess scholars argue that thealogy should speak in terms of Goddesses rather than the Goddess.[4] The "one or many" debate in thealogy is related both to the issue of matriarchal prehistory and to disputes about the realist nature of Goddess-talk.[5] A narrative that presents the possibility of a universal Goddess-centered worldview that predates patriarchy can be seen to be linked to an understanding of the Goddess as monotheistic but revealed in many aspects. At the same time, however, the notion of plurality is central to the resacralization envisioned by thealogy. Goddess, as the sacred immanent in the natural world, expresses the teeming biodiversity of all forms of life and death. Furthermore, in expressing the sacred as female, Goddess embodies the change, flux, and lateral systems of women's experience as opposed to the singular, linear quest of the heroic male. Issues of naming are therefore not simply matters of ontological debate but relate to the sociopolitical implications of Goddess-talk.

A further, crucial factor of these debates is that they appear to offer binary oppositions such as one/many. Many thealogical commentators have argued that such a dualistic model is itself challenged by the refiguration generated by Goddess-talk. Asphodel Long, for instance, argues that the use of the phrase "the Goddess" has never implied monotheistic assumptions.[6] The narratives of many Goddess feminists reinforce this opinion. A typical example is provided by a respondent in Cynthia Eller's influential survey of Goddess spirituality in America.

I don't make those kind of distinctions that you hear about, they don't make any sense to me. You can say it's the Great Goddess, and that's one Goddess, but she's also all of the many goddesses, and that's true. And she's everywhere. She's immanent in everything, in the sparkle of the sun on the sea, and even in an animistic concept. I think certain objects can embody force and power. So I worship the Great Goddess, and I'm polytheist and pantheist and monotheist too.[7]

A fluidity of thought, which speaks in terms of the singular and the plural as mutually inclusive, is also apparent in the narratives of the women with whom I was in conversation during my research. Thealogy's ability to embrace diversity and ambiguity makes it difficult to define but also provides it with the capacity to respond to challenges of a postmodern world. On the other hand, it could be argued that thealogy's roots are placed firmly within feminism as an emancipatory movement and are therefore inherently related to modernist ideals of progress and liberation. The possible tensions between the postmodern and modernist aspects of Goddess feminism have been identified by Melissa Raphael.[8] In my own research, I encountered such tensions, but I approached their exploration from a different direction from the one taken by Raphael. I do, however, echo Raphael's view when, after voicing some of her reservations about thealogy as an effective feminist project, she nevertheless suggests:

It must be a matter of celebration that, perhaps for the first time since the rise of Christendom in the West (and perhaps long before that), women are able to perceive and treat the material world as the locus of a self-generating divine value and power that can be experienced as something indivisible from themselves as women. It is still too early to assess to what extent and in what ways the reverberations of this shift will change the landscape of western religion and culture.[9]

With Raphael, I argue that the Goddess movement can offer enormous potential for the refiguration of narratives of the sacred. It is my contention, however, that much of that potential has not been realized and that Goddess-talk offers the opportunity to carry further the metaphoric process set in motion by thealogical reflections upon the language of the divine. In my research I was therefore arguing that the "small narratives" of radical thealogical reflection should be heard as well as the views that are presented as a "metanarrative" by a few spokespersons of the Goddess movement and most of its critics.[10]

My research explored further possibilities for the role of thealogy in transforming the religious symbolic. My interest was in the role of "Goddess" as metaphor and in the function of Goddess-talk. This process included a focus on the work of Carol P. Christ. A significant reason for this was the influence of Christ's work on the personal journey in which my research was rooted. Furthermore, Christ's work, especially "Why Women Need the Goddess,"[11] is recognized as a "foundational" text for the development of Goddess-talk and relates specifically to the questions of language, symbol, narrative, and experience. Christ occupies a particular position in the development of thealogy in that she bridges the world of academic feminist theo/alogy and the popular Goddess movement. Christ is also distinctive in that she addresses explicitly the epistemological implications of the paradigm shift generated by feminist approaches to the study and practice of religion. Her analysis of epistemological and methodological issues informed the approach of my thesis and its heuristic stage in particular. Furthermore, Christ's focus on language, experience, and knowing has led her, in her later work, to address, specifically, issues of "realist" or symbolic understandings of the Goddess. Christ's thealogy, rooted in her own experience, has developed to provide insights from process thought to present understandings of the Goddess as personal presence.[12] My own line of thought, however, led me in a different direction to consider the possibilities of postrealist narratives of the sacred framed by Goddess-talk.

In order to pursue these possibilities, I inter-viewed[13] with a group of nine women who located themselves on a spiritual journey that focused on or was related to feminism and/or the Goddess. Some, but not all, of these women identified themselves as Pagan. This heuristic aspect of my research was significant not because it claimed to provide ethnographic research of feminist spirituality but because it reflected some of the epistemological implications of feminist perspectives on the study of religion. Such perspectives validate the embodied knowing expressed in women's own accounts of their narratives. My intention was to investigate the possible trajectory of developments in the perceptions of spirituality and the sacred generated by feminist approaches to the study and practice of religion. My sources for such an exploration were, primarily, in the literature produced by feminist theorists and theo/alogians. My reflections upon this material were, however, informed by the conversations I have had with other women and with other scholars.

My own location and connections determined the choice of respondents. The nature of the group and my interaction with them was also affected by my own relationship with Goddess feminism. Two of the respondents were very well known to me, two I knew slightly and have since come to know well, five were referred to me by others. I contacted these women through connections I had made with other Goddess feminists, some of whom were within the interview group. This intentionally small-scale research was, therefore, not intended to be "representational" of the Goddess movement nor did I claim it to be a statistically accurate sampling of Goddess feminists. In her influential study of the Goddess movement in America, Eller makes the same point about her interview group of thirty-two women. She provides a disclaimer about the numerical and geographical limits of the range of her interviewing group and maintains that the primary source for her research is the literature of the movement, alongside participant observation. She is, nevertheless, intending to provide sociological research of feminist spirituality as a religious movement in a way that I am not.[14]

My intention was to interact with women's spoken narratives, as well as with written texts, in order to explore the possibilities of Goddess-talk for generating new understandings of the concept of spirituality and of notions of the sacred. I therefore spoke to women who, in some way, identified themselves as being on a feminist spiritual journey and/or used Goddess imagery to express the Divine. I chose to be in conversation with women who were willing to explore their ideas with me. Even within such a small group, there is a wide range of perceptions and understandings of the term "Goddess" and of the role of feminist spirituality. As with other "sample groups" of Goddess feminists, however, this diversity of opinions is not mirrored by a wide range of ethnic or social backgrounds.[15] The interviews took place between March 1999 and July 2000. I interacted with the women's ideas during the interview. The women provided informed consent for their views to be used in my own interpretations of Goddess-talk; they also had access to the transcripts of the inter-views.

I approached this process of interpretation by relating the function of Goddess-talk, as demonstrated in the women's narratives, to that of the "figurations" and "heteroglossia" called for by feminist theorists such as Rosi Braidotti[16] and Donna Haraway.[17] Furthermore, I discovered, in the work of Catherine Keller,[18] an example of the means by which Goddess narratives can function to express subjectivity as process and to present images which reflect positive strategies for responding to difference. In the resulting conclusions and suggestions offered by my research, I offered possibilities for the ways in which Goddess-talk could convey a postrealist understanding of the sacred as performative and grounded in a sense of relation with all forms of life. I also argued that such Goddess-talk could relate to postmetaphysical expressions of embodied spiritualities that reflect an acceptance of the plurality of subjectivity as process.

2. Setting the Contours of My Research: Comments on Sources and Method

My research was set within an epistemological and methodological framework that was informed by feminist approaches to the study and practice of religion. These approaches were explained, explored, and interrogated during the course of my thesis. The impact of feminist analysis has generated a paradigm shift in academic discourse, which determined my use of sources and methods.

2.1 Feminist Epistemology and Embodied Knowing

I adopted the use of the first person throughout my thesis and employed the imagery of a journey to convey the research process. In doing so, I reflected the epistemological bases of the content and method of my research, relating these to the implications of feminist approaches to the research of religion that challenge a notion of "objectivity" based upon Cartesian dualism and modernist claims for rationality.[19] Feminist critiques of androcentric traditions led to an awareness of the perspectival nature of all knowledge. It could therefore no longer be possible to retain the "Archimedean point" of Enlightenment rationalism where the universal knower can stand in order to view "true" reality, free from the "distortion" of individual "bias." Further challenges now face feminist discourse. Feminism made the understandable move to place the narratives of previously silenced and subjugated groups at the center of theories of knowledge. This now raises the question, however, of how it can be argued that, in such perspectives, "the subjectivity of the oppressed" can be taken as "normative" and not be treated as a situated perspective alongside any other.[20] Furthermore, there is a growing realization that attempts to place groups such as "women" at the center of epistemological process replicate modernist universalizing tendencies, and there is a call for the recognition of "difference." I attempted to take account of these challenges in the method and exploration of my research. Drawing on the insights that have informed feminist theo/alogies, I therefore worked within a paradigm that acknowledges the perspectival and situated nature of all knowledges. Indeed, such a paradigm challenges the concept of "knowledge" itself and posits instead a focus on the process of "knowing." In particular, I drew upon Carol Christ's theory of "embodied knowing," which recognizes the interaction between our own lived experience and our intellectual process. I therefore made no attempt to assume a position of neutrality and I acknowledged my own position within the text. I used the travel analogy to signify the relationship between my own experience and the research that my thesis represented.

2.2 Language and Narrative

The primary and most compelling feature of feminist epistemologies is the recognition of the connection between knowledge, language, and power. This is not just in the sense that further education enables fuller participation and empowerment but, more radically, that the legitimation of knowledge-claims is inherently linked to networks of domination and exclusion. In a move parallel to that taken by postmodern theories, this recognition has led to a deconstruction of the role of language in framing, sanctioning, and reifying the power structures which determine patterns of oppression. The term "narrative" encompasses the many means by which language and discourse produce perceptions of reality, constructions of "how things are." Feminist approaches to the research of religion revealed the extent to which the overarching theories of religious worldviews excluded and denigrated female experience. Such analysis generated an interrogation of the far-reaching and disabling effects of religious symbolism and the reconstruction of new or reclaimed forms of language. This process of analysis and transformation informed the direction and expression of my research. The language and terminology therefore reflected a deconstructive and creative approach to the function of words and phraseology.

Following Mary Daly, I made unconventional use of hyphens to signify the means by which words convey different layers of meaning, reclamation, and exclusion.[21] This is illustrated by such words as "re-search," "dis-cover," and "re-member." Daly also created new terms such as "biophilia" to express the life-affirming energy of women-centered processes. Feminist discourse makes use of plays on words to reveal androcentric assumptions of privilege disguised by ostensibly inclusive terms: hence, for instance, references to "malestream" rather than mainstream schools of thought.

2.3 Feminist Theologies

In drawing on feminist methodologies, I could not ignore the many problems that come along with such terminology. I am aware, for instance, of the problems surrounding the universalizing tendencies inherent in the term "feminist." I acknowledge the claims of womanist, mujerista, latina, and women-defined movements from the Majority World to express their own distinctive and context-generated expressions of theology. I recognize the danger of producing a "list" or an inevitably selective array of contextual, women-defined theologies and then pretending to subsume them all into the continued use of the blanket term "feminist." If I do so, I am in danger of reinscribing the process by which women of color and women of the Majority World are unrecognized, rendered invisible and silent. If I retain the word "feminist," it cannot be just a shorthand indication of wider diversity but more an expression of hope in the potential of feminist critiques and reconstructions for sociopolitical transformations. At the same time, I recognize the powerful and painful reality that the term has also been instrumental in the marginalization and negation of many women. In using the term, I also acknowledge that I speak from the position of a privileged, white, Western woman. I can speak from nowhere else but my own location but this must not, however, serve to provide a comfortable excuse for my inherent collusion with the structures that demean and disadvantage the wo/men whose labor, poverty, and suffering furnish my privilege. This advantage does, however, give me a voice and I am, at least, able to use that voice to challenge and critique my own privilege. Within these many qualifications, disclaimers, and constraints, I continued to use the term "feminist."

2.4 Qualitative Research Methodology

The epistemological assumptions[22] underlying the feminist methods examined and employed in my research require qualitative rather than quantitative approaches to the heuristic stage of its research.[23] Furthermore, the epistemological "shifts" generated by feminist scholarship, demonstrated by the work and reflections of Carol Christ,[24] which reveals the perspectival, situated, relational, and embodied nature of knowing, run parallel with the interpretive turn taken by the further development of qualitative research methods.

An overview of the development of qualitative research methods illustrates its relevance to theories explored in my research. The issues identified in such an overview relate to theories of knowledge and experience encountered and employed throughout my research. In their influential "handbook,"[25] Denzin and Lincoln identify five "moments" in the history of twentieth-century qualitative research.[26] It is not possible in this chapter to explore fully the issues raised by an examination of the growth and scope of qualitative approaches to research. Denzin and Lincoln summarize the chief challenge facing contemporary researchers as being that of reconciling the crisis of representation with a crisis of legitimation. While concerned to ensure that too much self-reflection does not stifle the qualitative research project completely, they see the need to "return the author openly to the . . . text."[27]

The methods of qualitative research can hold even more potential for a heuristic approach to the narratives of feminist spirituality than is expressed in the approaches advocated by Denzin and Lincoln. Some of the epistemological implications raised by the "fifth moment" of qualitative research are carried further by Margot Ely and others in their collection *Doing Qualitative Research: Circles within Circles*.[28] According to Ely et al., qualitative research means being "engaged in in-process, recursive analysis, meaning-making and reporting." In a move that reflects the imagery of feminist spiritualities, they employ metaphors of circles and spirals to emphasize the importance of *process* in qualitative research. They frequently emphasize the role of *experience* in the process of meaning-making that they view as the goal of qualitative research. This challenge to the myth of objectivity and recognition of the embodied nature of any knowledge means that Ely et al. also challenge some of the assumptions about subject/object and power relations in research. In their understanding of qualitative research, the role of researcher is one of "collaborator in research."

The approach advocated by Ely et al. has many points of contact with Christ's theories of embodied knowing and her arguments for a methodology of empathy. Christ argues for the recognition and declaration of personal perspectives in scholarship as the means to counter the myth of objectivity employed to screen unacknowledged androcentrism. She maintains that this is also a safeguard against feminist scholars employing false absolutes and universalisms. Christ emphasizes the affective dimension of knowledge. She relates scholarship to eros because it stems from

> a passion to connect, a desire to deepen our understanding of ourselves and others and to preserve or transform the world. . . . Within the ethos of eros the scholar remains firmly rooted in her or his body, life experience, history, values, judgements and interests. Not presuming to speak universally or dispassionately, the scholar speaks from a standpoint that is acknowledged to be finite and limited. But rather than remaining "narrowly personal," "merely confessional," "self-referential" or "self-indulgent"—discrediting terms taken from the ethos of objectivity—erotic scholarship moves from personal passion to empathy.[29]

When considering a rationale for the methods adopted in my approach to my interviews with the women who agreed to take part in my research, I needed to employ a methodology which fully recognized the epistemological implications of the relationship between narrative, experience, and knowing. Such a recognition has contributed to the growing impact of narrative analysis upon the methods of interviewing in qualitative research. Catherine Kohler Riessman explains the "narrative turn" taken by all the social sciences in terms of the realization that "individuals become the autobiographical narratives they tell about their lives."[30] Riessman demonstrates how such an understanding has emerged from the growing challenge to a view of language as a transparent medium, unambiguously reflecting stable, singular meanings. A critique of such realist, positivist assumptions about the relationship between language and knowing provides the philosophical underpinning for narrative studies. Skepticism about a correspondence theory of truth leads to an understanding of language as "deeply constitutive of reality, not simply a technical device for establishing meaning." Riessman's recognition that women's stories about their lives are constantly changing, being reedited and reinterpreted, reflects an understanding of identity as subjectivity in process. Riessman argues that "informants' stories do not mirror a world 'out there.' They are constructed, creatively authored, rhetorical, replete with . . . assumptions and interpretive."[31] An important implication of this for my research was an awareness that any attempt to analyze narratives is an attempt *to interpret interpretations.*

The methods of narrative analysis explored by Riessman employ a structured approach that attempts to provide some form of representation, albeit based on notions of "trustworthiness" rather than "truth."[32] My own approach was informed by case studies of research that pursue further the role of dialogue in qualitative interviewing. I therefore drew on the methods explored by Casey, Roseneil, and Kvale in order to underpin my own approach to the women's narratives.

2.5 Narratives, Discourse, and Heteroglossia

Kathleen Casey understands the life history narratives of the women she interviewed as texts.[33] When attempting to interpret these texts, however, she found the techniques provided by academic sociology wanting. Casey asked her interviewees to provide their own versions of their life narratives. As a result their narratives did not always address issues that a quantitative method would stipulate. Casey wanted an analysis of the texts that allowed her to appreciate the pattern of the women's own priorities. In order to do this she turned instead to a framework based on Bakhtin's theory of discourses. It was therefore a central feature of Casey's methodology that she began her analysis with an autobiographical account of her own identity as a woman teacher working for social change. She also included autobiographical references in her interpretation of the life narratives.

In her work with women from the Greenham Peace Camp, Sasha Roseneil takes further the issues raised by women's narratives, autobiography, and by the relationship between "insider" and "distant" approaches to qualitative research. She maintains that central to a feminist methodology of research is a focus on women's own interpretations of their experience, a rejection of value-neutrality and a commitment to reflexivity, locating the researcher on the same critical plane as the researched. Roseneil's own commitment to this last principle led her to explore the role of her own subjectivity in constructing her research product. She understands a vital aspect of this process to be the writing of her "intellectual autobiography."[34] Indeed, so strongly does she feel the methodological importance of this principle that Roseneil felt it necessary to reveal the impact on her research of her own lesbian identity. Central to Roseneil's methodology was the significant principle that the interviewees must participate in the theorizing. She makes explicit her desire not to theorize *about* Greenham women but theorize *with* them.[35] Having established this theoretical approach, Roseneil is, however, honest about the remaining power issues to be considered. Despite the dialogic nature of the interviews, she acknowledged that in the end, it was *her* analysis that was used to interpret the views of other women and *she* retained the power of authorship. She therefore took steps not to abuse this power, including the establishment of "informed consent."[36]

2.6 Inter-views

The methodologies explored by Casey and Roseneil made many points of contact with the theoretical issues presented by my own research. I was not proposing to engage in ethnographic research in a manner comparable to these researchers, but I wished to employ a similar approach to the use of interviewing and the dialogue with women's narratives. When exploring the role of interviewer in qualitative research, however, I found it very helpful to draw on the insights provided by Steinar Kvale.[37] His approach highlights the epistemological issues raised by qualitative approaches to research. He presents two contrasting metaphors in order to illustrate the implications of different understandings of the research process.[38] The interviewer can be understood either

as a miner or as a traveller. As a miner, the researcher seeks to extract objective facts or nuggets of meaning. Knowledge is waiting in the subject's
interior, waiting to be uncovered, uncontaminated, by the miner. These
precious facts are then "purified"—by transcribing their meaning into
written text. Finally, the value of the end product—its degree of purity—
is determined by correlating it with an objective, external real world or to
a realm of subjective, inner, authentic experiences. Kvale rejects this perception in favor of a traveller metaphor. This metaphor resonated with
my own approach to the process of knowing and to my interaction with
other women's narratives.

As a traveller, the interviewer sets out upon a journey that leads to a
tale to be told upon returning home. The interviewer/traveller "wanders
through the landscape and enters into conversations with the people encountered." Kvale draws attention to the fact that should the traveller
choose to follow a *method*, it would be in the original Greek meaning of
"a route that leads to a goal." He also points out that when the traveller
asks questions of the local inhabitants that lead the subjects to tell their
own stories of their lived world, then the traveller is conversing with
them in the original Latin meaning of *conversation* as "wandering together with." Kvale is therefore happy to acknowledge that this journey
might not only lead to new knowledge, but also to a process of change in
the traveller.

In favoring the model of the traveller, Kvale is opting for a postmodern constructive understanding of knowledge that involves a conversational approach to social research. Kvale stresses the interconnectedness of
the practical issues of the interview method and the theoretical issues of
the nature of interview knowledge(s). He maintains that

> The qualitative research interview is a construction site for knowledge.
> An interview is literally an inter view, an exchange of views between two
> persons conversing about a theme of mutual interest.[39]

There is, Kvale maintains, an alternation between the knowers and the
known, between the constructors and the constructed.

> The conception of knowledge as a mirror of reality is replaced by knowl-
> edge as a social construction of reality. Truth is constructed through di-
> alogue; valid knowledge claims emerge as conflicting interpretations and
> action possibilities are discussed and negotiated among the members of
> a community.[40]

2.7 Developing a Methodology

Following the epistemological implications of the theories of qualitative research, especially as explored by the scholars identified above, I approached the heuristic stage of my project understanding conversation as research and as a means of constructing knowledges. This allowed for a methodology that recognizes the relational and embodied nature of knowledge. With Kvale, I understood my research to be a process of "inter-views." I adopted a traveller metaphor for the role of researcher. With Casey, I understood women's narratives as texts with which I am in dialogue. I was attempting to ensure that my position as researcher, author, interpreter, and fellow traveller was clearly acknowledged in the text. I approached these narratives having already formed questions as a result of my own journey. I intended to adopt a hermeneutical approach to the analysis of the inter-views.[41] This method involved a process by which I shared my reflections during inter-views and allowed further questions and interpretations to emerge. I acknowledged a spiralling process of interpretation emerging from an ongoing conversation between the themes identified in my survey of the contemporary Goddess movement, the theories developed in dialogue with written texts, and the inter-views with women's spoken narratives.

Within the context of the theoretical issues explored in my dissertation and outlined above, I wished to explore the possibilities presented by Goddess-talk for new understandings of spirituality.

When considering the process of "verifying" and "reporting," therefore, I was pursuing the implications of Kvale's "traveller" epistemology further than his own, more linear model.[42] I was acknowledging my process of interpreting the women's interpretations. I was questioning whether it is possible to push the women's expressions of spirituality further along the trajectory of their own arguments. If the challenges to metaphysical dualism inherent in feminist Goddess-talk are pursued, what possibilities for new expressions of spirituality emerge? In other words, I was approaching the narratives with the question "What would happen if . . .?" In employing such a method, I was using a paradigm in which "knowledge" is "in process." This form of inter-viewing acknowledges the role of conversation in constructing knowledges. My conversation with the women's narratives continued in my further engagement with their ideas in relation to my own theorizing.

I wished to interrogate the implications of postdualistic spiritualities that take seriously the fluidity and plurality and relationality of subjectivity as process. I intended also to explore the role of Goddess-talk in the women's narratives. This exploration was informed by Nelle Morton's presentation of Goddess language as metaphoric process[43] and by an understanding of Goddess-talk as "figurations" within "political fictions" that generate possibilities for positive and effective responses to devalued difference.[44]

In wishing to theorize *with* and not *about* the women with whom I con-verse, I was recognizing, with Roseneil, that "in researching my sisters I am researching myself." I acknowledge that this does not exempt me from declaring the ethico-political issues involved in the power relations of research. Indeed, an acknowledgment of my role as interpreter brings with it serious ethical implications. It was therefore essential that my research demonstrated that the women with whom I am theorizing operate within a context of informed consent.

3. Possible Directions for Goddess-Talk

The ways in which the women with whom I was in conversation expressed their understanding of the term "Goddess" reflected the fluidity of thought that is characteristic of spiritual feminism. As Christ and several other commentators have been eager to maintain, this is not just the result of "sloppy thinking." The willingness to affirm several propositions simultaneously, some of which appear mutually exclusive, is part of thealogy's conscious challenge to the dualistic thinking that has determined theological orthodoxy for two millennia. Christ makes this explicit in her attempt to produce a "systematic" thealogy. Here she argues that the requirement to clarify issues such as whether the Goddess is transcendent or wholly immanent or whether thealogy is monotheist or polytheist is predicated upon the acceptance of a dualistic paradigm that presents the "one" and the "many" as irreconcilable. Christ demonstrates that a Goddess-oriented worldview challenges such assumptions as false, drawing on process theology to illustrate that it is not invalid to attempt a philosophical argument that presents immanence and transcendence, one and many, as compatible.[45]

Another important aspect of thealogy's conscious affirmation of ambiguity and plurality is its tendency to accept personal experience as a valid source of reflection about the nature of the divine. In doing so, thealogy is challenging another premise of dualistic thinking, the value of reason above embodied experience. Goddess-talk therefore abandons logocentric assumptions when expressing "reality" as it is encountered in the lived experience of individuals. This approach reflects the epistemological implications inherent in a feminist paradigm shift. When describing her experiences of the Goddess, Nelle Morton refused to accept a dichotomy between "experience" and "reality."[46] Morton was working within a paradigm in which the Goddess represented a "nonrealist" expression of the sacred. For Morton, this was an essential ingredient of the iconoclastic element of Goddess as metaphor. Morton rejected the notion of a transcendent sacred as the projection of a patriarchal worldview. She, nevertheless, maintained that her "experiences" of the Goddess were meaningful and revelatory. Morton found it pointless to respond to those who asked, "Did it really happen?" Morton has not provided further exploration of the implications of her apparent premise that the sacred can only be encountered in human experience and that to search for a "reality" beyond this is nonsensical. I, however, wished to follow the trajectory of Morton's thinking and explore the potential of Goddess-talk for postmetaphysical expressions of the sacred.

The emphasis on the embodied and experiential nature of reflections upon the meaning of the Goddess was apparent in the inter-viewees' responses. The women also demonstrated an acceptance of plurality and fluidity in their attempts to express their understanding of the Goddess. I am not suggesting that all the women consciously incorporated an epistemological critique of dualistic and logocentric paradigms into their narratives. However, I maintain that such a critique is implicit in many of the points that were made. All of the women, in diverse ways, expressed the need to abandon traditional, patriarchal images of the divine. The narratives' emphases on the sacred as immanent, spirituality as embodied, and experience as relational follow on from the women's rejection of conventional perceptions of the divine.

When discussing her perception of distinctive aspects of feminist spirituality's expressions of the divine, Eller focuses on the relationship between the Goddess and "the self."[47] Other commentators have recognized the close association between the notion of the Goddess and female identity as a significant feature of thealogy. For Asphodel Long, this is the primary focus of the Goddess movement, which she expresses in the phrase "in raising Her we raise ourselves and in raising ourselves we raise Her."[48] Long maintains that this experience of the Goddess as self-empowerment preceded all thealogical reflection. As a result, the apparent ambiguity of expression, for instance between Goddess as the "one" or "the many," can be understood in this context. Raphael maintains that a distinctive aspect of feminist spirituality is the sense of an "ontological continuum" between women and the Goddess.[49] Notions of "Goddess-as-self" were very apparent in the women's narratives. Alongside these affirmations of the Goddess as coterminous with the women's own sense of identity, is a recognition of movement and process in that sense of identity. The expressions of spirituality found in most of the women's accounts are related to narrative and identity. The women frequently referred to their understanding of the Goddess and of themselves in terms of a journey, pathway, or process of evolution. In these accounts of their "travels," the women freely acknowledged that their configurations of the Goddess have changed as their knowledge and experience developed and that such a process is often linked to their own psychological as well as spiritual development. One respondent voiced her belief that all religious expression was the product of psychological development or change and was "embedded in each person's personal story." She recognized that the more she studied the more her views about Goddess changed.

In their accounts, inter-viewees were often open to the idea that their personal journeys were without a destination. When discussing her spiritual journey, one woman was anxious to stress that she did not understand "progress" in terms of a "a straight line." Another also wanted to emphasize that her "pathway" was not a process of "discovering who I am" but an ongoing journey, recognizing that she has different needs at different times in her life. She, therefore, was happy to understand herself as being on a journey where she is "not going to get there." Instead, she was "uncovering layers" of herself, but did not expect to "get to the core" of her self. When discussing her "journey," another inter-viewee also stated that she "doesn't think she will ever arrive any where."

At the same time, however, there seemed to be very little willingness to relinquish a notion of the unified self. Only one respondent touched upon this possibility when she expressed her sense of identity as having many layers. On the whole, however, despite the close relationship between the Goddess and the women's own sense of identity, there was sparse evidence that the women were prepared to associate the readily accepted plurality inherent in Goddess with a recognition of plurality in their own subjectivity. On the contrary, many of them retained an allegiance to the notion of reincarnation, whereby some aspect of a presumably "eternal" self transmigrated into another life.

I therefore argue for the identification of tensions between this and the affirmation of embodied spirituality. Similarly, many of the women "reverted" to a metaphysical conceptual framework in order to articulate their notion of the sacred, despite an apparent affirmation of the Goddess as wholly immanent in the physical. This is not to recognize the validity of thealogical challenges to notions of immanence and transcendence as mutually exclusive.

Such challenges, however, still seem to operate within a metaphysical frame-work that posits a "realist" notion of Goddess. Postmetaphysical expressions of the religious symbolic must engage with questions of "realism."[50] I share with Morton a profound skepticism of the extent to which such an under-standing of the sacred can function to disrupt images of hierarchical du-alisms.[51] The starting point for nearly all the respondents was the symbolic function of Goddess-talk. Only one respondent, however, was prepared to present an unequivocally nonrealist understanding of Goddess.

In travelling with these narratives, I wished to move further along the direction of the nonrealist implications of Goddess-talk. This led me not only into new figurations of the sacred but also into further explorations of identity and subjectivity. As a result, I wished to argue that if feminist approaches to the study of religion are to move beyond Augustinian and Cartesian dualisms, they need to question symbols of the fixed, unified, self-authenticating "self" as well as those of the immutable, immortal, and disembodied "spirit." As a result I propose an understanding of *spiritual-ity as process*, which reflects the insights produced by poststructural chal-lenges to Cartesian theories of the unified self. This understanding can be seen as a necessary aspect of the "shift in paradigm" required in order to provide alternatives to a God-talk that is embedded in representations of the fixed, transcendent Absolute. Instead, we can develop an understand-ing of the *sacred as performative*, in which sacrality is recognized as a process of relation. I believe such reimaginings can have far-reaching so-ciopolitical implications. I hope that such a paradigm shift might gener-ate challenges to hierarchical notions of the Other and enable more positive strategies for responding to difference, strategies that address the assumptions underpinning the discourse and structures of oppression.

Notes

1. Mantin 2002.
2. See e.g., Adler 1979, Goldenberg 1979, Harvey 1997, Jayran 1999, King 1989, Long 1994, Raphael 1999a, Rountree 2004, Spretnak 1982, Starhawk 1989.
3. See e.g., Christ 1996, Clack 1999, Long 1994, 1997; Mantin 2000; Raphael 1996.
4. See e.g., Culpepper 1987, Downing 1990, Harvey 1997.
5. It could be argued that a realist/nonrealist debate is more apparent in British thealogical circles (e.g., Raphael 1999b and Clack 1999) whereas in America the focus is on issues of matriarchal prehistory.
6. Long 1997.

7. Eller 1993, 132–33.
8. Raphael 1996, 1999a, 1999b.
9. Raphael 1999a, 163.
10. See e.g., Davis 1998, Eller 2000.
11. Christ 1979.
12. Christ 1996.
13. My use of this terminology relates to the methodology advocated in Kvale 1996.
14. Eller 1993.
15. Eller 1993, 18-21; Raphael 2000, 25.
16. Braidotti 1994.
17. Haraway 1990.
18. Keller 1986.
19. Lennon and Whitford indicated in the introduction to their anthology, *Knowing the Difference*, that although challenges to traditional theories of knowledge are inherent to feminist thought there was not a great deal of material which dealt explicitly with feminist contributions to contemporary epistemological debates (Lennon and Whitford 1994, i). Since then, more has been produced in this area, e.g., Linda Alcoff and Elizabeth Potter, *Feminist Epistemologies* (New York: Routledge, 1993) and more recently, Jan Duran, *Worlds of Knowing: Global Feminist Epistemologies* (New York: Routledge, 2001).
20. Lennon and Whitford 1994, 3; also Jantzen 1998, 215.
21. Mary Daly was one of the first feminist theorists of religion to identify the crucial role of the relationship between language and power in oppressing women and other subjugated groups. In *Beyond God the Father* she wrote "To exist humanly is to name the self, the world and God. The 'method' of the evolving spiritual consciousness of women is nothing less than this beginning to speak humanly—a reclaiming of the right to name" (Daly 1973, 8). Since writing this, Daly has become far more radical in her approach and has advocated that other women discard the "semantic baggage" of her earlier ideas (Daly 1985, xxiii). Daly no longer uses the term "God," referring instead to Goddess as Verb. Daly has continued to develop her process of renaming, producing a whole "wickedary" of new or reclaimed words (Daly and Caputi 1987).
22. For example, Christ 1989, 1996; Davaney 1987a, 1987b; Lennon and Whitford 1994.
23. See e.g., Warren 1988.
24. See e.g., Christ 1987, 1989, 1991, 1996. In the development of qualitative research methodologies, feminist researchers also encountered issues of androcentrism masquerading as "objectivity" (Roberts 1989).

Feminists, in stressing the need for a reflexive sociology in which the sociologist takes her own experiences seriously and incorporates them into her work, expose themselves to challenges of a lack of objectivity from those of their male colleagues whose sociological insight does not enable them to see that their own work is affected in a similar way by their experiences and their view of the world as men. (Roberts 1989, 16)

25. Denzin and Lincoln 1994.
26. Denzin and Lincoln 1994, 6–15.
27. Denzin and Lincoln 1994, 578.
28. Ely, Anzul, Friedman, Garner, McCormack, and Steinmetz 1991.
29. Christ 1996, 30.
30. Riessman 1993, 20.
31. Riessman 1993, 4–5.
32. Riessman 1993, 64.
33. Casey was researching the ways in which women teachers worked for social change within their everyday lives in the United States. Casey 1993.
34. Roseneil 1993, 181.
35. Roseneil 1993, 202.
36. Roseneil 1993, 203–5.
37. Kvale 1996.
38. Kvale 1996, 3–5.
39. Kvale 1996, 1.
40. Kvale 1996, 239.
41. Kvale, 46–50.
42. Kvale 1986, 229.
43. Morton 1985, 143–45.
44. Braidotti 1994, 4–8.
45. Christ 1997, xiv.
46. Morton 1985, 147.
47. Eller 1993, 141–43.
48. Long 1994, 17.
49. Raphael 1996, 131.
50. In feminist theology, Ruether's foundational work, *Sexism and God-talk* (1983), represents a serious consideration of the implications of a postmetaphysical framework for new expressions of theological concepts. As a result, Hampson "accuses" Ruether of abandoning theism (Hampson 1990, 29).
51. Morton 1985, 217.

References

Adler, Margot
  1979 *Drawing Down the Moon: Witches, Druids, Goddess-Worshippers and Other Pagans in America Today.* Boston: Beacon Press.

Alcoff, Linda, and Elizabeth Potter
  1993 *Feminist Epistemologies.* New York: Routledge.

Braidotti, Rosi
1994 *Nomadic Subjects: Embodiment and Sexual Difference in Contemporary Feminist Theory.* New York: Columbia University Press.

Casey, K.
1993 *I Answer with My Life: Life Histories of Women Teachers Working for Social Change.* London: Routledge.

Christ, Carol P.
1979 Why Women Need the Goddess: Phenomenological, Psychological, and Political Reflections. In *Womanspirit Rising: A Reader in Feminist Religion,* 273–87. San Francisco: Harper and Row.

———.

1987 Towards a Paradigm Shift in the Academy and Religious Studies. In *The Impact of Feminist Research in the Academy,* edited by Christine Farnham, 53–76. Bloomington: Indiana University Press.

———.

1989 Embodied Thinking: Reflections on Feminist Theological Method. *Journal of Feminist Studies in Religion* 5(1): 7–16.

———.

1991 Mircea Eliade and the Feminist Paradigm Shift. *Journal of Feminist Studies in Religion* 7(2): 75–94.

———.

1995b *Odyssey with the Goddess: A Spiritual Quest in Crete.* New York: Continuum.

———.

1996 Thealogy Begins in Experience. *Metis* 1 (Spring): 1–16.

Clack, Beverley
1999 The Many-Named Queen of All: Thealogy and the Concept of the Goddess. In *Is There a Future for Feminist Theology?* edited by Deborah Sawyer and Diane Collier, 150–59. Sheffield, UK: Sheffield Academic Press.

Culpepper, Emily
1987 Contemporary Goddess Thealogy: A Sympathetic Critique. In *Shaping New Visions: Gender and Values in American Culture,* edited by Clarissa Atkinson, Margaret Miles, and Constance Buchanan, 50–60. Ann Arbor: University of Michigan Press.

Daly, Mary
1973 *Beyond God the Father: Toward a Philosophy of Women's Liberation.* Boston: Beacon Press.

———.
1985 *The Church and the Second Sex; with the Feminist Postchristian Introduction and New Archaic Afterwords.* Boston: Beacon Press.

Daly, Mary, and Jane Caputi
1987 *Websters' First New Intergalactic Wickedary of the English Language.* Boston: Beacon Press.

Davaney, Sheila G.
1987 Some Problems with Feminist Theory: Historicity and the Search for Sure Foundations. In *Embodied Love: Sensuality and Relationship as Feminist Values,* edited by Paula Cooey, Sharon Farmer, and Mary E. Ross. New York: Harper and Row.

———.
1987b The Limits of the Appeal to Women's Experience. In *Shaping New Visions: Gender and Values in American Culture.* The Harvard Women's Studies in Religion Series, edited by Clarissa Atkinson, Margaret Miles, and Constance Buchanan, vols. 1–2, 79–95. Ann Arbor: University of Michigan Press.

Davis, Philip
1998 *The Goddess Unmasked: The Rise of Neopagan Feminist Spirituality.* Dallas, Tex.: Spence.

Denzin, Norman K.
1997 *Interpretive Ethnography: Ethnographic Practices for the 21st Century.* Thousand Oaks, Calif.: Sage.

Denzin, Norman K., and Y. S. Lincoln, eds.
1994 *Handbook of Qualitative Research.* Thousand Oaks, Calif.: Sage.

Downing, Christine
1990 *The Goddess: Mythological Images of the Feminine.* New York: Crossroad.

Duran, Jan
2001 *Worlds of Knowing: Global Feminist Epistemologies.* New York: Routledge.

Eller, Cynthia
1993 *Living in the Lap of the Goddess: The Feminist Spirituality Movement in America.* New York: Crossroad.

———.
2000 *The Myth of Matriarchal Prehistory: Why an Invented Past Won't Give Women a Future.* Boston: Beacon Press.

Ely, M., Anzul, M., Friedman, T., Garner, D., McCormack, and Steinmetz, A.
1991 *Doing Qualitative Research: Circles within Circles.* London: Falmer Press.

Goldenberg, Naomi R.
1979 *Changing of the Gods: Feminism and the End of Traditional Religions.* Boston: Beacon Press.

Hampson, Daphne
1990 *Theology and Feminism.* Oxford: Blackwell.

Haraway, Donna
1990 A Manifesto for Cyborgs: Science Technology and Socialist Feminism in the 80s. In *Feminism/Postmodernism,* edited by L. Nicholson, 190–233. London: Routledge.

Harvey, Graham
1997 *Listening Peoples: Speaking Earth.* London: Hurst.

Jantzen, Grace M.
1998 *Becoming Divine: Towards a Feminist Philosophy of Religion.* Manchester, UK: Manchester University Press.

Jayran, Shan
1999 Western Goddess Spirituality Thealogy in Social Context. Unpublished paper.

Keller, Catherine
1986 *From a Broken Web: Separation Sexism and Self.* Boston: Beacon Press.

King, Ursula
1989 *Women and Spirituality: Voices of Protest and Promise.* Houndmills, UK: Macmillan Educational.

Kvale, Steinar
1996 *InterViews: An Introduction to Qualitative Research Interviewing.* Thousand Oaks, Calif.: Sage.

Lennon, Kathleen, and Margaret Whitford, eds.
1994 *Knowing the Difference: Feminist Perspectives in Epistemology.* London: Routledge.

Long, Asphodel
1992 *In a Chariot Drawn by Lions: The Search for the Female in Deity.* London: Women's Press.

———.
1994 The Goddess Movement in Britain. *Feminist Theology* 5 (January): 11–39.

———.
1997 The One or the Many: The Great Goddess Revisited. *Feminist Theology* 15: 13-29.

Mantin, Ruth
2000 "The Journey Is Home": Some Thealogical Reflections on Narrative Spirituality as Process. *Journal of Beliefs and Values* 22(1): 157–67.

———.
2002 Thealogies in Process: The role of Goddess-talk in Feminist Spirituality. Unpublished doctoral thesis, Southampton University.

Morton, Nelle
1985 *The Journey Is Home*. Boston: Beacon Press.

Newman, Fred, and Lois Holzman
1997 *The End of Knowing: A New Developmental Way of Learning*. London: Routledge.

Raphael, Melissa
1996 Truth in Flux: Goddess Feminism as a Late Modern Religion. *Religion* 26: 199–21.

———.
1999a *Introducing Thealogy: Discourse on the Goddess*. Sheffield, UK: Sheffield Academic Press.

———.
1999b Monotheism in Contemporary Feminist Goddess Religion: A Betrayal of Early Thealogical Non-Realism? In *Is There a Future for Feminist Theology?* edited by Deborah Sawyer and Diane Collier, 139–49. Sheffield, UK: Sheffield Academic Press.

Riessman, Catherine, K.
1993 *Narrative Analysis*. Sage University Paper series on Qualitative Research Methods, vol. 30. Newbury Park, Calif.: Sage.

Roberts, Helen, ed.
[1981] 1989 *Doing Feminist Research*. London: Routledge.

Roseneil, Sasha
1993 Greenham Revisited: Researching Myself and My Sisters. In *Interpreting the Field: Accounts of Ethnography*, edited by D. Hobbs and T. May, 177–208. Oxford: Clarendon Press.

Rountree, Kathryn
2004 *Embracing the Witch and the Goddess*. London: Routledge.

Ruether, Rosemary Radford
1983 *Sexism and God-talk: Toward A Feminist Theology*. Boston: Beacon Press.

Spretnak, Charlene, ed.
1982 *The Politics of Women's Spirituality Essays on the Rise of Spiritual Power within the Feminist Movement*. Garden City, N.Y.: Doubleday.

Starhawk
[1979] 1989 *The Spiral Dance: A Rebirth of the Ancient Religion of the Great Goddess.* San Francisco: Harper and Row.

Warren, Carol A. B.
1988 *Gender Issues in Field Research.* Sage University Paper series on Qualitative Research Methods, vol. 9. Beverly Hills, Calif.: Sage.

CHAPTER TEN

LIVING WITH WITCHCRAFT

Ronald Hutton

Two concepts that have recently become very prominent in the social sciences are reactivity and reflexivity. Reactivity is the effect produced on a social group by the scholar who is studying it. In the course of the twentieth century it became very obvious how much the process of making such a study can alter, significantly and permanently, the people who are being studied. Reflexivity is the readiness of scholars to be openly aware of the prejudices, preoccupations, instincts, emotions, and personal traits that they bring to their studies, and the ways in which these can influence the latter. It can also include the impact of the process of study itself upon the personality and attitudes of the scholar.[1] Neither concept has so far made much impact upon the professional writing of history. Reactivity is naturally barely relevant to the latter, for the obvious reason that in most cases the people being studied are dead and therefore presumably beyond the reach of any influence exerted upon their beliefs and lifestyles by academics. Reflexivity should have a much more obvious application to the work of historians of all kinds, but they have as yet hardly begun to recognize the need for it. Where it is assayed among them, it is still liable to be termed "self-indulgence." Both, however, became issues of quite acute importance to me when I was engaged in the writing, and observing the reception, of the book to which I gave the title of *The Triumph of the Moon: A History of Modern Pagan Witchcraft.*[2]

This chapter is reproduced with minor alteration from Ronald Hutton, "Living with Witchcraft," in *Witches, Druids, and King Arthur* (London: Hambledon and London, 2003). Copyright © 2003 by the author. Reprinted with permission from Hambledon and London.

When I wrote the last part of that book, in October 1998, I intended to include a relatively long section reflecting on those issues. I drafted this, and then, after some thought, excised it. As I stated in the preface, I found much of what I had to write too painful and personal for publication. At the same time I left open the possibility that the pages concerned might be published in separate form at a later date, when I was more distanced from the experiences concerned. When I wrote those words I had no idea whether they would attract any attention or interest at all. Since the book appeared, I have repeatedly been made aware, both in reviews and in private conversation, that they have provoked a great deal of both. In some cases this was the result of pure curiosity, but in most it very clearly proceeded from a belief that the missing section would have aired important issues concerning the conduct and implications of academic research. I am still not altogether sure that this is correct, but enough time has passed to make me willing to consider, in a public setting, the matters which were originally designed to be discussed in the missing part of the book's conclusion.

The reason why the book raised these matters for me in such an acute form must be obvious enough. I was attempting to become the first person to write the history of one of the most sensational and radically countercultural of the world's mystery religions, which had taken to itself the glamour and fear associated with the traditional stereotype of the witch. My reasons for undertaking this work were fully expressed in the book's preface, and were largely based on a wholly conventional set of scholarly instincts and ambitions. During the course of writing my three previous major works, one on the pagan religions of the ancient British Isles and two on the history of the ritual year in Britain, I had become aware of how much the existing scholarship in both fields had been conditioned by the ways in which paganism and magic in general had been discussed in Britain since 1800. I wanted to write a study of attitudes to both phenomena during that period, and to use the history of modern pagan witchcraft as a microhistory of them. The project presented me with two obvious challenges. The first was that it automatically turned me into a pioneer, undertaking the history of a subject which had never been attempted in depth before, at least by an academic scholar. The other was that it involved trying to reconstruct the story of the origins and development of a mystery religion, relying in large part on records in private hands, records which the custodians were committed by tradition to keeping secret. I could not write about pagan witchcraft unless I possessed the confidence and support of pagan witches. In attempting to gain or to build upon this, I had to reckon with a legacy of distrust created by my own professional world. In part this derived from a general problem: that the traditional history of pagan witchcraft, in which many of its adherents had believed, had diverged sharply over the previous couple of decades from that taught and written within the academy.

What, then, of reflexivity? It may be remembered that the concept embodies two different meanings, the first being the need of scholars to be openly aware of the prejudices, personal characteristics, and other conditioning factors that they bring to their researches. On the positive side of this balance, I brought certain advantages and areas of competence to this particular study. The simplest and most fundamental was that I had myself been brought up as a Pagan, although not in any formal or initiatory tradition, nor one associated with witchcraft, nor one which involved any profound personal religiosity. This gave me some common ground with pagan witches, and indeed I had been acquainted with the latter since my adolescence. Their world was therefore not unfamiliar to me, and my various friendships had already given me some experience of functioning as a mediator and communicator between conventional society and some of its less conventional subcultures. I was deeply interested in cultural politics, although not in national or party political issues, and this too chimed well with the attitudes of many witches. I enjoyed and empathized with the spectacle of ritual and possessed a long-standing love of poetry. My professional interests overlapped heavily with the concerns of pagan witches: most obviously in the fields of ancient paganism, prehistoric archaeology, folk customs, and medieval and early modern attitudes to witchcraft. All this provided a set of points of contact between myself and the people whose history I would be attempting to write. I did not enter the world of pagan witchcraft simply to complete a research project; I was already connected to that world, and, as I progressed through the various degrees of the religion, I did so with a genuine curiosity concerning the experiences which they provided, and a desire to give and take as much as possible in them which reflected my hunger for life in general.

My greatest single predeterminant of behavior and perception—which might have functioned as a distortion—was that I was an academic. It is with only a limited measure of irony that I regard the academy as the greatest mystery religion of the modern Western world, with its imposing shrines, its three degrees of initiation with their gorgeous robes, its long, hidden processes of training, and its claim to place its initiates to some

measure in contact with the truths of the universe. I honor, extol, and attempt to augment its achievements, and my acute sense of its limitations
and errors has only sharpened my tendency to praise what it does do well.
As a result it was possible that I consistently overestimated the importance
of academic publication to the history of modern pagan witchcraft, and
overvalued written or printed records preserved from the past in relation
to remembered tradition. It is also possible that I did not do so, and that
dominant norms of the treatment of evidence in any case left me little
choice; but the danger remains. More generally, I entered upon the research with a natural gratitude to Pagans who value academic scholarship
and a proportionate antipathy to those who rejected or derided it.

This, then, was the prior intellectual and emotional equipment that I
brought to the work, the acknowledgment of which corresponds to one-
half of the process of reflexivity. What of the other half, a recognition of
the impact of the study upon my own attitudes? Here there is no doubt
that I found the experience of dealing with witches, and in particular with
Wiccans, very much easier and more pleasant than I might have expected
it to be. The great majority responded to my researches with a remarkable
warmth, generosity, and fair-mindedness. Many accepted me as a bringer
of information that, if not always palatable, was worth having. More still
exploited me joyfully as a source of raw historical data from which invocations and other ritual motifs could be fashioned. As I said above, on entering the field I was automatically adopted as an ally by one tendency
within pagan witchcraft, but even those who opposed the latter generally
accorded me a hearing, treated me with courtesy, and debated according
to the empirical rules of evidence. I soon became aware that pagan witchcraft encourages qualities of loyalty, dedication, comradeship, and trustworthiness, which endow many of its adherents with a gift for friendship.
It was soon equally obvious to me that it attracts personalities who tend
to be independent, self-confident, enquiring, creative, dynamic, and highly
literary: for an academic, the mindset associated with ideal students and
colleagues. The lack of a dogmatic framework to the religion, its playfulness, its sense of a true priesthood of all believers, and its disinclination to
impose a common and literal acceptance of the existence of set deity-
forms, all soothed my prejudices against both established religion and
charismatic sects and cults. As I recorded in the final chapter of my book,
I never encountered anything among its members that seriously offended
my sense of propriety or compromised my adherence to the law. The aes-
thete in me was delighted by most of its rites, while the historian was
pleased by the creative use to which old forms were put, and the romantic

in me responded to the recognition of beloved texts and figures from literature spanning the whole time from the ancient Egyptians and Greeks
to the Edwardians. The only determined and embittered hostility that I
met with directly was from noninitiatory Pagans who treated the label of
Paganism largely as a garnish for radical politics rather than as an expression of religiosity. Even this was small in quantity and decreased over time.

In understanding my reactions to the experience of what witches actually do, it is important to appreciate a point that I emphasized in the book:
that modern pagan witchcraft is not a religion of faith, or of salvation, or
of doctrine, or of evangelism, and so the whole language of conversion experience, applied to religious traditions that have those characteristics, is irrelevant to it. What it does do, as I tried to make equally clear in my book,
is provide a set of ritual practices intended to induce personal transformations and the sensation of contact with divine forces. The question of what
is actually happening in those experiences, and of the literal existence of
spirits or divinities, is generally left up to the individual to determine, or to
leave open. Among witches I encountered reactions to this question along
all parts of a spectrum extending from complete personal belief in particular deities and devotion to them, to a conception of divine powers as human constructions, symbols, or projections.

What I did gain unequivocally from participation in these rites was a
powerfully reinforced sense of the latent powers within human beings. I
was repeatedly provided with examples, to a greater extent than ever before, of the majesty, wisdom, eloquence, and creative power of otherwise
ordinary people, and the capacity of religious ritual and ritual magic to ex-
ert powerful transformative effects upon them. I was even less inclined
than before to think that specific deities should be venerated by all humans, or even that most people should believe in any. I did not lose my
hitherto automatic distaste for established religions, or those which demanded an active profession of faith or placed a premium on the conversion of others, but my former anticlericalism began to dissolve in the face
of a new understanding of how priesthood operates. Having carried out
research into the history and nature of modern pagan witchcraft, I felt
better able to understand at least some aspects of religious experience in
general, and in doing so perhaps became more effective both as a member
of the present world and as a historian.

When considering the second aspect of reflexivity, therefore, the balance sheet of my experiences with witches was overwhelmingly positive.
The subject itself proved to be so interesting and so revealing of many
broader aspects of culture, and the company of the people connected to it

was so pleasant and supportive, that had I only needed to deal with them alone, I would gladly have remained in the field longer and perhaps made an enduring speciality of it. I had reckoned, however, without the rest of society.

The review of the book that excited the most widespread interest and comment—at least for a time—was the first to appear, and the most critical. It occupied two-thirds of a page in *The Times*, and was by Marina Warner,[3] a celebrated member of the metropolitan literary world who had produced a range of fictional and nonfictional works, including some major studies of aspects of cultural history. The latter brought insights taken from feminism and literary criticism to bear upon well-known images and figures of Christian religiosity, reflecting the author's own compound of attitudes and beliefs. The quality of her work had been sufficient to ensure her a succession of visiting posts in various universities over the three decades in which it had been published. Like the other reviewers, her overall judgment on the book was positive, proclaiming that it had "a very interesting story to tell, . . . which puts a richly peculiar slant on Victorian values and on their Edwardian successors."

However, her review did beg some tremendously important questions about current attitudes to objectivity, personal belief, and participant observation in the relevant academic disciplines. Ironically, in history itself, as in theology, the question of a scholar's ideological position or personal relationship with the subject matter has not seemed to be particularly problematic. In a recent historiography of the English Reformation, for example, the undoubted facts that Jack Scarisbrick and Eamon Duffy are devout Roman Catholics, that Geoffrey Dickens had as patent an evangelical Protestant faith, and that Patrick Collinson came from a background in Protestant dissent and Diarmaid MacCulloch from one in Anglicanism, have never been regarded as a matter for concern. It is blatantly clear in every case that these personal beliefs or spiritual inheritances have conditioned the attitudes of the historian concerned to the data, but such differing perspectives are regarded as providing the most useful possible range of approaches and intepretations. The difference with Wicca, of course, is twofold. It is virtually impossible to obtain contrasting perspectives upon the latter from informed observers, because only somebody who has got inside it can write about it with authority; and to many people it is not regarded as a "legitimate" religion in the manner of denominations of Christianity.

Here again Marina Warner opened up a critically important issue while making a travesty of it herself, by claiming that I seemed to recognize that anthropologists observe the activities of the people whom they study, but do not participate in them. This has not been true since the 1930s at the latest, when a pioneer like Evans-Pritchard could, famously, settle down to study the cattle-rearing Nuer of the Sudan by getting himself a herd of cattle. The crucial distinction was that although anthropologists could behave like natives, they were not supposed to think like them, but to interpret their thought and behavior in terms of Western knowledge and concepts, which were automatically supposed to be superior. As the colonial empires gave way to independent states, and as Western societies themselves became more multiethnic and culturally diverse, so attitudes began to soften and blur. From the 1960s a new emphasis was placed upon the ability of the anthropologist to immerse herself or himself so completely in the culture or subculture under study that it became possible to understand its deepest instincts and reflexes. In 1967 George Devereux could already confront the professional demand for "objectivity" with the assertion that "informed subjectivity . . . is the royal road to an authentic, rather than fictitious, objectivity."[4] Eleven years later, Benetta Jules-Rosette spoke of social science as a "journey towards becoming the phenomenon," in which the practitioner "attempts to assume the competence of the subject studied."[5]

By the early 1980s this approach was producing some notable successes. David Hayano, writing about poker players in American society, recorded that "after several years I had virtually become one of the people I wanted to study."[6] Liza Dalby, examining the culture of the geishas of Japan, worked as one herself until she learned how to behave and think automatically as they did.[7] The most relevant work of this sort for scholars of witchcraft was Jeanne Favret-Saada's account of traditional beliefs concerning bewitchment in the countryside around Mayenne in western France, published in French in 1978 and translated into English in 1980. She stated roundly that in the nexus of witchcraft beliefs "there is no room for uninvolved observers." In order to understand them properly, she had to engage in them, by being taken for and behaving like a bewitched person herself, befriending those who thought themselves similarly afflicted, and seeking relief from local "unwitchers." In 1990 Favret-Saada reconsidered the implications of her research and reinforced them, with the declaration that "'participant observation' is an oxymoron." "If I tried to 'observe,' that is to keep my distance, there would be nothing left for me to observe."[8]

The new orthodoxy declared in all this work was that the anthropologist had to "go native," in action and thought; but not to *stay* native. Hayano did not remain a poker player nor Dalby a geisha, while Favret-Saada never took up the work of an unwitcher herself and never adopted a literal and personal belief in witchcraft. The ideal was now that the anthropologist should assume a cultural role like an actor taking on a part, and then shed it when the work was done and the time came to write up the study. It was this ideal to which Tanya Luhrmann felt obliged to adhere; her study was in that sense a classic product of 1980s anthropology.

Even during that decade, however, it was already obvious that this template of behavior had serious drawbacks. It was designed, like its more overtly imperialist and conformist predecessor, for scholars from "developed" societies studying more traditional peoples. It was not easily applied by academically trained writers from non-Western societies occupied in studying their own societies, and these were starting to appear in significant numbers during the 1980s. It was particularly ill-suited to female, and even less so to feminist, anthropologists who were seeking to express the experiences of women in such cultures.[9] By the end of the decade some practitioners were starting to realize that it had weaknesses that made it questionable in virtually any conditions. One was that it retained the assumption that the beliefs and attitudes of the people studied were valueless in themselves, and that the anthropologist would accordingly suffer no loss in shaking them off at the end of the project. The second was that it turned the researcher into a form of impostor, an undercover agent for a different culture who acted out membership of a group before leaving it and throwing off the disguise. This aspect of Luhrmann's own work was, it may be remembered, criticized explicitly by a professional colleague, Katherine Ewing, in 1994. Ewing included this specific expression of doubt in a general attack on the philosophy of research that underpinned Luhrmann's approach: "By creating a blind spot, by placing a taboo around the possibility of belief, anthropologists have prevented themselves from transcending the contradictions embedded in a situation in which the imposition of one's own mode of discourse interferes with the project of representation." More bluntly, she declared that "the taboo against 'going native' results from a refusal to acknowledge that the subjects of one's research might actually know something about the human condition that is personally valid for the anthropologist: it is a refusal to believe." She was able to cite by that date four colleagues who had already published their acceptance that they had learned something valuable from the peoples whom they had studied.[10] Three years beforehand, another American, Philip Peek, had edited a collection of essays on native African divination systems by a dozen contributors, presented as a concerted attempt "to understand their sources of knowledge." This was, significantly, offered as an explicit breach with British anthropologists, "who treated divination with great derision."[11]

The key text in this movement was probably another American collection that appeared in 1994, and represented ten anthropologists who all believed that Westerners needed to give serious attention to non-Western beliefs concerning the spirit world. All, to some extent, had been altered in their own attitudes by studying those of other cultures with regard to meaningful dreams, visions, and other "extraordinary experiences" for which their own society had no explanation and which indeed it refused to recognize: a problem to which I referred earlier. The editors began with the declaration that "because of the fear of ostracism, an entire segment of cross-cultural experience common to many investigators, is not available for discussion and scientific investigation." They went on "to entertain the notion that what is at first seen as an 'extraordinary experience' is in fact the normal outcome of genuine participation in social and ritual performances through which social realities are generated and constituted."[12] This was Tanya Luhrmann's "interpretative drift," but reformulated in such a way as to suggest that by drifting away from the interpretations made by mainstream rationalist Western culture, scholars could learn something genuinely valid and useful about the nature of the world. In practice, the contributors to the volume differed widely as to the meaning of the phenomena concerned, on a spectrum ranging from Charles Laughlin, who thought that they could be satisfactorily explained by neurology, to Edith Turner, who accepted the literal existence of spirits. In fact, being convinced that she herself had seen a spirit-form emerge from the back of a patient during a healing rite in Zambia in 1985, she had gone on to make a literal acceptance of what Westerners commonly call magic. In a separate publication, this very renowned and respected anthropologist declared her certainty that trance states could give humans access to "nonempirical healing, clairvoyance and accurate divination." She went on to call for a new anthropological methodology of "radical participation."[13] Such a methodology had already been developed by feminist anthropologists and those native to the cultures under study, who could hardly avoid applying it and who produced a notable body of important work in the course of the 1990s.[14]

Over the same period parallel developments were occurring in a different discipline, that of religious studies. This discipline consists, essentially, of the application of techniques drawn from the social sciences to the study of religions, involving participation by the scholar in groups practising the beliefs concerned, "without prejudice and with sympathetic understanding." It was not considered necessary, or even desirable, for the scholar actually to embrace the religion under study with full personal commitment: instead the duty of the researcher was to seek to suspend personal judgments, and to represent as faithfully as possible what the members of the religion believed, how they expressed these beliefs, and (as far as possible) why they held them.[15] By the 1990s this model was running into trouble, for much the same reasons that it was being questioned in anthropology. David Hufford could complain that "disinterest is urged on scholars of religion, but disinterest is impossible in religious issues."[16] Two different initiatives developed in response to this dilemma. The first was an increasing tendency to credit members of a religion who happened to have academic training and affiliations with at least as much ability to speak of it in scholarly terms as nonbelievers: a privilege, of course, that had always been extended to practitioners of faiths that Western intellectuals regarded with respect, such as established Christianities, Judaism, Islam, and Buddhism. By 1997 Elizabeth Puttick, considering new religious movements in the West, could observe that the "insider as researcher" position was becoming increasingly common in the discipline.[17] The other initiative was to urge nonbelievers who chose to carry out participant observation within religious groups to do so with still greater tact and willingness to suspend personal opinion. Jone Salomonsen, a Norwegian studying pagan witches in California, coined the expression "compassionate anthropology" to describe the study of such groups "from the inside of lived reality." She expected anthropologists henceforth to share in their religious life not simply behaviorally, or even emotionally, but congnitively, to seek to share what the other members of the group were experiencing, as far as it was personally possible to do so.[18]

My own investigation of the history of pagan witchcraft was undertaken alongside the work of no less than five scholars based in university departments of anthropology, archaeology, or religious studies, who were working in the same or related fields according to these two new models for research. All took their projects to successful conclusion. One was Amy Simes, who produced a doctoral thesis on Paganism in the northeast Midlands in a fashion that was a direct practical anticipation of Salomonsen's "compassionate anthropology."[19] Another was Joanne Pearson, who has already been mentioned as studying Wicca itself and running up against just that legacy of distrust and suspicion left by Tanya Luhrmann that I noted myself. Her position was explicitly that of an "insider" to the religion, and she challenged the whole prejudice against "going native" by suggesting that a privileged position for research was available to one who was a "native" already.[20] The third was Susan Greenwood, whose subject consisted of pagan witchcraft and ritual magic in the London area, ten years after Luhrmann's work there. She was also, inevitably, obliged to contend with the results of that work, and did so by establishing the theoretical position that concepts of scientific truth and academic objectivity should no longer be set up in opposition to the insights gained by full participant observation; rather, spiritual experience should be accepted as a source of knowledge in its own right.[21] The fourth was Robert Wallis, who looked at shamanism among modern Western pagans, and its relationship with archaeology. He endorsed the concept that beliefs are best studied by holding them sincerely, and condemned the traditional concept of scholarly objectivity as itself a dogmatic intellectual position based on outmoded colonialist and monocultural attitudes.[22] The fifth scholar was Graham Harvey, who published a general survey of paganisms in contemporary Britain. It was characterized by a constant sympathetic representation, which amounted at moments to a warm endorsement of the ideals of the people under study.[23]

The only professional historian in Britain who worked on anything like a related field during the time of my own research was one who only intermittently operated within the academy. This was the expert on early modern and modern astrology, Patrick Curry, who wrote that it was impossible to produce an "impartial" history of the subject. Ever since the eighteenth century, its practitioners had been undermined, marginalized, and silenced by mainstream scholarship, and so to seek to understand them—to show the consistency and integrity of their beliefs as well as those of their critics—was to affirm the legitimate consideration of more than one version of the truth. This automatically conflicted with the hitherto dominant mixture of Christian monotheism and universalist secular humanism that had characterized western intellectuals and so represented an engagement in a debate between two opposed views of reality that was still under way.[24]

By now it must seem to some readers that I have been using Marina Warner as an Aunt Sally, if indeed she was so wildly wrong about so many things. It must be obvious from the above that far from abandoning the accepted criteria for academic research, and so betraying my profession, I had actually been working within the mainstream of developing theory and practice in all the disciplines related to my own research: history, anthropology, and religious studies. Indeed, I did not depart as far from traditional scholarly constraints as many of the anthropologists cited above. I did not affirm the reality of spirits, or even insist that the "extraordinary experiences" associated with ritual magic, divinatory systems, or the reception of visions might tell us something valuable about the cosmos. This was not just because the "reality" of witchcraft was not part of my concern, but because I simply did not have extraordinary experiences of that kind. My interpretation of the history of pagan witchcraft was wholly compatible with a rationalist and humanist view of the world, although it did not depend on one or deny the possibility of others. I did not recommend pagan witchcraft as a system of practice and belief, being content to explain and explode traditional misrepresentations of it that have circulated in society at large and to explain why its practitioners found it attractive and (to some extent) what they were like. These targets released me from the need to describe and analyze its actual rites in detail, and that release enabled me to keep faith with members of what is, after all, a mystery religion, by leaving them some privacy after writing so much about them in other respects.

Once again, however, things are not that simple, and Warner picked up on a significant point, even though I reject both her understanding and her employment of it. My work was not equivalent to that of the anthropologists, sociologists, and specialists in religious studies who had considered forms of modern paganism; I was leaning in the opposite direction to them. As their starting point was to portray the nature of the religions considered, from what was at least some form of participant observation, they had to signal very firmly what it was that gave their work some academic quality: in other words, what distinguished it from that of the "natives" in general. Each did so by using a framework of analysis and a set of methods that were intelligible to fellow scholars and provided insights into the religions concerned that neither outsiders nor most or all of the practitioners would have spotted, left to themselves. My starting point needed no such distinction. I was already well known for having rejected the traditional historiography of pagan witchcraft, and I was at best enlisted as an ally in a division of opinion that had already taken place within it. There was no way in which, given my reputation and the direction of my work, I could readily be mistaken for a straightforward convert to it by anybody who knew anything about it. My task, as said, was to write a history of that witchcraft that was as accurate as possible while still leaving it dignity as a religion, and that could not be used as a weapon by those determined to deny it any such status. Whereas other scholars needed to distinguish themselves in some fashion from other members of the groups and traditions under study, I was striving to ensure that my work had any value for the latter.

Furthermore, Patrick Curry was right; it is impossible to write sympathetically about subjects such as divination, magic, and witchcraft in modern history without automatically taking sides in at least one major, and often bitter, cultural debate. When I characterized the recent models of "radical participation" and "insider position" as the cutting-edge methods of anthropology and religious studies, I neglected to make clear how much their proponents have felt themselves to be opposed to ingrained prejudice and hostility within their own disciplines. It must be admitted that no body of literature has yet appeared to articulate that opposition, in sharp contrast to the outpouring of works that propound the new approaches, but the assumption of controversy and hostility is still significant. When Jone Salomonsen defined "compassionate anthropology," she insisted that its practitioners, however seriously they took the beliefs of the people under their study, should never become "scholarly converts and proselytisers."[25] The trouble with this superficially impeccable distinction is that in the eyes of a critic as hostile as Marina Warner, any sympathy and compassion is liable to be condemned as conversion and proselytization. There *was* an evangelical ideology embedded in my book, which extended, by implication, to proselytization. It was an assumption that the best condition for a future Britain would be as a formally secular state in which its members are free to follow an effectively infinite range of religious traditions, or none, according to their own spiritual inclinations and needs. Each of these religions, old or new, should be regarded with equal respect and tolerance by those who do not belong to it, only providing that it does no clear and obvious harm to its own members and to others. The last clause, of course, leaves room for plenty of accusation and disputation in itself; but even to articulate that basic, liberal, and humanist position is to pit oneself against the beliefs of a great many people in contemporary British society. My book was not intended to be a propaganda piece for witchcraft, but it embodied a sociopolitical ideal of religious tolerance and equality that itself could be regarded as polemic.

My position amid these cultural cross-currents has become rather more comfortable since the book was published, because for anybody prepared to read it attentively, my actual relationship with pagan witchcraft is now clear and need no longer be made a subject for speculation and gossip. Both Pagans and non-Pagans, moreover, are growing increasingly accustomed to treat me as one of those individuals whom they employ as a mediator and interpreter for mutual benefit. The police, the judiciary, lawyers, the caring services, and schools have all come to regard me as a useful source of objective information concerning Pagans, and the latter have repeatedly engaged me in turn to represent them to these authorities. My performance of the same role in the mass media has, of course, steadily increased since the book made its impact. One lesson that has been reinforced for me, however, is that makers of television and radio documentaries are a different sort of person from investigative journalists and feature-writers. My only difficult experiences have been with the latter, commencing with a man who telephoned me in early 2000 claiming to work for one of Scotland's most reputable newspapers, *The Scotsman*. He had become interested in witchcraft because of a conference on the early modern trials due to be held at Edinburgh, at which I was a speaker. When he contacted the organizers and expressed an interest in modern witches, they referred him to me and I summarized some of the data in my book. The result was that a set of different local Scottish newspapers published a story sold on to them by him, in which he attributed to me either a misheard or an invented statement condemning the Church of Scotland. This ran exactly counter to my own views, and earned me a string of angry and distressed responses from pious Scots, to whom I had to explain that we had both been gulled.

Much worse was the result of the genuine approach that I received from an equally respected English national Sunday newspaper, hitherto generally admired by liberals, to give an interview to a feature-writer who wanted to produce a piece based on my book. I agreed, and during the conversation I was asked how the paper might meet any witches. I recommended that it contact the main national body that represents Britain's Pagans, the Pagan Federation. It did, and duly interviewed, among others, its Youth Officer, the person responsible for formulating policy toward approaches from young people and monitoring the place of Paganism in school courses on religious studies. He happened to be a schoolteacher himself, and here the paper spotted an angle for a eye-catching story. Contrary to the promises made by its journalist, it published a piece which named him and included a photograph of him, to "alert" the nation to the plans of witches to put their message across to young people. It was careful to contact two hostile clergyman and the local Conservative MP, and to enter their warnings and expressions of outrage beneath the report; and the teacher was suspended pending a disciplinary hearing. I am pleased to say that I was subsequently able to play a minor part in providing the evidence that got him reinstated; but since then I have given no more interviews to the press.

Such experiences, and the general implications of my mediatory role, have had some impact on the writing of this essay. Some readers may feel disappointed that I have not written more of my own attitudes, experiences, and relationships when engaging with pagan witches. I acknowledge that to have treated the latter in more depth might have had some value, but apart from concerns about self-indulgence or breaches of confidence concerning the activities of a mystery religion, to do so might well compromise my apparent position as an honest broker and referee. As the latter seems to have such clear value to witches as well as to so many agencies and interest groups who seek information on them, and as real issues of human happiness and safety are at stake, I prefer to maintain this appearance of reticence and detachment until circumstances change. In that sense, an opportunity for complete reflexivity is not yet open to me.

One further thing which the experience of this research brought home to me more vividly than before is the emotive power of language, and in particular of the process of labelling. In this case the significant words were "pagan" and, above all, "witch." In the period since completing the book, I have worked (among other projects) on the historical associations of two other traditions within the constellation that make up modern paganism, shamanism and Druidry. Both have beliefs and practices that overlap with those of pagan witchcraft, while modern Druidry in particular has absorbed a number from it. Both can likewise be characterized as countercultural forms of religious or spiritual behavior. I have found, however, that neither word triggers reactions of alarm, hostility, prurient curiosity, or savage derision among people who do not belong to the traditions concerned. On the whole, "shaman" has connotations of tribal spirituality (generally neutral, and often positive), while "Druid" now has associations of homegrown amiable eccentricity, at least when it is made clear that the modern manifestations of the image are under discussion. There seems to be little doubt that a researcher working on either has a much easier time than one concerned with pagan witchcraft.

In general, I believe firmly that a scholar should enter into an area of research not merely with the ambition of extracting as much as possible from it, for the benefit of oneself, one's colleagues, and one's public, but with that of leaving it in the best possible condition for the next researcher: much as a good guest leaves a bedroom or hotel room as tidy as possible on departing. This means dealing with documents as delicately as is practicable, providing all references as clearly as may be done so that they can be followed up, and treating people who are the subjects of research or custodians of archives in such a manner as to encourage them to take a good view of scholars and inclined to welcome the next to come their way. That is what I tried to do in the case of pagan witchcraft, and having attempted it, I am content now to let my own work in the field itself dissolve into history.

Notes

1. These concepts have been especially prominent in recent American scholarship, and have tended to filter through to British academics from that source. Notable works in the genre have been Jay Ruby, *A Crack in the Mirror: Reflexive Perspectives in Anthropology* (Philadelphia: University of Pennsylvania Press, 1982); James Clifford and George E. Marcus, eds., *Writing Culture: The Poetics and Politics of Ethnography* (Berkeley: University of California Press, 1986); Victor W. Turner and Edward M. Bruner, eds., *The Anthropology of Experience* (Urbana: University of Illinois Press, 1986); and Renato Rosaldo, *Culture and Truth: The Remaking of Social Analysis* (London: Routledge, 1989). I am very grateful to Sabina Magliocco for recommending these titles.

2. Consistently in the text, the word "pagan" will be put in lowercase when it is used as a descriptive term imposed by myself to define areas of belief, such as "modern pagan." It will be put in uppercase when used of the self-image of practitioners of modern pagan religions, to describe their membership of those traditions.

3. Marina Warner, "Scholar Who Was Seduced by the Pagan Rituals of Witchcraft," *The Times* 25 November 1999, 46.

4. George Devereux, *From Anxiety to Method in the Behavioural Sciences* (The Hague: Mouton, 1967), xvi–xvii.

5. Benetta Jules-Rosette, "The Veil of Objectivity," *American Anthropologist* 80 (1978), 549–70; quotation on 550.

6. David Hayano, *Poker Faces* (Berkeley: University of California Press, 1982), 149.

7. Liza C. Dalby, *Geisha* (Berkeley: University of California Press, 1983), *passim*.

8. Jeanne Favret-Saada, *Deadly Words: Witchcraft in the Bocage* (Cambridge: Cambridge University Press, 1980), 10, 12; "About Participation," *Culture, Medicine and Psychiatry* 14 (1990), 190, 192.

9. Classics of this genre are Lila Abu-Lughod, *Veiled Sentiments: Honour and Poetry in a Bedouin Society* (Berkeley: University of California Press, 1986); and

Kirin Narayan, *Storyteller, Saints and Scoundrels: Folk Narrative in Hindu Religious Teaching* (Philadelphia: University of Pennsylvania Press, 1989). I am grateful to Sabina Magliocco for these references.

10. Katherine Ewing, "Dreams from a Saint," *American Anthropologist* 96 (1994), 571–83; quotations on 571–72.

11. Philip M. Peek, ed., *African Divination Systems: Ways of Knowing* (Bloomington: University of Indiana Press, 1991); quotation on 9.

12. David E. Young and Jean-Guy Goulet, eds., *Being Changed by Cross-Cultural Encounters: The Anthropology of Extraordinary Experience* (Peterborough, Ontario: Broadview Press, 1994); quotations from 8–9.

13. Edith Turner, "The Reality of Spirits," *Revision* 15(1) (1992), 28–32; quotation from 28.

14. For example Kirin Narayan, *Mondays on the Dark of the Moon: Himalayan Foothill Tales* (Oxford: Oxford University Press, 1997); Ruth Behar, *The Vulnerable Observer: Anthropology which Breaks Your Heart* (Boston: Beacon, 1996); Ruth Behar and Deborah Gordon, eds., *Women Writing Culture* (Berkeley: University of California Press, 1995); Lila Abu-Lughod, *Writing Women's Worlds: Bedouin Stories* (Berkeley: University of California Press, 1993). I am very grateful to Sabina Magliocco for supplying these references.

15. This is taken from one of the foundation texts of the discipline, Ninian Smart, *The Religious Experience of Mankind* (London: Collins, 1981); quotation on 12.

16. David J. Hufford, "The Scholarly Voice and the Personal Voice," *Western Folklore* 54 (1995), 57–76; quotation on 60.

17. Elizabeth Puttick, *Women in New Religions* (London: Macmillan, 1997), 6.

18. Jone Salomonsen, "Methods of Compassion or Pretension?', *The Pomegranate* 8 (1999), 4–13.

19. Amy Simes, "Contemporary Paganism in the East Midlands" (Nottingham University Ph.D. thesis, 1995); "Mercian Movement," in Graham Harvey and Charlotte Hardman, eds., *Paganism Today* (London: Thorson, 1996), 169–90.

20. Joanne Pearson, "Religion and the Return of Magic," 90–94; "Going Native in Reverse," *passim*.

21. Susan Greenwood, *Magic, Witchcraft and the Otherworld* (Oxford: Berg, 2000).

22. Robert J. Wallis, "Autoarchaeology and Neo-Shamanism" (Southampton University Ph.D. thesis, 2000), esp. 1–11.

23. Graham Harvey, *Listening People: Speaking Earth: Contemporary Paganism* (London: Hurst, 1997).

24. Patrick Curry, "Astrology on Trial, and Its Historian," *Culture and Cosmos* 4 (2000), 47–56.

25. Jone Salomonsen, "Methods of Compassion or Pretension?", 10.

Part Four
RE-LOCATING THE RESEARCHER

CHAPTER ELEVEN

BETWEEN THE WORLDS: AUTOARCHAEOLOGY AND NEO-SHAMANS
Robert J. Wallis

[G]iven the current place of shamans and shamanisms in spiritual movements and cultural commentary, it is incumbent on ethnographers to attend to the wider conversations both popular and academic, not only to
devise new ways of being heard but also to engage reflexively these contemporary inventions. (Atkinson 1992, 321)

Between the Worlds

"Shamanisms" have held a fascination for the Occident since "first
contact" with Siberian shamans in the seventeenth century (e.g.,
Flaherty 1992, Narby and Huxley 2001, Hutton 2002). The origins of neo-Shamans,[1] modern Western people engaging with shamanisms past and present for personal and communal empowerment, may also
stem from this era when some Westerners, so captivated by shamans—a
classic example of otherness—identified themselves as shamans. Suitable
examples in Britain, the first geographical location for my research (e.g.,
Wallis 2002a), might include a nineteenth-century Welsh "cunning man,"
the design of whose costume may have been inspired by accounts of
"Siberian tribal shamans" (Hutton 1999, 90); and also, the "modern
Druid" Dr. William Price, "a natural shaman. . . . In wizard's robes topped
by a fox-skin head-dress he performed the seasonal Druid rites at his altar on the Pontypridd rocking stone" (Michell 1997, 6; see also Green
1997, 152). In the USA, my second case study (e.g., Wallis 2003), nineteenth-century ethnographers fit my description of early neo-Shamans:
Lewis Henry Morgan was in search of "authentic America" and in his
men's secret societies participants "played Indian"; they wore Indian

clothes, took Indian names, and claimed guidance from Indian "spirit guides" and "visions" (Deloria 1998, 79). And when studying the Zunis of New Mexico, Frank Hamilton Cushing assumed a "white Indian" identity (Deloria 1998, 119): he had to "be adopted, he had to be made into a Zuni, and this required that he undergo the same social and ritual procedures which all Zunis underwent" (Roscoe 1991, 127). Following this process, Cushing, as a "white" or "neo-" shaman, wrote his "Remarks on Shamanism" (1897). It is in the last two decades, though, that "how I became a shaman," has solidified, as Clifton suggests, as "a distinct literary category" (Clifton 1994, frontispiece). The "Mind Body Spirit" shelves of bookstores across Britain and North America are filled with the autobiographical accounts of shamanic and neo-Shamanic practices and practitioners, which themselves encourage readers to become shamans.

In response to this—what might be called a neo-Shamanic revival—anthropologists have begun to study neo-Shamans as sources of valid ethnographic data. In over a decade, however, very few have done so with the reflexivity Atkinson advocates as essential to such analysis in the quotation opening this chapter. A small number of scholars have been developing "new ways of being heard" and fashioning reflexive methodologies (e.g., Alvesson and Sköldberg 2000, Blain 2002, Salomonsen 2002; and, now, papers in this volume) including collaborative work (e.g., Pettigrew and Tamu 2002) showing that where the researcher is not a member of the indigenous or shamanic community, there are still ways to represent "voice." It is, none the less, rather unsettling that these approaches have more often been eschewed in favor of monolithic deconstructions and sneering criticisms of neo-Shamans, usually aimed at Michael Harner's (1988, 1990) "core-shamanism"—as I have argued elsewhere (e.g., Wallis 2003) and set out below. Such approaches, which sweepingly suggest all neo-Shamans romanticize, decontextualize, and psychologize indigenous and prehistoric shamans, for example, are inappropriate.

First, the evidence—the diversity of neo-Shamanisms—resists such metanarratives; second, monolithic stereotypes are thoroughly outmoded in a postmodern era with its incredulity toward metanarratives; and third, such recent (over the last decade) theoretical and methodological developments in the field as self-reflectivity, autoethnography, anthropology at home, and interventions permeating the insider/outsider divide, engage with a more sensitive and nuanced approach. As such, while these postmodern directions—advocated strongly here for researching neo-Shamanisms and other Paganisms—are moving into the mainstream, only a few scholars have applied them to neo-Shamanisms and wider Paganisms. There have been a number of timely studies of Pagans by Pagan academics from a variety of disciplines, from the perspectives of anthropology (e.g., Greenwood 2000, Blain 2002) to religious studies (e.g., Harvey 1997, Letcher 2001, Pearson 2003) and history (e.g., Hutton 1999). It remains, however, not only that serious self-reflexive academic studies of neo-Shamanisms are lacking and that such studies of other Paganisms are still sparse and in their formative years—hence this volume—but also that even reflexive anthropologists (or nonpagan ones, at least) have yet to take neo-Shamans and Pagans seriously. This does not mean that only insiders—Pagans—can produce quality research on Pagans; it does mean that to date, in the early years of researching Paganisms, practitioner/academic research has been the most productive.

Neo-Shamans do not only engage with indigenous shamans, with implications for anthropologists and scholars of religion, however; they also attend to shamanisms past, raising issues for archaeologists and historians of religions. While anthropologists at least make occasional discussion of neo-Shamanisms—albeit most often with derogatory remarks—archaeology has yet to recognize many of the implications neo-Shamanisms have for its discourse. Following in the vein of many anthropologists, archaeologists tend to regard the New Age, and Paganisms and neo-Shamanisms—as with all "alternative" archaeology—negatively (but see Finn 1997, Denning 1999)—if, that is, they recognize them at all. As occupational atheists, and all too often "shamanophobes" (coined by Dowson 1996), archaeologists have only just begun to study world religions (e.g., Insoll 2001), let alone new or unconventional religions and archaeology, or their own religious experiences and the effects of these on their work. This neglect of research does not reflect an insignificant research area. On the contrary, neo-Shamanic engagement with the past is considerable and, likely, given the marked increase in Pagan numbers in recent years (e.g., Weller et al. 2001), accelerating.

My own position, then, as a Heathen neo-Shaman with training in archaeology and anthropology, puts me in a personal, idiosyncratic, and situated position from which to research the interface between these disciplines and neo-Shamanisms. During my Ph.D. I became a culture broker, and, to borrow a term often used by neo-Shamans (borrowed from anthropologists who themselves borrowed from indigenous shamans), I needed to walk "between the worlds" of academia and Paganism. In traversing a new field, and to avoid the off-the-cuff monolithic criticisms of neo-Shamans made by some scholars, I applied and developed a careful and considered interpretative framework—an approach I have termed "autoarchaeology" (e.g., Wallis 2000, 2003). Such a strategy for researching Paganisms, and specifically neo-shamans and neo-Shamanic elements of Paganisms, which I introduce and discuss in this chapter, facilitates a more sensitive and nuanced assessment beyond the derision of previous critics.

Toward "Autoarchaeology"

First, it seems appropriate to offer some context for how I arrived at "autoarchaeology." Writing as an academic/practitioner, I offer this personal, biographical narrative as ethnographic description of my initial involvement in both worlds, of how this dual location was first compromised and later negotiated, and with the intention that such transparency evidences my positionality as "between the worlds."

We arrived at the woods soon after 10 P.M. The mid-November cold was biting but an expectant mood motivated us and we headed along the footpath, torches leading the way, into the night. The sacred site we frequented consisted of two fallen but still living Yew trees which formed a v-shape, sloping down-hill. Each of the six of us touched a fist to his heart, a mark of respect to the trees and the place, before crossing over the barrier one Yew formed to enter the space. . . .

Shadows danced across Yew-bark as the well-tended fire crackled, real ale was swilled to alter consciousness, and talk of runes and the Anglo-Saxon "shamanic" god Woden filled the chilled night air. As an emerging Heathen group, we had all agreed that the runes were the mainstay of our practice, a means of engaging with Wyrd to steer our directions in life. We had also agreed that the personal use of a crystal sphere aided the "kenning" process—understanding the meanings of rune-casts. But we were still undecided on many things. Should we have galdr ("spoken spells") to invoke the gods and goddesses? Ought we to use gandr (wands) to "sign and send" runes in magickal workings? Might we use runes for healing as well as divination? Would deep trance states facilitate direct possession by deities and engagement with other nonhuman beings? For my part, I was keen to offer thoughts and suggestions. But I was a newcomer to this group and there had already been whisperings that perhaps the only reason I was present was to gather information and use this to further an academic career. In the woods, among these Heathens, I was "outed" as an academic. . . .

Late into the night, accompanied by jangling rattles and thudding drums we rowed the Yew boat to the otherworld; at the center of the Yggdrasil tree we cast runes, descried the "other" worlds of Norse cosmology, and then, as Woden himself had done, "fell back from there."

I was "out" in another way too. Sitting with my Ph.D. supervisor in his office the following day, we talked about the insider/outsider divide in anthropology and ways in which postmodern thought had contested the validity of the outsider's proclaimed objectivity. He encouraged me to be upfront about my being a Heathen neo-Shamanic practitioner in my academic work, as he had outed his own situated position as a gay man and archaeologist. But I felt that it was one thing to be known as an academic researching Paganisms among Pagans, and quite another to be "outed" as a Pagan among academics. The situation seemed compounded in this instance; I was already having difficulty convincing orthodox archaeologists that researching Paganisms was of importance—even in the postmodern theory- and reflexivity-driven climate of the discipline, many colleagues had their (often unspoken) reservations.

Theoretical and Methodological Considerations

On a day-to-day basis, these experiences among Pagans and among academics created many tensions for me. How was I to resolve being Pagan and retain my academic credibility, and indeed resolve being an academic and retain trustworthiness among Pagans? Already, the group I was working with—primarily with a spiritual imperative that persists to this day, but also in order to provide "data" for my research—or one member at least, had reservations about my involvement as an academic. I could not ignore the way in which I, the researcher, was having an effect on the group, my "informants." It was on recognizing this, combined with the support of my Ph.D. supervisor, that I found resolution: I could not pretend to not be involved, as an academic or a Pagan; I could not claim that my position as a scholar would not have an effect on my informants; I could not be entirely "rational" and "objective" as a Pagan when conducting this academic research. What I could be was honest and upfront about my own partiality and location(s) as an academic/practitioner. In so doing, I was drawing on the theoretical and methodological resources offered by a relatively recent postmodern shift in anthropological thought that, for many fieldworkers, has replaced misleading notions of scientific objectivity, complete impartiality, and metanarrative, with issues of reflexivity, diversity, and difference (e.g., Lyotard 1986).

The aim of detached scientific impartiality is no longer deemed tenable by many scholars, especially in social "science" and the humanities, since the sociopolitical background of the researcher inevitably influences and determines how data is interpreted and interpretations presented. In consequence, the worlds of archaeological and anthropological inquiry are now considered by many protagonists not to be neutral and objective, but partial and relational. These postmodern considerations have prompted researchers to be politically self-conscious and self-reflexive in their approaches (e.g., Denzin 1997, Davies 1999). Crapanzano (1980), as a pioneering example, found himself implicated as a subject during his study of a Moroccan spirit-worker; but rather than compromising the integrity of the research, this situation produced other, significant results that challenged orthodox ethnographic methods. One benefit of such critical self-reflection and reflexivity has been an increased permeability of boundaries between disciplines and transdisciplinary methodologies, which Geertz (1983) terms "blurred genres" and Strathern (1987a) refers to as "pastiche." The blurring of boundaries between archaeology, anthropology, and religious studies, and perhaps history and sociology, in this chapter and other papers in this book, promotes such an attitude.

The terms auto-, self-, experiential, reflexive, and self-reflective anthropology/ethnography, though different in their own ways, have been coined to exemplify this shift and enable a "political standpoint which at the same time will articulate and challenge the assumptions framing not only the standpoints they challenge but also those they occupy. . . . Standpoint specificity should be regarded as a resource, not a liability" (Wylie 1995, 268–70). This reflexive theme has been prominent in the theoretical and methodological stances of the autoresearcher, a position I have utilized and refined for approaching neo-Shamanisms. Indeed, examining the alterity of neo-Shamanisms requires a markedly alternative methodology.

Producing ethnographic insights into, or "fragments" of neo-Shamanisms[2] as an academic/practitioner myself involved qualitative auto/ethnography (see papers in Reed-Danahay 1997, particularly Motzafi-Haller; also Ellis and Bochner 2000; Blain 2002) and autoanthropology, methodologies described as "anthropology carried out in the social context which produced it" (Strathern 1987b, 17) or "anthropology at home" (Jackson 1987). At the essence of this "new ethnography" is the opportunity for experimental writing (e.g., Ellis and Bochner 1996), with a "self-consciously critical purpose." This does not result in fabricated ethnographies, but rather, these approaches provide the methodological tools for examining one's own culture ethnographically. Indeed, there has been a strong move for "insider research," the "self-as-subject" (e.g., Marcus and Fischer 1986), in the social sciences, including in studies on religion. As Blain (2000) has argued, though, simply adopting the "auto-"

insider position, "'going native,' total cultural immersion, in itself is not enough" since "critical awareness and reflexivity" with regards to this position are not necessarily intrinsic to the insider's position but are, of course, paramount for quality scholarly research. Autoanthropology reflexively problematizes the insider's standpoint and in place of a binary "insider" or "outsider" position, questions the dualism of the insider-outsider paradigm. In this volume Harvey argues for a "third position" that I might situate "between the worlds." In turn, experiential anthropology alters radically the field technique of participant observation by bringing into question not only the notion of "going native," but also the seriousness with which we take the beliefs and practices of our "informants" (more sensitively termed "collaborators" or "research assistants"), in a movement toward new and different engagements with them.

Armchair Ethnographies and the Insider-Outsider Divide

Taking our informants seriously and regarding the relationship as a collaborative one has other ramifications, including the production of otherwise irretrievable data. Academic literature on neo-Shamans consistently reflects an "armchair" approach, comprised of documenting neo-Shamanic practices and practitioners based only on written accounts. Such researchers tend to keep practices and practitioners at a distance, simply reading neo-Shamanic books, flyers, and workshop outlines, perhaps in an attempt to keep the perceived "fringe" at a suitable distance lest they become contaminated by alterity. In these instances, though many pertinent criticisms are raised, each researcher's monosyllabic voice intones the same stereotypes (e.g., Johnson 1995, Root 1996, Deloria 1998, Kehoe 2000), in which neo-Shamanisms are summarily deconstructed and belittled. Few researchers actually engage with their subjects, but while those that do tend to have a more "balanced" perspective, they tend to explore only one group of neo-Shamans, consistently producing "single-sited" ethnographies (e.g., Lindquist 1997 on Seidr in Sweden; and Jakobsen 1999 on core-shamans vis-à-vis the Greenlandic Angakkoq) or slim overviews (e.g., Harvey 1997).

The risk here is of short-sighted interpretations that extend laudable localized interpretations to a larger scale, thereby stereotyping neo-Shamanisms writ large. Not all neo-Shamans are core-shamans (who tend to refer to themselves as "shamanic practitioners," not "shamans"), not all neo-Shamans are romantic in their understandings of shamans, and not all neo-Shamans psychologize the world of spirits into Jungian metaphors (as

I have argued elsewhere, e.g., Wallis 2003). There is, for example, Philip "Greywolf" Shallcrass, until recently Joint-Chief of the British Druid Order (now the Druid Network), who reports suffering an initiatory sickness and a "calling" from the spirits (see below), which has, today, resulted in community-embedded healing and empowering Druidic practices. And there is "Runic John," a Heathen neo-Shaman, who describes possession experiences by the Northern god Frey and who believes that his relationship with the Anglo-Saxon god Woden enables him to divine the future and locate the sources of sickness in the clients that seek his help. Clearly a more nuanced approach to neo-Shamans is due, which takes into account and examines the diversity of practices and practitioners. But while taking neo-Shamans seriously and engaging with them directly is an important step towards this end, these directions have their own challenges.

In her seminal study of witchcraft in western France's Bocage, Favret-Saada argues that the idea of ethnographic "neutral positioning" is challenged in situations where experience is everything: "one must make up one's mind to engage in another kind of ethnography" (Favret-Saada 1980, 12). This "experiential anthropology" blurs the insider/outsider divide by suggesting that anthropologists treat their own experiences as valid data (Turner 1994, 72; 1989). In the past this might involve the risk of "going native" with a concomitant "fear of ostracism" (Young and Goulet 1994, 8) from one's academic colleagues who might deconstruct one's research in terms of its "subjectivity." Today, it is just as agreeable and more methodologically sound to take one's own experiences seriously, as valid data, and to disrupt the perceived impartiality of participant observation. Participant observation has never been an entirely satisfactory "scientific" field technique since "direct observation" is an impossible ideal, indicative of "pretension," and there are no checks and measures to "specify accurately the kind of participation required" (Salomonsen 1999, 8). Indeed, the extent to which one participates is also not stipulated and it is no small challenge to occupy a space that is "detached" during an intense shamanic ritual, for instance—a claim of "unaffected objectivity" is indeed logically impossible.

This is equally the case in a Western setting where, as I have experienced at neo-Shamanic rituals, involvement is all or nothing—being present necessitates taking part. Neo-Shamanisms are comprised of experiential "spiritualities" wherein modes of verification depend on personal insight, so that "journeys" to the world of spirits cannot easily be "observed" or "revealed." At the *Harner Method* "Way of the Shaman" Basic Workshop, for instance, it was not appropriate in my experience to sit on the edge, outside the circle of participants, and take notes or audio recordings—it is not the right of the ethnographer to impose a "right" to "intrude" and "record." For one thing, I would have been disrupting the setting inappropriately: my fellow participants were here to learn Harner's "shamanic journeying" techniques for often very personal reasons, and sometimes painful ones, shared emotionally with the group. A participant observation method of pretension would not only have disrupted this sensitive atmosphere, but this in turn would have colored my "results" and challenged my own practices as a Heathen neo-Shaman—I felt I could not legitimately claim to be an academic outsider at this workshop, only to be an insider as a Heathen neo-Shaman on leaving.

I made the decision to take part, to make shamanic journeys myself, and to take my own experiences and those of my workshop colleagues seriously. Salomonsen refers to this as a "method of compassion" that demands "embodiment rather than disengagement," insisting that such an approach promises a healthy component of reflexivity in which constructive critical comments can be made (Salomonsen 1999, 9–10; see also 2002, 17–21), thereby revising the impartialist strategy of going native behaviorally ("participant observation"), even emotionally ("empathy"), but not "cognitively" (Salomonsen 1999, 7). As Jackson points out:

> To break the habit of using a linear communicational model for understanding bodily praxis, it is necessary to adopt a methodological strategy of joining in without ulterior motive and literally putting oneself in the place of other persons; inhabiting their world. Participation thus becomes an end in itself rather than a means of gathering closely observed data which will be subject to interpretation elsewhere after the event. (1989, 58)

This is a process of "testing the limits of ethnography" (Marcus 1995, 95). A number of current anthropologists, ethnographers, archaeologists, and scholars of religion, are, then, adopting a "queer" methodology that disrupts normative methods of inquiry. Queer theory (which I have discussed in greater detail elsewhere, e.g., Wallis 2000, 2003), disrupts normativity, thereby not only "reordering the relations among sexual behaviours, erotic identities, constructions of gender" but at the same time "forms of knowledge, regimes of enunciation, logics of representation, modes of self-constitution, and practices of community" (Halperin 1995, 62). In this way, it "acquires its meaning from its oppositional relation to the norm. Queer is by definition whatever is at odds with the normal, the legitimate, the dominant" (Halperin 1995, 62) and queer theory is thus open to "anyone who feels their position (sexual, intellectual or cultural) to be marginalised" (Dowson 1998, 84).

Pitched in response to the "mainstream" (of society and/or academy), my identity as a Heathen neo-Shaman confers the sort of marginalization Halperin refers to and which is prerequisite to utilizing queer theory. This "Heathen neo-Shaman" identity is not fixed, however, but fluid and, along with the rest of my identity—as with that of anyone else's—as it is constituted in cognitive dissonance, shifts and responds to different people, circumstances and places. Thus there may be multiple "queer" locations from which to "see" in opposition to the norm, and to be seen as "queer." With my involvement in neo-Shamanisms and as a trained archaeologist, for instance, I have often felt torn between two irreconcilable opposites. I began my research feeling incredibly uneasy when trying to write an "objective" account of a "fringe" religion. But of course this subject area resists "objective" analysis and is sufficiently beyond mainstream research to foil my writing about it in a conventional academic way. On approaching my "informants" I felt further uneasiness, being too academically (objectively) minded to engage with them in as intimate a dialogue as I would have liked. I have been able to resolve conflicts such as these by unloading the needless baggage of perceived scientific objectivity, by being upfront about my own positionality to both academics and neo-Shamans, and transparent about other "hangups" and biases which constitute my identity (as intended by the section "Toward Autoarchaeology," for example). This has thwarted my conversations with some academics, but perhaps more importantly has opened up my relationship with neo-Shamans and more liberal academics considerably.

Through a somewhat painful transformation into an autoarchaeologist, I have found that my perspective does not fall in either archaeological or neo-Shamanic camps, nor midway between the two, but marks a different position altogether. As an autoarchaeologist, I am claiming my own voice. Just as I cannot speak only as a "neo-Shaman," to speak only as an archaeologist would downplay neo-Shamanic influences in my narrative. And to claim an objective standpoint from either position would ignore the influence of my work on neo-Shamans themselves. Scholars researching contemporary Paganisms, particularly those that are Pagan, are finding their research is agentic in Pagan (and in my case neo-Shamanic) understandings and constructions of themselves; this is a fascinating state of affairs and it is incumbent upon these researchers to be self-reflectively responsive in their involvement in the construction and development of Pagan identities. Having briefly referred to my own experiences in researching contemporary Heathen shamanic practices and Harner's core-shamanism, and the effects these engagements have had on the way I have conducted my research, I close my discussion by examining in more depth this important issue of the effects of academic-Pagan relations on Paganisms themselves.

Impacting Paganisms

One of my principal neo-Shaman informants, as remarked earlier, is "Greywolf." In one interview, I asked him to clarify the ways in which his practices might be approached as "shamanic." He responded:

> I avoid using the term shamanism wherever possible since it is, or at least should be, a culturally specific term for spirit workers in Siberia who have particular understandings of the universe and particular ways of working within that understanding. The kind of Druidry I practice works with the spirits of the land, is of the creatures who inhabit the land, of the gods and of our ancestors. The work we do is about communication, seership, healing, rites of celebration, rites of passage and teaching. . . . I sometimes use a drum as an adjunct to moving myself and/or others into altered states of awareness. I use a rattle for calling spirits, for cleansing ritual space or individuals' psychic space or for tracking spirit paths. I use incense for cleansing and purification. . . . I journey into the spirit world to find healing for people. I look to the spirit world for guidance and information.

This quote demonstrates Greywolf's sensitivity to the issues of his practices vis-à-vis those of indigenous shamans, since he evidently draws a distinction between his own (neo-Shamanic) practices and those of the Siberian shamans from which the modern term "shaman" derives. It also indicates, none the less, similarities between Greywolf's neo-Shamanic practices and those of indigenous shamans: in particular, Greywolf alters consciousness in a variety of ways to engage with a spirit world for the purposes of journeying and healing, within personal and community contexts—all consistent elements of shamanisms agreed on by a variety of academics (see footnote 1). Further, this quote evidences, I think, Greywolf's familiarity with academic theorizing of the term "shaman" and discussions on how shamanisms are constituted.

My own approach to shamanisms and neo-Shamans (e.g., Wallis 2002b, 2003), following Brown (1989) considers the "dark side of the shaman," such as battling with evil spirits and death threats, which is an integral part of some shamanic vocations (e.g., Jakobsen 1999). In contrast, at the core-shamanism basic workshops I attended, participants were instructed not to accept insects, reptiles, or carnivores as "spirit-helpers" or "power animals," perhaps due to the negative connotations associated with these creatures in the West—understandably, but unlike indigenous shamanisms, core-shamanism recommends less dangerous creatures to ensure beginners feel "safe."[3] I reflected on these experiences in a discussion with Greywolf, and he suggested:

> [T]he traditional shaman often fights against the calling, kicking and screaming all the way, and usually undergoes extremely painful experiences to learn. The neo-shaman signs up for a course of workshops and listens to New Age music. This obviously oversimplifes, but, from experience I know that there is a good deal of truth in it. My own path into spirit work has more parallels with the traditional than the neo approach. As a child, I used to fight demons who flew in through my bedroom window. I was the archetypal misfit/outsider. I spent some years driving myself to the edge of psychospiritual endurance and beyond. I suffered a major breakdown at the age of eighteen, complete with "initiatory" visions. The only things I lacked were a culture that understood in any meaningful way the nature of the experiences I was going through and a living teacher who could offer guidance. The pain of the path is something very little stressed. . . . The benefits are expanded awareness to an extent that can be positively ecstatic and the ability to help others. The harm is the potential for egomania, madness or death.

Again, these comments indicate a sensitive approach to and detailed understanding of native shamanic practices and relations between Greywolf's experiences and those of such indigenous shamans. Clearly, this neo-Shaman reflexively reworks his approach to shamanisms based on academic theorizing and ethnographic accounts. Commenting on postmodernity, Giddens suggests "in a reflexive world, we are all knowledge producers" (1995, 276) and more specifically Atkinson argues the "romantic engagement of shamans in popular culture forces anthropologists to rethink their own roles and discursive stances vis-à-vis shamanic practice . . . [an example of] the predicament facing contemporary ethnography" (Atkinson 1992, 323). Greywolf, along with other neo-Shamans and Pagans, is an active agent in the construction of knowledge, bringing coherency to personal and community worldviews and practices in a variety of ways. Academic analyses of these emerging networks of interaction, and of the roles of academicians in the productions of these, is in the vein of what Fabian terms "anthropology as interpretive discourse" (1983, 27).

It is interesting, for example, that widening Pagan networks are providing inspiration for new community practices. After meeting practitioners of the Heathen neo-Shamanic practice of oracular seidr (aspects of contemporary seidr are critically appraised by, for example, Blain 2002, Blain and Wallis 2000; see also Blain this volume), Greywolf commented:

> [I]t struck me as strange that the seidr tradition should be undergoing such a dramatic and widespread revival, yet no one in the Druid community seems to be taking a similar approach to the practice of *awenyddion*. I think this situation should change and wonder if maybe we can help that process along?

Greywolf suggests *Awenyddion* is a "Druidic" oracular practice described by Giraldus Cambrensis in his *Description of Wales* of the twelfth century:

> [A]mong the Welsh there are certain individuals called Awenyddion who behave as if they are possessed. . . . When you consult them about some problem, they immediately go into a trance and lose control of their senses. . . . Words stream from their mouths, incoherently and apparently meaningless and lacking any sense at all . . . and if you listen carefully to what they say you will receive the solution to your problem. When it is all over they will recover from their trance, as if they were ordinary people waking from a heavy sleep. . . . They seem to receive this gift of divination through visions which they see in their dreams. (n.d.)

The extent to which Giraldus' statement is evidence of "Druid" traditions or a reflection of reality in twelfth-century Wales is not of concern to me here; what is interesting when researching Paganisms from an interpretative ethnographic point of view is how these Heathen and Druid members of the Pagan community are engaging with one another and, inspired by each other's trance practices, developing new ones. The current reconstruction of Awenyddion marks the development of a Druidic neo-Shamanic practice that is communally empowering—as seidr has been and continues to be for Heathens. Such reconstructions have significance for academics other than anthropologists of new religions: archaeologists and historians in particular ought to engage with such "alternative histories" (e.g., Schmidt and Patterson 1995), not only because of the challenges they may present to orthodox discourse, but also because of the contributions they may make to academic understandings of the past. In this light, Hutton opines, optimistically,

It is a classic case of a situation in which the experts are feeding the public with information while leaving it free to make such imaginative reconstructions as it wishes. . . . Druids are well placed to take advantage
of it . . . indeed, it is almost a duty on their part to do so, for the more
people who are involved in the work, and the broader the range of plausible pictures imagined, the healthier the situation. (1996, 23)

Arguably, Hutton stands alone as a senior academic historian who takes contemporary Paganisms and their alternative histories seriously (e.g., Hutton
1996, 1999). Rather than leaving Pagans "free" to make their "imaginative reconstructions" then, it might be a case of other "expert" historians simply neglecting or ignoring Pagans, or simply not knowing they exist at all.

While the issues are dealt with better by anthropologists and scholars
of religion, the situation in current archaeology is analogous to that in historical studies. Scholars have begun to work collaboratively with local/
indigenous communities and found that such engagements, including the
incorporation of "other" perspectives, enrich and transform the archaeological exercise itself and facilitate "insights into how the past is experienced, and how it is negotiated and understood in the present. . . . [A]s
archaeologists we benefit from a more diverse understanding of the past"
(Moser et al. 2002, 243). Ironically, these community archaeologies engage with indigenous people abroad but have failed to recognize Pagan
communities in Britain and their interactions with the archaeological past.
Many Pagans regard archaeological sites as "sacred" places, with each new
religious/celebratory and intrinsically engaged encounter at sites
(per)forming meanings well beyond the detached "visitor experience"
marketed by the heritage bodies (see especially reports by the Sacred Sites,
Contested Rights/Rites Project, e.g., Wallis and Blain 2003, and see
www.sacredsites.org.uk). These Pagans, at the "honeypot" sites of Avebury
and Stonehenge in Wiltshire, and at smaller less frequented sites in Penwith, Cornwall, and elsewhere across Britain, campaign actively with regards to site management and presentation (e.g., Norfolk 1998, Prout
1998, Latham and Norfolk 1998/9, Fleming 1999), and may offer alternative (to the archaeological orthodoxy) interpretations (e.g., Cope 1998;
Gyrus 1998, 2000)—all of which tend (with some exceptions, e.g., the
National Trust Guardianship at Avebury and roundtable negotiations over
access to Stonehenge) to be regarded negatively by archaeologists (e.g.,
Price 2001; Pryor 2001) or ignored altogether.

So, indigenous communities outside the British Isles have to some extent been involved in community archaeology projects, with the result that

there is "analysis of the ways in which 'others' have themselves translated and subverted Western [academic] discourses" (Moser et al. 2002, 234). This is a reflexive and dialogic situation "where archaeologists not only educate affected cultural groups . . . but also *become* educated" (Moser et al. 2002, 225). Yet for their part, British archaeologists have ignored their own "new-indigenes," contemporary Pagans. This presents a potential archaeopolitical time bomb, given the pressures Pagans are now putting on heritage bodies. I anticipate "alternative community archaeologies" coming to the fore in British archaeology in the next few years, as archaeologists increasingly yield some of their power over knowledge about, and hitherto exclusive access to, the past, and ways in which the past and its monuments are curated. From an autoarchaeological perspective, this will mark a sea change in orthodox archaeological research methods towards explicitly, reflexively, taking Pagans and their engagements with the past seriously.

Conclusion

Tanya Luhrmann is well known for her research into British Wicca (e.g., Luhrmann 1989). She has been praised for:

> preserving her anthropological integrity. "The anthropologist," she writes, "is meant to become involved but not native" (320). Immersing herself in magical practices, she has nonetheless succeeded in preserving her identity as an anthropologist. . . . Anthropology at its very best. (Flaherty 1991, 154–55)

In his review, Flaherty misses the point: since Luhrmann was initiated into witchcraft and conducted rituals, she did go native; but in ceasing to be a coven member or solo practitioner after fieldwork, she is perceived to have "come back" again. Contra Flaherty, I argue that Luhrmann would have produced an equally critical ethnography of Wicca had she remained "native." Indeed, by not being upfront about her academic agenda with her subjects, Luhrmann's research had a serious negative impact on some of them, who claimed their traditions had been damaged by her releasing of initiate-only knowledge in published form. In being politically explicit about my research with the Heathens I practiced with and who have since become my closest friends, as well as my other neo-Shamanic informants such as Greywolf and Runic John, initial tensions over my being an academic were resolved: over time we reached mutual respect and understanding; the relationship was cooperative and never exploitative. In turn,

I consider my writings on neo-shamans to be more sensitive and critically nuanced as a result of this collaboration.

Pearson, a recent Wiccan academic/practitioner, asserts, following in the vein of established "auto-" research, "I do not . . . consider myself to have broken the anthropological taboo against 'going native,' for I already was native. The situation has in fact been quite the reverse, 'insider going outsider, going native in reverse'" (Pearson 2001, 8). The situation may, in reality, be more complex, more dissonant, and less black-and-white than this, but never the less Pearson's approach demonstrates how the Pagan academic becomes a "broker," negotiating ways of presenting the "insider" view in ways that the "outsider's" discourse can understand (Blain 1997), and inhabiting both worlds, indeed multiple worlds, simultaneously. Operating within the "global village" necessitates a "multiple-positioning" on the part of the researcher (see papers in Fardon 1995) to enable the "peripatetic, translative mapping of brave new worlds" (Marcus 1995, 114). More than being a single "boundary crosser" with "dual identity" (Reed-Danahay 1997, 3), though, I, as a multisited autoarchaeologist of neo-Shamanisms, have had multiple lines to cross and consciousness to inhabit.

It might be argued that postmodern discourse of this kind is at risk of judgmental relativism in which "anything goes," where "reality and fact are no longer certain" (Doty 1990, 269), also termed "epistemological hypochondria" by Geertz (1988, 71). It has therefore become imperative that researchers move from a "perhaps self-destructive position, into an era of self-confidence" (Ahmed and Shore 1995). Lindholm is convincing in this regard:

> [P]ostmodernism has led, in the worst cases, to self-indulgent personal accounts [and] a kind of journalistic anthropology in which both theory and data are eschewed in favour of self-congratulatory literary flourishes. But the best practitioners have paid heeded attention to previously ignored alternative narratives and have developed a healthy critical stance towards the validity of anthropological research. These are constructive contributions worth emulating. (1997, 753)

Autoarchaeology has voiced alternative narratives and made contributions to anthropological and other research methods rather more than it has become a subjective, self-obsessed "literary flourish" without serious value to academia. The balances and checks in this area are provided by peer review, a method considered—quite appropriately—the mainstay of academic credibility. In effect, it does not matter how close researchers get to their "subjects" so long as their findings express the level of insight and constructive, critical evaluation that one's academic peers require for acceptable scholarship. In assessing my own work (Wallis 2003), Hutton has stated:

> His writing is marked by an uncommon generosity and empathy to academic scholars, indigenous peoples and neo-Shamans alike, and that his stance as somebody who is both a university-based scholar and a neo-Shaman genuinely has enabled him to understand both worlds and to treat both with justice and respect. (Review submitted to the publisher.)

If Hutton's peer review is agreeable, then it is possible to not only "go native," but moreover to be native and produce quality scholarly work. This does not mean traditional ethnography is outdated and has no place in anthropology today, and it does not mean that one has to be an "insider"— a Heathen neo-Shaman for example—to glean insights into neo-Shamanisms and neo-Shamanic aspects of Paganisms; it does mean autoethnography is at least as valid as the conventional approach and that "being changed" (e.g., Young and Goulet 1994) by one's ethnographic experiences is not only part of the job but also brings new, particular insights to one's research. As such, this paper demonstrates that being "between the worlds" of academia and neo-Shamanism, indeed in both worlds simultaneously—and more accurately in a different autoarchaeological position altogether—results in important insights into neo-Shamanisms and the research process itself that might not otherwise be obtained.

Despite these benefits, the self-avowed and theorized academic/practitioner position has not become the norm—and nor should we expect it or want it to become so. Furthermore, at the time of writing, I have not reconciled all of the uncertainties and tensions I confessed to when opening this chapter—and similarly this is a situation I have come to accept as a necessary and important one. If the research methods for researching Paganisms are to continue to develop, refine, and gain coherency, then it is not imperative that the academic/practitioner position becomes mainstream and "establishment." Indeed were it to become so, its foregrounding of plurality, multivocality, and difference would be compromised—it would cease to be queer and gain insights from a standpoint which is in opposition to the norm, with the consequence that it might then misrepresent Pagan voices as homogenous, not discursive. In turn, were all the uncertainties I experience in my research to become resolved or sublimated then my queer, discursive standpoint would perhaps be compromised—I would cease to be a broker, between the worlds. It is not essential to be an academic/practitioner to produce insights into contemporary Paganisms/neo-Shamans, but alongside other chapters in this volume, this paper argues that Pagan studies by Pagan scholars have been invaluable in the formative years of researching Paganisms.

Notes

1. For full discussion of this term, its orthography, my reasoning for using it over such terms as "Urban Shamans," "Modern Shamans," "White Shamans," and "Western Shamans," its relation to "indigenous shamanisms," and connections between neo-Shamans and contemporary Pagans, see Wallis 2003, 30, 32–33. Given the subject of this volume I should make clear that I use the term "neo-Shamans" to also examine pervasive shamanistic aspects in contemporary Paganisms (e.g., Wallis 2000, 2002a, 2003).

2. Ethnographers today recognize that it would be arrogant to assume a complete or comprehensive ethnography is possible and speak of partial and situated knowledges (e.g., Marcus 1995, Blain 2002). I follow in this vein by using "ethnographic fragments" here as a shorthand disclaimer.

3. Ironically, the most common animal helpers and power animals practitioners tend to identify with are, in my experience, those superior in the food chain, from wolves, bears, and lions, to ravens, eagles, and dolphins; only rarely do such organisms as slugs, worms, beetles, and mice enter neo-Shamanists' animal-helper repertoire. This may indicate an overtly romantic slant in the approaches of some practitioners, not to mention a misunderstanding of what constitutes a "carnivore," but whatever the influences, accepting these animals as helpers is a clear contradiction of advice given at the core-shamanism basic workshop and in Harner Method literature that often comprises many neo-Shamans' first point of contact.

References

Ahmed, A. S., and C. Shore
1995 Introduction: Is Anthropology Relevant to the Contemporary World? In *The Future of Anthropology: Its Relevance to the Contemporary World*, edited by A. S. Ahmed and C. N. Shore, 12–45. London: Athlone.

Alvesson, M., and K. Sköldberg
2000 *Reflexive Methodology*. London: Sage.

Atkinson, J. M.
1992 Shamanisms Today. *Annual Review of Anthropology* 21: 307–30.

Blain, J.
1997 On the Knife-Edge: Seidr-Working and the Anthropologist (Unpublished paper presented at Re-Enchantment: An International Conference on

Contemporary Paganism and the Interface Between Nature and Religion(s), King Alfred's College, Winchester, UK).

———.
2000 Speaking Shamanistically: Seidr, Academia and Rationality. *Diskus* 6. Available online: http://www.unimarburg.de/religionswissenschaft/journal/diskus/blain.html

———.
2002 *Nine Worlds of Seidr-Magic: Ecstasy and Neo-Shamanism in North European Paganism.* London: Routledge.

Blain, J., and R. J. Wallis
2000 The "Ergi" Seidman: Contestations of Gender, Shamanism and Sexuality in Northern Religion, Past and Present. *Journal of Contemporary Religion* 15(3): 395–411.

Brown, M. F.
1989 Dark Side of the Shaman. *Natural History* (November): 8–10.

Clifton, C. S.
1994 Shamanism and Neoshamanism. In *Witchcraft and Shamanism: Witchcraft Today, Book Three,* edited by C. Clifton, 1–13. St. Paul, Minn.: Llewellyn.

Cope, J.
1998 *The Modern Antiquarian: A Pre-Millennial Odyssey through Megalithic Britain.* London: Thorsons.

Crapanzano, V.
1980 *Tuhami: Portrait of a Moroccan.* Chicago: University of Chicago Press.

Cushing, F. H.
1897 Remarks on Shamanism. *American Philosophical Society Proceedings* 36: 183–92.

Davies, C. A.
1999 *Reflexive Ethnography: A Guide to Researching Selves and Others.* London: Routledge.

Deloria, P. J.
1998 *Playing Indian.* New Haven, Conn.: Yale University Press.

Denning, K.
1999 Archaeology and Alterity. Paper presented in the Method and Theory 2000 session at the Society for American Archaeology Annual Meeting, Chicago.

Denzin, N. K.
1997 *Interpretive Ethnography: Ethnographic Practices for the 21st Century.* Thousand Oaks, Calif.: Sage.

Doty, W.
1990 Writing the Blurred Genres of Postmodern Ethnography. *Annals of Scholarship: Studies of the Humanities and Social Sciences* 6 (3–4): 267–87.

Dowson, T. A.
1996 Review of *The Hunter's Vision: The Prehistoric Rock Art of Zimbabwe,* by P. Garlake. *Antiquity* 70: 468–69.

———.
1998 Homosexualitat, teortia queer i arqueologia (Homosexuality, Queer Theory and Archaeology). *Cota Zero* 14: 81–87. (In Catalan with English Translation).

Ellis, C., and A. Bochner
2000 Autoethnography, Personal Narrative: Reflexivity Researcher as Subject. In *Handbook of Qualitative Research,* edited by N. K. Denzin and Y. S. Lincoln, 733–69. Thousand Oaks, Calif.: Sage.

———, eds.
1996 *Composing Ethnography: Alternative Forms of Qualitative Writing.* Walnut Creek, Calif.: AltaMira.

Fabian, J.
1983 *Time and the Other: How Anthropology Makes Its Object.* New York: Columbia University Press.

Favret-Saada, J.
1980 *Deadly Words: Witchcraft in the Bocage.* Cambridge: Cambridge University Press.

Fardon, R., ed.
1995 *Counterworks: Managing the Diversity of Knowledge.* London: Routledge.

Finn, C.
1997 Leaving More than Footprints: Modern Votive Offerings at Chaco Canyon Prehistoric Site. *Antiquity* 71: 169–78.

Flaherty, G.
1992 *Shamanism and the Eighteenth Century.* Princeton, N.J.: Princeton University Press.

Flaherty, R. P.
1991 T. M. Luhrmann and the Anthropologist's Craft: Differential Identity and the Ethnography of Britain's Magical Subculture. *Anthropological Quarterly* 64: 152–55.

Fleming, S.
1999 Psychic Vandalism. *The Right Times* 5 (Spring Equinox): 12–14.

Geertz, C.
1983 Blurred Genres: The Refiguration of Social Thought. In *Local Knowledge: Further Essays in Interpretive Anthropology*, 19–35. London: Fontana.

———.
1988 *Works and Lives: The Anthropologist as Author*. Stanford, Calif.: Stanford University Press.

Giddens, A.
1995 Epilogue: Notes on the Future of Anthropology. In *The Future of Anthropology: Its Relevance to the Contemporary World*, edited by A. S. Ahmed and C. N. Shore, 272–77. London: Athlone.

Green, M.
1997 *Exploring the World of the Druids*. London: Thames and Hudson.

Greenwood, S.
2000 *Magic, Witchcraft and the Otherworld: An Anthropology*. Oxford: Berg.

Greywolf
n.d. *Awen: The Holy Spirit of Druidry*. Available online: www.druidorder .demon.co.uk/Awen.html

Gyrus
2000 *On Prehistoric Rock Art and Psychedelic Experiences*. Available online: http://home.freeuk.net/rooted/2cb.html

Gyrus Orbitalis
1998 *The Goddess in Wharfedale*. Available online: http://www.suresite.com/ oh/v/verbeia/

Halperin, D. M.
1995 *Saint Foucault: Towards a Gay Hagiography*. Oxford: Oxford University Press.

Harner, M.
1988 What Is a Shaman? In *Shaman's Path: Healing, Personal Growth, and Empowerment*, edited by G. G. Doore, 7–15. Boston: Shambhala.

———.
[1980] 1990 *The Way of the Shaman*. London: HarperCollins.

Harvey, G.
1997 *Listening People, Speaking Earth: Contemporary Paganism*. London: Hurst.

Hutton, R.
1996 Introduction: Who Possesses the Past? In *The Druid Renaissance*, edited by P. Carr-Gomm, 17–34. London: Thorsons.

———.
1999 *Triumph of the Moon: A History of Modern Pagan Witchcraft*. Oxford: Oxford University Press.

———.
2002 *Shamans: Siberian Spirituality and the Western Imagination*. London: Hambledon.

Insoll, T., ed.
2001 *Archaeology and World Religion*. London: Routledge.

Jackson, A., ed.
1987 *Anthropology at Home*. London: Tavistock.

Jackson, M.
1989 *Paths toward a Clearing*. Bloomington: Indiana University Press.

Jakobsen, M. D.
1999 *Shamanism: Traditional and Contemporary Approaches to the Mastery of Spirits and Healing*. Oxford: Berghahn Books.

Johnson, P. C.
1995 Shamanism from Ecuador to Chicago: A Case Study in Ritual Appropriation. *Religion* 25: 163–78.

Kehoe, A. B.
2000 *Shamans and Religion: An Anthropological Exploration in Critical Thinking*. Prospect Heights, Ill.: Waveland Press.

Latham, C., and A. Norfolk
1998/9 A Press Release on Behalf of the Genius Loci of West Penwith. *The Druid's Voice: The Magazine of Contemporary Druidry* 9 (Winter): 27.

Letcher, A. J.
2001 The Role of the Bard in Contemporary Pagan Movements. Unpublished Ph.D. thesis, School of Cultural Studies, King Alfred's College, Winchester, UK.

Lindholm, C.
1997 Logical and Moral Dilemmas of Postmodernism. *Journal of the Royal Anthropological Institute* 3: 747–60.

Lindquist, G.
1997 *Shamanic Performance on the Urban Scene: Neo-Shamanism in Contemporary Sweden*. Stockholm Studies in Social Anthropology no. 39. Stockholm: University of Stockholm.

Luhrmann, T. M.
1989 *Persuasions of the Witches Craft: Ritual Magic in Contemporary England.* Cambridge, Mass.: Harvard University Press.

Lyotard, J.-F.
1986 *The Postmodern Condition.* Manchester, UK: Manchester University Press.

Marcus, G. E.
1995 Ethnography in/of the World System: The Emergence of a Multi-Sited Ethnography. *Annual Review of Anthropology* 24: 95–117.

Marcus, G. E., and M. M. J. Fischer
1986 *Anthropology as Cultural Critique: An Experimental Moment in the Human Sciences.* Chicago: University of Chicago Press.

Michell, J.
1997 Stonehenge: Its Druids, Custodians, Festivals and Future. *Druidlore* 1: 4–6.

Motzafi-Haller, P.
1997 Writing Birthright: On Native Anthropologists and the Politics of Representation. In *Auto/Ethnography: Rewriting the Self and the Social,* edited by D. E. Reed-Danahay, 195–222. Oxford: Berg.

Moser, S., D. Glazier, J. E. Philips, Lamya Nasser el Nemr, Mohammed Saleh Mousa, Rascha Nasr Aiesh, S. Richardon, A. Conner, and M. Seymour
2002 Transforming Archaeology through Practice: Strategies for Collaborative Archaeology and the Community Archaeology Project at Quseir, Egypt. *World Archaeology* 34(2): 220–48.

Narby, J., and F. Huxley, eds.
2001 *Shamans through Time: 500 Years on the Path to Knowledge.* London: Thames and Hudson.

Norfolk, A.
1998 Cornish Sacred Sites and Their Protection. *Pagan Dawn: The Journal of The Pagan Federation* 128 (Lughnasadh): 15–18.

Pearson, J.
2001 Going Native in Reverse: The Insider as Researcher in British Wicca. Paper presented at BASR (British Association for the Study of Religion) Annual Conference: Religion and Community. Faculty of Divinity, University of Cambridge.

———.
2003 *Wicca: Magic, Spirituality and the Mystic Other.* London: Routledge.

Pettigrew, J., and Y. Tamu
2002 Healing Here, Healing There and In-Between: A Tamu Shaman's Experience of International Landscapes. In *Practitioners, Practices and Patients: New Approaches to Medical Archaeology and Anthropology*, edited by G. Carr, 109–24. Oxford: Oxbow.

Price, N.
2001 An Archaeology of Altered States: Shamanism and Material Culture Studies. In *The Archaeology of Shamanism*, edited by N. Price, 3–16. London: Routledge.

Prout, C.
1998 Saving Sacred Sites. *The Right Times* 2 (Summer Solstice): 6–7.

Pryor, F.
2001 *Seahenge: New Discoveries in Prehistoric Britain*. London: Harper-Collins.

Reed-Danahay, D. E., ed.
1997 *Auto/Ethnography: Rewriting the Self and the Social*. Oxford: Berg.

Root, D.
1996 *Cannibal Culture: Art, Appropriation, and the Commodification of Difference*. Boulder, Colo.: Westview.

Roscoe, W.
1991 *The Zuni Man-Woman*. Albuquerque: University of New Mexico Press.

Salomonsen, J.
1999 Methods of Compassion or Pretension? Anthropological Fieldwork in Modern Magical Communities. *The Pomegranate* 8: 4–13.

———.
2002 *Enchanted Feminism: The Reclaiming Witches of San Francisco*. London: Routledge.

Schmidt, P. R., and T. C. Patterson, eds.
1995 *Making Alternative Histories: The Practice of Archaeology and History in Non-Western Settings*. Santa Fe, N.Mex.: School of America Research Press.

Strathern, M.
1987a Out of Context: The Persuasive Fictions of Anthropology. *Current Anthropology* 28(3): 251–81.

———.
1987b The Limits of Auto-Anthropology. In *Anthropology at Home*, edited by A. Jackson, 16–37. London: Tavistock.

Turner, E.
1989 From Shamans to Healers: The Survival of an Inupiaq Eskimo Skill. *Anthropologica* 31: 3–24.

———.
1994 A Visible Spirit Form in Zambia. In *Being Changed by Cross-Cultural Encounters: The Anthropology of Extraordinary Experience*, edited by D. E. Young and J.-G. Goulet, 71–95. Peterborough, Ontario: Broadview Press.

Wallis, R. J.
2000 Queer Shamans: Autoarchaeology and Neo-Shamanism. *World Archaeology* 32(2): 252–62.

———.
2002a Waking the Ancestors: Neo-Shamanism and Archaeology. In *Shamanism: A Reader*, edited by G. Harvey, 402–23. London: Routledge.

———.
2002b The *Bwili* or "Flying Tricksters" of Malakula: A Critical Discussion of Recent Debates on Rock Art, Ethnography and Shamanisms. *Journal of The Royal Anthropological Institute* 8(4): 735–60.

———.
2003 *Shamans / Neo-Shamans: Ecstasy, Alternative Archaeologies and Contemporary Pagans*. London: Routledge.

Wallis, R. J., and J. Blain
2003 Sites, Sacredness, and Stories: Interactions of Archaeology and Contemporary Paganism. *Folklore* 114(4): 307–21.

Weller, P., A. Feldman, and K. Purdam
2001 *Religious Discrimination in England and Wales*. Home Office Research Study 220. Available online: www.homeoffice.gov.uk/rds/pdfs/hors220.pdf

Wylie, A.
1995 Alternative Histories: Epistemic Disunity and Political Integrity. In *Making Alternative Histories: The Practice of Archaeology and History in Non-Western Settings*, edited by P. R. Schmidt and T. C. Patterson, 255–72. Santa Fe, N.Mex.: School of America Research Press.

Young, D. E., and J.-G. Goulet
1994 Introduction to *Being Changed by Cross-Cultural Encounters: The Anthropology of Extraordinary Experience*, 7–13. Peterborough, Ontario: Broadview Press.

CHAPTER TWELVE

TRACING THE IN/AUTHENTIC SEERESS: FROM SEID-MAGIC TO STONE CIRCLES

Jenny Blain

Introduction: Becoming a Heathen Researcher

For researcher/practitioners in any field, boundaries between "participation" and "life" are necessarily blurred. For those who "work" shamanically, the fuzzy boundaries between multiple worlds are what they live with on a daily basis. So, I sit at my computer writing about reflexive research and new directions for twenty-first-century ethnography, distracted by the voice of an ivy-clad tree outside my window and the raindrops that gleam in sunlight on its branches, and the e-mails from first-year students wanting help with assignments, thinking of the journey I have been on, and how it continues.

Unlike several of the researchers in this volume, I was already a practitioner before I started writing about pagan spiritualities. My Ph.D. research, involving ethnographic interviews with men and women as parents, was a different kind of "insider" research. It led me into discussing feminist methodologies, Dorothy Smith's (e.g., 1987) concepts of institutional ethnography and "sociology for women," poststructuralism, reflexivity, and "voice," and introduced me to discourse analysis. Increasingly, the discourse analysis began to take over. How and why did people say what they did? Where did their ideas, concepts, terms, and phrases come from? How did discourse inform practice, and practice become both content and context for discourse? How was hegemony—and resistance—constructed through discourse? Was theorized transformation—the hope of critical feminist research—possible?

The Ph.D. over, I found myself able to spend some time on myself, and indeed needed to do so. I'd moved to Canada from Scotland with my then partner, when our first child was a toddler. My time was spent dealing with young children; graduate school at Dalhousie University, taking an M.A. within sociology/anthropology, and the Ph.D. through the School of Education; trying to earn a living through contract research; and, increasingly, teaching. Spirituality—previously focusing mostly on reading mythology, archaeology, and ethnographic accounts of "indigenous" religion, and relating these, in my own mind at least, to political and environmental action—had necessarily taken a back seat in the intensity of "writing up" the Ph.D. But now a chance encounter led me to a new pagan discussion group starting up in Halifax, and I was able to share knowledge with other interested people. My knowledge tended to be in European mythologies and feminist theory, including some Goddess spirituality but more notably the various tellings of the "Matter of Britain," the Mabinogi, and the "northern" mythologies of the Eddas, and my general reading had delved into Wiccan and other ritual forms. Now I had some kind of community in which to identify my Paganism, leading to the formation of a women's ritual group. The Internet led me to discover other people interested in Heathenry—though mostly known as Ásatrú, "Northern Tradition," or "Norse Paganism"—and I began to find, to my joy, that many, indeed most, were not the racists I had feared. (Some discussion of ethnicity and spirituality will emerge later in this chapter: theorizing tensions between "nationalisms" and "ancestors," within constitutions of self through imagined or invented "pasts," is a focus of my present research.) Blending feminist/academic and pagan interests as a follower of "Germanic" and "Celtic" goddesses—and having recourse to several university libraries—I started to investigate Old English healing charms until a ritual use of the Nine Herbs Charm (see e.g., Pollington 2000) resulted in a form of self-dedication to a god rather than a goddess.

Meanwhile, I had been furthering my thoughts on discourse analysis, and turning my Ph.D. into conference papers and journal articles. For personal reasons I jettisoned my intention to turn my thesis into a book, despite having done a considerable amount of work on this project. At a meeting of the developing local CUUPs group (Covenant of Unitarian Universalist Pagans) an acquaintance, Judith, asked where my research would go next, and I replied that I was looking for a project. "Why not research *this*?" she asked. But researching paganism did not then seem, well, valid. The thought was, however, planted: and on receiving the shocking news of Judith's sudden death I knew what I should do. An application to my university's internal research fund generated "seed money" to permit interviewing and some transcription assistance; and this in turn generated a further, successful application to the Social Sciences and Humanities Research Council of Canada. I was now a researcher of people's accounts of their spirituality, dealing with issues of "voice" and "representation" and increasingly turning to my own participation, and to ethnographic methodologies, in developing the nature and focus of my research into identities and discourses of Paganisms.

My teaching commitments had enabled some reconnection with interests in physical anthropology and prehistory, from hominid evolution, through cave art and shamanism via a summary paper by Lewin (1995) I'd given my class, to the prehistory of Nova Scotia. An opportunity had arisen in 1994 for a family holiday in Britain, when I took my children to some of the places that had meant much to me as a child, discovering others during the visit (see Blain 2001). Returning to Canada and to discussions of indigenous Mi'kmaq spirituality, I found that I was increasingly examining my own engagement with place and representation. Northern Europe with its grey skies began to call through three years of researching Heathen communities in Canada and the U.S.—during the course of which I stumbled across the reemergence or reconstruction of Northern shamanic practice, or seidr, and realized that here I had a focus for my research and my own personal quest for meaning. A conference presentation in Canada gave an opportunity for an article in a research methods textbook (Blain 1998) and detailed e-mailed discussions of practitioner meanings with Winifred, the first seidworker I saw in action. A chance search of the Internet led to discovery of the 1997 Re-enchantments conference in the U.K., and hence to meetings with other researchers of Paganism, with whom collaborations and friendships have grown, some of whom present their work in this book, and the first steps on my journey home.

In this chapter I will sketch the areas—Heathenry, neo-Shamanism,[1] and "sacred sites"—in which I am attempting to move from a description of practice to a theorizing of identity: seeing Paganisms as discursively constituted within a host of cultural/societal concepts of self, other, "superstition" versus rationality, and what constitutes "religion," against the ever-present model of hegemonic Christianity. I do so in ways that attempt to draw on the complexities of reflexive ethnography (on which generally see Alvesson and Sköldberg 2000) and the ethics and epistemologies of representational research (see James, Hockey, and Dawson 1997).

First, some methodological and epistemological context: for some time, Denzin (1997) and others have called for traditional ethnography to garner a new lease of life by "coming home"—by turning the anthropologist's detailed gaze on everyday life in Western societies, and by rendering the familiar "unfamiliar," examining constructions of meaning and practice. Recent developments within ethnography have continued the critique by examining ethical implications of representing the "other," and discussing possible alternatives, especially autoethnography (Reed-Danahay 1997, Blain 2002a), so that the concept of the exotic "other" studied objectively by the Western anthropologist is misplaced—though "Paganisms" still seem "exotic" to many of the audiences whom I address. Yet even within autoethnography the task is to render the familiar unfamiliar (Denzin 1997), and turn a critical and inquiring gaze on oneself, and one's own contexts which are problematized (and to some extent destabilized) by that gaze. While continuing to speak of "ethnography coming home" and gleefully using the term "autoethnography," I take on board Cohen and Rapport's critique that "the very nature of their enquiry means that anthropologists are never 'at home,' for their enquiry consists in asking questions, or in making questionable what those whom they study do not question" (1995, 10). That "self" inherent in "autoethnography" too is problematic: who is the "Jenny Blain" who speaks in the context of this book or a pagan ritual or in dealing with the details of everyday life, relationships, feelings, and motivations? Giddens' (1991) concept of the reflexive self goes some way to providing a framework for theorizing self, but as Cohen (1994) and Cohen and Rapport (1995) point out, it assumes a separation of self and context: "he depicts the self as engaging with a world which is somehow independent of it—and therefore has to be seen as not of its making" (Cohen and Rapport 1995, 7). Yet in attempting to examine my own involvement with Paganisms and sacred sites, I am required to examine the process in which I become conscious of this involvement, and through my consciousness to not merely react, but actively accomplish meaning and change. And consciousness, as Kapferer (1995, 150) has it, "while embodied, nonetheless extends beyond its physical confines into the world which is fundamentally and inseparably part of the dimensionality of consciousness." My knowing is inherently bound up with the situation I know and the situation from which I know, and—to return to a feminist critique—the power relationships and structures within which my embodied consciousness is constituted and the processes within which I create relationships or rituals.

My work therefore draws on concepts of "situated knowledges" and agency, on reflexive ethnography, and critical discourse analysis. In pursuing authorings of identity and sacredness, I am persuaded by Marcus' arguments of the need to "follow the people . . . the metaphor . . . the story . . . the conflict" (Marcus 1998, 90–95), tracking my own biography as well as those of others, problematizing my own agency and finding myself changed through my own authorship. Willis (2000, 68) argues: "the post-postmodern task, especially of the ethnographic imagination, is to analyse and depict the practices through which the structures of discourse, culture and communication find new articulations with, or dialectical uptake within, the structures of material and institutional life." Whether we define autoethnography on the practice and politics of Paganisms as "postmodern" or "postpostmodern" or as something else entirely, such analyses and depictions of change, spirits, and meaning challenge forms of expression and representation. This book is perhaps too academic a format, but for the moment, at any rate, it will serve.

Reconstruction and the Community

First, description. This requires some thoughts on "reconstruction"—how and of what—and on how and where reconstruction meets shamanistic practices of today. I will then move to my involvement with Heathenry and seidr, and attempt to develop autoethnographic understandings of practice and meaning. In later sections I will return to the issue of researching "sacred sites."

To the outsider, "Paganisms" may appear very similar. Within today's practice there is distinct diversification, in theology and philosophy, in ritual format, in practitioners' relationships with Earth, spirits, and deities, and in the extent to which practitioners or groups draw on source material from outside Paganisms. People's practices and relations to their paganism have arisen within, from my observation, four modes: those of goddess spiritualists, Wicca and eclectic groups who use the format of Wiccan rituals, shamanic practitioners, and reconstructionists. While many individuals work within one of these broad modes, others move between them. Communities structured within each, therefore, have some overlap.

The term "reconstructionist" is problematic on a number of levels, but used by many within the communities. Basically, "reconstructionists" work from the principle that documents or artefacts from "the past" hold clues to religious or spiritual practice, and that this practice can be used meaningfully in today's world. Confusion may exist between reconstruction and reenactment: within reenactment the purpose is to display the forms or processes of the past, for a number of purposes. Today's practitioners point out that they are attempting to reach what they consider the centrally important points of religion—for instance an understanding of how people approached their deities—and work with this to create something that "works" within today's environment. The extents to which they base practice on "evidence" (from literature or archaeology) vary considerably. The reconstructionist groups I've engaged with are mostly Heathen, with some input from Celtic and Roman reconstructionists. The Heathens are drawing on material from Northern Europe, the Icelandic Eddas and sagas, English healing charms, archaeology, and folktales from Britain and Scandinavia. As part of their practice they have come across references to seidr, a type of magical practice referred to in the sagas and possibly reflected in some of the Eddic poems. This appeared to be a way (or set of ways) in which "ancestors" connected with deities and spirits: some argued about whether seidr was "good" magic, as it is usually described as performed against the hero of the sagas; some argued about precise meanings of the term (differentiating "seidr" from "spae" as in the Scottish "spaewife"); some became exceedingly worried by inherent ambiguities of gender and sexuality that appear in some of the descriptions (see e.g., Blain and Wallis 2000a, Meulengracht Sørensen 1984); and some others simply attempted to "reconstruct" seidr practices, for protection, for healing, and notably for divination, which they called "oracular seidr." It rapidly became evident that I had my own relationship to the practices involved, and indeed that my understandings were constituted within my own involvements with "seeing," gods, and spirits. To describe and analyze the practices of others meant a detailed engagement with and appraisal of my own involvement, on several grounds: including not only understanding of "experience" and analysis of an interwoven perception/experience/discourse but also my understanding of anthropological obligation. I was investigating the practices of "others," people who, while not the exotic "other" of conventional ethnographic description and hence postcolonial critique, were those who chose to distance themselves from mainstream rationality by claiming contact with ancestors, gods, and spirits. As a practitioner and an ethnographer, it behooved me to examine the ethics of the situation, and to reflect on how my words and works impacted on those who had given me their time and their trust. Later I found that others (e.g., Ellis and Bochner 2000), in very different circumstances, had come to similar conclusions, and I had a word for my writing: autoethnography.

My book, *Nine Worlds of Seid-Magic* (Blain 2002a), is a contribution to the literature on shamanism and neo-shamanism, and on Western Paganisms today. It also discusses understandings of medieval literature, the "texts" on which "reconstructionist" practitioners draw. It engages with feminist theory and queer theory, and issues of appropriation. It is written from an autoethnographic stance, as my understandings of practice, and indeed the central chapter—described by a colleague and advance reader as not only central physically, but theoretically and spiritually, to the book—describes my own experiences and understandings within the seidr altered consciousness, and subsequently it develops my own understanding of some source literature and my engagement with Icelandic poetry. Yet because of the exigencies of "academic" analysis, I cut some sections from that central chapter, because they were too revealing of my own explorations of Heathen shamanic practice.

Oracular Seidr

The most complete description in the sagas comes from *Eiríks saga rauða*. A farm in Greenland faces famine; a seeress is invited to prophesy, and comes to the farm. Her costume is described in detail, her cloak, her staff, even her eating utensils and the laces on her shoes. A special meal is made for her, and a platform (hjallr) prepared on which she will sit to prophesy. The next day she makes what preparations she needs, sits on the seidhjallr, and a woman sings to call the spirits. The seeress speaks of the end of the hard times, prosperity for the community, and prophesies also for individuals, notably the young woman who sang so beautifully that more spirits attended than ever before, enabling clearer vision or more detailed knowledge. Some, both heathens and academics (e.g., Borovsky 1999) have considered that the seeress would not only "see" future prosperity, but work actively with the spirits, to create it.

One thousand years on, within "reconstructionist" Ásatrú, a woman was searching for "something for the women to do" when the men were playing "Viking games" at festivals or other events. She knew the description of the Greenland seeress, and with a group of friends began to attempt the reconstruction. The details were, of course, missing: what song was sung, how the ritual was structured, what "preparations" the seeress made. She and some other group members had experience with other forms of shamanistic practice—for instance, from workshops run by anthropologist-turned-neo-Shaman Michael Harner (see Harner 1990)—and so they filled in what they could, using drum and chant, writing a song to summon the spirits. They set the central "seeing" within a ritual that included calling upon land-spirits, and Ódhinn and Freyja, the deities who are described in the old texts as making seidr; and when the first seeress sat on the "high seat," a raised chair to represent the seidhjallr, she "saw" for the community and the individuals within it. Experimenting further, they found songs to call spirit animal helpers, and built in "safety" measures to protect audience members who might venture onto unfamiliar territory. The oracular seidr ritual they have developed takes all participants on a "guided meditation" that explores part of the cosmology and ends at the gates of Hel's realm, the place of the ancestors, where wild hemlock flowers year-long, at the East Gate where Ódhinn summoned a völva to answer from her grave, but there the audience stops and waits while the seeress journeys further, in a deeper level of trance, to seek answers for participants' questions.

Diana Paxson, who did much of the initial work, has described the experience of being a present-day practitioner of seidr within a non-shamanic culture: her own rationalistic worldview wars with her seidr experiences (personal communication), and in describing the experiences she falls back on the discourses of archetypes, symbols, and the collective unconscious. Other seeresses, possibly with less exposure to psychological explanations, are more direct. Rauðhildr, working within Heathen cosmology of the well of wyrd, the Norns, and the tree Yggdrasill, dealing with the beings of all the nine worlds, describes her own initiation—by spirits, not by humans—which appears as a classic shamanic experience of death-and-dismemberment. She went, naively she says, to visit the Maurnir—female giants or etins, the oldest ones who live in a cave. They have much wisdom and knowledge from earliest times. She asked, again naively, if they would share with her their wisdom. No, said they, but she could become part of the wisdom—and when she agreed, they ate her, throwing aside the bones. Her bones were lying on the cave floor when Loki—a Trickster deity, regarded somewhat suspiciously within Heathenry—appeared, dancing what she described as "a shaman dance," and calling on the gods to put her back together. Once re-membered, she thanked him, to which he replied, "once, you gave me a drink," that is, by honoring him in a blót, a heathen ritual. She did not discuss what might have been the outcome had Loki not appeared.

Others report their own experiences: for instance, Bil, in New Mexico, discusses a severe illness lasting two years, and recovery in which he came to recognize that his life was no longer his own, but was coordinated by a team of "helper" spirits. He is not an oracular practitioner: his work is chiefly with bringing balance to specific situations involving humans and spirits, and much of his work is with those who are dying. Malcolm, in Scotland, engages with healing. Winifred puts people in touch with deities. Thus, people report specializing in specific areas of practice. Their spirit helpers differ also: Bil works with animal and plant spirits, and local spirits or deities relating to place. Rauðhild speaks with ancestors, aided by her fylgja or familiar. In my own experience, there may be deal-ings with remote ancestors, but images or simply "knowing" are brought by animal helper spirits.

The processes—of oracular seidr as "performed" by Rauðhild, or heal-ing seidr by Bil—were deliberately constructed: they seem to work for others who create their own versions, or come to this practice from other perspectives (e.g., from core shamanism). One Western shamanic practi-tioner who has learned seidr from a different source describes it as the most ecstatic practice she engages with: she has also taken part in a Hea-then-style seidr, which equally "works." "Ecstasy" in this shamanic/ anthropological sense implies being "taken out" of oneself, losing self within an altered consciousness process—though from a practitioner's point of view "reconstituting self" as infinite potential within another place or dimension may be as accurate. For myself, the experience of sit-ting, staff in hand, within two worlds, with difficulty moving my lips to speak what I "see" and having such "seeing" recognized by those who seek knowing or healing, is profoundly ecstatic and emotional. Descriptions emerge in poetry or painting, as much as in narrative or academic prose.

The Inauthentic Seeress

Within academic and Heathen/pagan communities, seidr "reconstruction" is critiqued: for instance, that the practices were not, and are not now "shamanism"; and that in any case, what happens today is not the seidr (or spae-working) of the past—the details are wrong. These criticisms depend on a view of both past and present, it seems to me, as fixed, bounded, and "true." An examination of them leads into an interweaving of theories of identity and Shamanism/neo-Shamanism, as the seidwoman sits leaning on her staff looking to both *past* and *present*, and from these speaking po-tential *futures* as she constructs them within her own community and her own being, embedded within contexts of time and "lore."

First—yet easily overlooked—the practice is important to the practi-tioner. "Getting it right" matters, though "getting it right" is evaluated in the seeress' terms, not necessarily those of the academic onlooker. Seid-folk want something that "works." Different practitioners find their own ac-commodations with the descriptions in the literature and within what seems possible and practical today. The seeress of Eiríks saga rauða had a hat of black lambskin lined with white catskin—at which most practition-ers would draw a line. Diana Paxson suggests that for purposes of today's costuming, rabbit fur and catskin can be seen as interchangeable. Fine, say others, if what you want is costuming, but the passage may refer to the seer-ess' association with an animal spirit; the catskin may link her with her fyl-gja (animal ally, fetch, or familiar). Yet others see the description as simply that of a woman of substance in the community: when doing seidr, they dress in whatever helps them fit the part, not the outward form but the in-ner mindset that helps them access the otherworld of spirit helpers. The staff described in Eiríks saga rauða has a knob, decorated with brass and stones. Some use this description; others make for themselves, again, what works—perhaps a connection with a particular tree, or they may not use a staff while prophesying. Some "show" may assist in dealing with the human community present, marking the seidkona as apart from her "audience": other elements assist spirit communication, and in the end each makes their own compromise. A dark cloak may serve both purposes, while help-ing to block the light and hence assist alteration of consciousness.

Here, practicality, performance, community, and identity come to-gether. "Authenticity" is important for many within reconstructionist reli-gion, while shamanistic practitioners are more apt to go with "what works." Seid-folk, attempting to derive and use shamanistic practice within a particular reconstructionist-cosmological framework, may like-wise have concerns for authenticity, but these are tempered by inspiration and by drawing on other (e.g., indigenous) sources—and in particular, by practicalities. What works today?

Second, what "works" does not refer to the human audience or to in-dividual clients. Seidr is not a "performance" put on for human consump-tion (Blain and Wallis, in prep.); rather, "performance" aspects of the process relate to creation of a relationship between human and nonhuman inhabitants, within a specific cultural/cosmological framework; and, as the relationships are being created today, the techniques and tools used have to make sense for today's practitioners. Consciousness is altered through a variety of techniques (potentially by the will of the seer, who then uses en-vironmental stimulae, sounds and so forth, to achieve something through the altered state) (Blain 2002a, 2002b), usually including song, drum, nar-rative, or all of these. To an outside ethnographic observer, the "perfor-mance" is judged on how it looks or sounds; to the practitioner, it is judged by whether it works: Is she able to use the altered consciousness to obtain information that "makes sense" to querants? To an audience member, though, the criterion may be simply, is the *information* of direct use.

In another sense, though, the ritual can be viewed as a performance that must be sufficiently convincing to members that they join in: the en-ergy of the singing becomes a vehicle which the seeress uses to meet her spirits and gain knowledge from them. This phenomenon, of "shamanistic performance" being a community involvement, has been described elsewhere, notably by E. Turner (1994, personal communication).[2] With sufficient involvement and energy supplied by others, the seeress loses "self" to find a new focus for identity in the immediate community (often the spirit community) and the negotiation that implies. In other forms of seidr practitioners report dissociation of self, and a sense that what they do or say is the product of a communication or negotiation process; at times they report "possession" experiences (usually by a deity, although one practitioner gave me a story of possession by a malevolent ancestral spirit, which his helper spirits advised him how to expel). Indeed, deity possession may be a way to give community querants answers to their questions.

Third, what "works" is not guaranteed. Recent e-mail discussions—I am a member of several e-mail lists devoted to seidr practice—have focused on this point, with several practitioners attempting to demonstrate, to those who had not directly engaged with either oracular or healing seidr, the uncertain nature of the process and their doubts and qualms about future or upcoming events. Nonpractitioners attempted to address this in terms of "confidence"; practitioners spoke of the unpredictability of spirit help, and the sense that, because the efficacy of the "performance" is not due only to them, they do not know whether—or when—helper spirits may eventually refuse help.

Fourth, seidworkers are aware of tensions within the community, differences in interpretation of the old material, an "evil" reputation of seidr, and (see Blain forthcoming) pejorative comments against men who make seidr, today or in the past, and even debates over terminology in today's practice. Yet the debates on practice present or past indicate something about its flexibility, and its association with spirit help. One criticism persistently raised is that "this is not shamanism." This, however, may be a matter of opinion. It all depends on what definition of "shamanism" you adopt. The derivation of "shamanism" from the Tungus/Evenki "sama:n" via Russian and German explorers and the curiosity of a Western public seeking to romanticize while differentiating themselves from a "primitive" "other" has been discussed elsewhere (Flaherty 1992, Wallis 2003, Blain and Wallis 2000a). Some attempted, and competing, definitions have been more persistent than others: the "master of spirits" (e.g., Shirokogorov 1935, Jakobsen 1999) versus Eliade's "Archaic techniques of ecstasy" (1964). Each of these has relevance—for some places, and some times—and Merkur has pointed out (1992) that all definitions of shamanism exclude some people who by others' definitions—including those of practising shamans—are "shamans."

Rather than definition, we can seek "shamanisms" in the accounts of both shamans and anthropologists, as processes and relationships by means of which specific people work in specific ways for specific communities, to connect past and present, spirits and people, ancestors and those of today. Within anthropology, Greene (1998) discusses South American practitioners' "appropriations" of what works—a shaman works creatively and inventively, and Western medical practice becomes drawn upon by indigenous practitioners. Taussig's (e.g., 1987) locating of Colombian shamans within politics and history serve as a reminder that their practices cannot be regarded only as individual "techniques of ecstasy": they and their practitioners are part of the processes of change, power, and resistance that structure and shape communities, and they have their own relationships to state and society. The locating of practitioners within Western structures may be less obvious but still pertains, particularly if we see societies of postmodernity as fluid, wherein boundaries are becoming permeable and identities dynamically constituted. Theories of "neotribalism" (based on Maffesoli 1996) suggest fluid and temporary adherence to discursively derived identities, with a sense of change and impermanence that drives many Europeans and Americans in quest of roots—with varying results that may often end, it seems to me, in the fixed, embattled identities of fear. Seidfolk, likewise seeking both identity and roots, may find themselves able to traverse place and time, and to accept change in both present and past.

Seidman Bil says of authenticity that "everything I do is authentic." More simply put, because he draws on a cosmology that he distinguishes as Heathen, based in part on the old literature and folklore, part on his own earlier experiences, and part on the countryside in which he lives and its spirits and legends, technique is not an issue. "Doing it right" relates not to reconstructing the past but to creating something that works for his clients and himself, today, where he is. In this and other ways seidfolk can draw on understandings from elsewhere—including from academia. Practitioner and academic constructions need not be at odds: where each learns from the other, something new is constructed, and at least some of today's practitioners of seidr and other "Western" shamanisms look to recent research not only for "facts" about artefacts or practices, but for discussions of the complexities of religion, shamanism, and culture.

Shamanism, Ethnography, and Seidr

"Shamanism" may be an overworked word and its definition is, necessarily in my view, unclear (see Blain forthcoming; Blain and Wallis in prep;

and notably the introduction in Thomas and Humphrey 1996). What I maintain is that approaching seidr past and present—and similar manifestations, such as the Welsh *Awenyddion* described by Giraldus (and discussed with me by druid-"shaman" Greywolf—see Wallis, this volume)—in ways that are informed by "shamanism" gives an ability to analyze and discuss what's going on without a need to fall back on symbols, "belief," and archetypes.

Today, seidworkers experience transformation of self and others, within negotiated relationships with spirits and with human members of their communities. They draw on understandings of cosmology and past practice, together with these negotiated relationships, to create their practices today. Their clients seek instruction on daily life in a complex urban society, once again informed by contemporary understandings of practices of 1,000 years ago that may combine the attraction of the exotic shaman "other" with nostalgia for a constructed past. Yet however audiences or clients view their work, seidworkers are not reconstructing the past, but shifting across 1,000 years to weave Wyrd[3] from past threads, in creating shamanic forms for the twenty-first century. They talk about fear and change, within meetings, the experience of trance, mingling everyday and "extraordinary," known and unknown. Seidfolk and others like them are constructing identity out of change, movement, and the unpredictability of the otherworlds. Within postmodernity, change and choice replace the older certainties. The ability to deal with unpredictability, but to ground it, root it in past, and relate it to future, goes beyond neotribalism into a weaving of meaning or reweaving of Wyrd, that may challenge conventions and representations, and with the challenges begins a new construction of community and practice.

Toward an Ethnography of Self

Such a description of seidr requires me as ethnographer to "take seriously" (Young and Goulet 1994) the reported experiences, emotions, and understandings of practitioners, and to go beyond this into a reflexive engagement with practices. I have previously used the examples of "shaman"-as-ethnographer and ethnographer-as-shaman (Blain 2002b). Each goes into relatively unfamiliar territory, explores practices and questions those (spirit or human) who seem "indigenous," and translates practitioner/spirit understandings into accepted discourse using what techniques and "props" they can (whether essays, photographic images, or the physical *ihamba* tooth described by Turner 1994) to represent the "other" to the community *for whom* they work.

When the ethnographer is also a "shamanic practitioner" things can become rather complicated. In particular, the boundaries between communities become very blurred. Thus, I have been asked to speak in both Pagan and academic forums as a practitioner, and I have written material for a practitioner audience. As such, I am personally implicated in the development of seidr practices, pagan understanding, and indeed of Heathenry on an international basis, as a practitioner who is regarded as some kind of "expert" in the techniques that I practice (a label that I would dispute—in this time none or few are expert and some are more experienced than me—but neither am I a beginner). I am a practitioner who walks, at times uneasily, in academic, practitioner, and other worlds, but who can never completely belong to one or another. This, however, leads to a consideration of how and where I practice, and how I understand myself, theorize my own identity/ies. Guédon has discussed her own situation as ethnographer among the Déné, spending years, even decades, in learning to "read" the landscape as do the people she was among, perceiving it "as a process and as an unfolding story" (1994, 47). To conclude this article I return to discussion of landscape, how I "read" it, and its importance for my own work and spirituality.

Stone Circles and the Sacred Sites Project

First, while my research on "sacred sites" and pagan appropriations of this may seem a separate study, it is not. Identities are focused and developed around place and community, authored in understanding of past and its development into present. In (re)turning to the stone circles of Britain, both theoretically and in terms of relocating there, my focus is not only on what people do there but on their convoluted development of meanings. Stonehenge at summer solstice is an outstanding case in point. A small selection of expressed meanings, from fieldwork at summer solstice 2001, includes:

"Wizard" This is the most magical place on earth. Bar none.
Man   I figure a lot more people are realizing what they are in the
          whole scheme of things and uh you know, this structure was
          built to kind of register and keep time on the bigger scale of
          things, with the planets and stuff, to keep people in check
          with the land . . . and be at least an equal part of it. And I
          think that really these sort of things are forgotten.
Man   [I]t's slight desperation as well really. A lot of people don't
          feel like they fit with, you know, society these days, and feel
          that like monuments like this are symbols of a really civi-
          lized society in a truer sense, purer sense, you know like

much more equality, much fairer, anyway people walking, treading lightly on earth. . . .

It's like an ancestral memory bit that's stored up, you know.

You're drawn here, quite simply the bottom line is you're drawn here.

Man   Stonehenge, for me, represents individual freedom. And the individual freedom of everyone here, who've all come for their own reasons, but it all represents that spark of individual freedom. That's what it means to me.

Woman   My mum always says that when she was a kid, she and her sisters come here for picnics and that, so I just thought that, wow you can't get close to the stones normally, so I just really would love to get actually really close to them. Get such a sense, this amazing feeling when you actually get in there. Yes, that's why I'm here!

Man   I think it's just a case, right, of just you're free away, right, it's an anarchy that's working, and you're free. Stonehenge used to have a festival here that was a month long, for maybe twelve years.

Man   I was conceived here twenty-three years ago today!

Woman   I've come 'cos it's part of my faith.

Man   I've been to these stones now probably about five times, and I've always been resenting, well not resenting but I've always been really unhappy about the fact that I can't come and touch them . . . and so I've come along to touch them, you know. Makes it seem more meaningful and real. And I can't get over how *huuuuge* they seem once you actually get in amongst them

Woman   I follow quite a solitary Wiccan path, really, so it fits in. . . . And my sort of ancestry back as well, like I can (be) remembering, as well, passing on. And, and celebrating change, again.

Man   [T]hey've become so symbolic, and so much that's about freedom now. Like the first thing that was to accord with me was about ten years ago when I saw this documentary on the battle of the beanfield, and the Levellers uh sort of did that song about it, you sort of heard about festivals and stuff, but they've become so much a part of what's about freedom and struggles and resistance against, against sort of rules, and you know, all that sort of stuff. I guess that's part of it as well, really. That's part of it that sort of becomes important. So again it's not just about a physical thing, but that in

        itself is—well I guess spiritual, in a sense, and cultural, you
        know, they've come to mean so much.
Woman   It's almost like a focus as well, for some people.

Not all meanings relate to personal spiritual quest—and not all those given above are from self-identified pagans. Some are explicitly political—the focus on freedom, on the recent history of conflict at the site. Pagan understandings emerge within contexts which are (increasingly?) contested; communities overlap and shift. Paganisms are neither monolithic nor uncomplicated. People are developing their Paganisms within physical, geographical, political, and spiritual contexts and communities. Travellers develop Paganisms that differ from those of middle-class suburbanites, and there is no single "Paganism" that is more valid than any other (despite the media's love for presentations of Witches and Druids). In coming to Avebury or Stanton Moor or Kilmartin—all locations of prehistoric monuments considered "sacred sites"—people bring their understandings of time, archaeology, and humanity, and they "read" the site, potentially engage with spirits there if they can hear them, and author their own engagements. As an anthropologist, I may consider some of their understandings silly, misplaced, bizarre, or overreliant on outdated archaeology (notably Gimbutas' concept of the "Great Goddess"—Gimbutas 1999, Blain 2003), but I cannot claim that the spiritualities so authored are invalid. What I can do is attempt to facilitate negotiations by, once again, walking in two worlds—using my credentials in each, as academic and as Heathen shamanic practitioner, to establish a basis for interactive communication—though knowing that by doing so I may compromise my own standing in either world in the eyes of some. While some pagans may regard my interventions as the "thought police," others seem willing to hear at least some ideas that (for instance) the proximity of heat and water damages sandstone megaliths at which "offerings" may also be made, and that local wights may—if listened for—not really regard tea-lights and their holders as the most fitting offering a pagan could make.

My own experiences of sacred sites—prehistoric monuments—inform my writing and my involvement with the Sacred Sites project (see Wallis and Blain 2003; http://www.sacredsites.org.uk). To me, these are places which hold their own, multiple, stories; where landwights and ancestors are more rapidly met with; places of healing and/or ecstasy; places where my own biography becomes interwoven with site and stones, and where the echoes of joy or despair feed future involvements; places where histories are played and replayed, and where multiple pasts are reinscribed with every "visitor." But "visiting," as one informant points out, is what you do in the home of another, and hence a large part of my writing becomes an attempt to present the tension between "visitor" and "householder" to all who use these places. For we all claim them as places where we—archaeologists, site managers, or pagans—are "at home," and yet such places are always also the home of another, including from my animist perspective the ancestors who dwell/dwelt there—and whom we may disturb.

> sally you just wait 'til we get home,
> one says, loudly, as the child
> stands, wailing, in the puddle at the gate.
> now you be quiet!
> as the row of biker engines rises
> above the cries, higher than shouting boy who runs
> around the great stone standing, or the plane above
> or children rolling cartwheels down the bank
> or whirring cameras as grandma poses,
> one hand on hip, the other touching cold
> stone—stephen you race your brother now, see who
> can stand on that stone first!
> until across the circle, one stands on the bank,
> arms waving, triumphant, he alone the conqueror,
> the undefeated by requests to please not
> tread on this stretch of turf just yet,
> while still here the tour group stands to hear of
> death that was (not) by stone-fall
> and I stand
> by broken ring-stone, viewing broken lives,
> and walk toward the ditch, to gaze
> on one jackdaw feeding
> where once lay covered a dwarf-woman's bones. . . .
> (Avebury, Easter Sunday 2001, J. Blain)

My engagement, therefore is not neutral or uninvolved, and I require to devise my own ethics of research/participation. As with researching Heathenry, my obligations go beyond the conventional ethics of non-malfeasance, beneficence, nondeception, and informed consent, into a need to consult as widely as I can and make my participation transparent and findings accessible (e.g., by publishing in popular journals [e.g., Blain and Wallis 2000b, 2002]). Representation of site, as well as of communities, is a major issue: and there is need to acknowledge my involvement and to present it both as a motivating force and as a way of knowing about place and time, as a central focus to my identity, which affects, in turn, those whom I meet or those who read my work, and the relationships I form. Ethnography is political. I seek to learn, analyze, understand, in the spirit of what George Marcus describes as a reemergence of comparison, not in the older sense of direct (controlled) comparing of points or categories, but as juxtaposition which emerges from

> putting questions to an emergent object of study whose contours, sites, and relationships are not known beforehand, but are themselves a contribution of making an account which has different, complexly connected, real-world sites of investigation. (1998, 186)

So, some of my "sites" are also "sacred sites" (just as the "neotribes" of analysis also describe themselves as "new-tribes"—for which the Sacred Sites project has coined "new-indigenes"), while others include the All Party Parliamentary Archaeology Group, and the several forums where heritage management discourses are presented and negotiated. My attention is now turning to the stories in the land, the living landscape as "mythscape," and ways in which these stories are told, juxtaposed, and contested to create and further meanings and practices today. Here, once again, discourses conflict and the describing and analyzing of "mythscapes" requires care. While the difficulties I face in representing meanings of cultural landscape are not so great as those detailed by Layton (1997)—my practitioners and heritage management speaking what is on the face of it the same language—meanings inherent in landscape are not necessarily readily translatable into heritage discourse, and can become obscure or risible for a rationalist-academic audience (2000). My task is not only to translate and analyze but to recontextualize.

Yet, finally, the focus on land and "neotribes" returns me to the disputed question of "whose land" and to the discourses of nationalism and/or racism that can appear in many guises. While many practitioners make plain that attachment to, for instance, Stonehenge can be made by anyone who feels drawn to the place, still there is a strand that suggests that some people—possibly "Celts" or even "Saxons"—have a greater claim than others. In a survey of pagan texts, Gallagher has remarked on the lack of contextualization or historical periodicity in much pagan discourse, and a concomitant assumption of inheritance, whereby our links to "the past" or "Ancient times" (Gallagher 1999, 20) become mystified as ancestry or possibly membership in "the Celtic nation." I have examined a specific instance (Blain 2001) where unexamined use of concepts of ancestry, place, and "spirit teaching" led to a decontextualized practice of "Celtic shamanism." The focus on indigeneity is a difficult one, associated as it is with the concept of living on specific land "from time immemorial" in Canada and other ex-colonial areas. To see nationalism and discourses of land and "rights" constructed within a history of colonialism, while it may fit in with postcolonial anthropology, requires a considerable amount of historical and political context.

The extreme claims of right-wing groups—whether "Celtic" or "Odinist"—run counter to the expressed views of most pagans (including all Heathens) with whom I have personally spoken. Nevertheless the discourses of nationalism easily permeate thought and inform action. Hage (2000) has implied (of racism in Australia) that having *someone* to point to as extreme racist enables much of the general public to maintain a low level of unthinking uncritical racism: so it seems to me that within Paganisms, the existence of a few obvious racists or nationalists enables finger-pointing, which rather than causing people to examine their own discourse, in general allows them to feel better and ignore potential problems.

For myself as autoethnographic researcher of Heathenry, sites, and Paganisms more generally, it becomes important to not only record practice and discourse, but see myself as involved in its creation. A few webpages, and my reputation within the Heathen and Pagan communities, attest to my earlier involvement against racism in the heathen community. A long-standing collaborative plan to examine this situation of nationalism has been postponed, time and again, due to work pressures. Now, within narratives of "sacred sites" and "sacred landscape," it may be time to bring this to the forefront. In moving to look at "mythscapes" I have to ask "Whose?" and "For whom?" in ways that open up this area. I have, therefore, to see my own practices, my poetry and my academic writing, as complicit in whatever developments result: and myself, my being, as implicated and intrinsic within the continued construction of Paganisms for today.

Notes

1. "NeoShamanism" is a problematic term. Some practitioners dislike it, and some use "Western Shamanic Practice" as more appropriate. Nevertheless it is useful. See Wallis (2003 and this volume) for details.

2. The community can equally destabilize "performance" as Schieffelin describes (1996 and 1998). This interweaving of community and shamanic accomplishment or meaning seems to be particularly important for any study of identity among paganisms, yet it is currently overlooked. The question of "performance,"

however, while useful anthropologically, is inherently problematic for many practitioners, as discussed by Blain and Wallis (in prep.).

3. "Wyrd" is a concept found in the medieval literature of North Europe, which has a meaning somewhat akin to "fate" or "destiny." However, wyrd appears not to have been fixed or static, but changing according to how people construct their lives and create their obligations: and not only people but gods, spirits or wights, communities, and worlds have their wyrd. So today for a researcher of postmodern spirituality, wyrd serves as a good metaphor for the complex reshaping of action, obligation, discourse, and understanding, in which personal and community agency, culture, history, biology, and political processes all have their part.

References

Alvesson, M., and K. Sköldberg
2000 *Reflexive Methodology*. London: Sage.

Blain, J.
1998 Presenting Constructions of Identity and Divinity: Ásatrú and Oracular Seidhr. In *Fieldwork Methods: Accomplishing Ethnographic Research*, edited by S. Grills, 203–27. Thousand Oaks, Calif.: Sage.

———.
2000 Speaking Shamanistically: Seidr, Academia, and Rationality. *DISKUS*. Available online: http://www.uni-marburg.de/religionswissenschaft/journal/diskus/blain.html

———.
2001 Shamans, Stones, Authenticity and Appropriation: Contestations of Invention and Meaning. In *New Approaches to the Archaeology of Art, Religion and Folklore: A Permeability of Boundaries?* edited by R. J. Wallis, K. Lymer, and S. Crooks. Oxford: British Archaeological Reports.

———.
2002a *Nine Worlds of Seid-Magic*. London: Routledge.

———.
2002b Magic, Healing or Death? Issues of Seidr, "Balance" and Morality in Past and Present. In *Practitioners, Practices and Patients: New Approaches to Medical Archaeology and Anthropology*, edited by P. A. Baker and G. Carr, 161–71. London: Routledge.

———.
2003 Review of *The Living Goddesses* by Marija Gimbutas, edited and supplemented by Miriam Dexter Robbins. *Nova Religio* 6(2): 390–93.

———.

In Press. "Now Many of Those Things are Shown to Me which I was Denied Before": Seidr, Shamanism, and Journeying, Past and Present. *Studies in Religion/Sciences Religieuses.*

Blain, J., and R. J. Wallis
2000a The "Ergi" Seidman: Contestations of Gender, Shamanism and Sexuality in Northern Religion Past and Present. *Journal of Contemporary Religion* 15(3): 395–411.

———.

2000b Seidr and Gender. *Idunna: A Journal of Northern Tradition* (Spring): 30–38.

———.

2002 A Living Landscape? Pagans and Archaeological Discourse. *3rd Stone: Archaeology, Folklore and Myth—The Magazine for the New Antiquarian* 43 (Summer): 20–27.

———.

In Prep. Ritual Reflections, Practitioner Meanings: Disputing the Terminology of Neo-Shamanic "Performance." Revision of paper given at BSA Study Group on Religion conference, Oxford, 2001.

Borovsky, Z.
1999 Never in Public: Women and Performance in Old Norse Literature. *Journal of American Folklore* 112(443): 6–39.

Cohen, A. P.
1994 *Self-Consciousness: An Alternative Anthropology of Identity.* London: Routledge.

Cohen, A. P., and N. Rapport
1995 Introduction: Consciousness in Anthropology. In *Questions of Consciousness,* edited by A. P. Cohen and N. Rapport, 1–18. London: Routledge.

Denzin, N. K.
1997 *Interpretive Ethnography.* Thousand Oaks, Calif.: Sage.

Eliade, M.
1964 *Shamanism: Archaic Techniques of Ecstasy.* New York: Pantheon.

Ellis, C., and A. P. Bochner
2000 Autoethnography, Personal Narrative, Reflexivity: Researcher as Subject. In *Handbook of Qualitative Research,* edited by N. K. Denzin and Y. S. Lincoln, 733–69. Thousand Oaks, Calif.: Sage.

Flaherty, G.
1992 *Shamanism and the Eighteenth Century.* Princeton, N.J.: Princeton University Press.

Gallagher, A.-M.
1999 Weaving a Tangled Web? Pagan Ethics and Issues of History, "Race" and Ethnicity in Pagan Identity. *The Pomegranate* 10: 19–29.

Giddens, A.
1991 *Modernity and Self-Identity: Self and Society in the Late Modern Age.* Oxford: Polity Press.

Gimbutas, M.
1999 *The Living Goddesses.* Edited by M. Robbins Dexter. Berkeley: University of California Press.

Greene, S.
1998 The Shaman's Needle: Development, Shamanic Agency, and Intermedicality in Aguarina Lands, Peru. *American Ethnologist* 25(4): 634–58.

Guédon, M. F.
1994 Dene Ways and the Ethnographer's Culture. In *Being Changed by Cross-Cultural Encounters: The Anthropology of Extraordinary Experience*, edited by D. E. Young and J.-G. Goulet, 39–70. Peterborough, Ontario: Broadview Press.

Hage, G.
2000 *White Nation: Fantasies of White Supremacy in a Multicultural Society.* London: Routledge.

Harner, M.
[1980] 1990 *The Way of the Shaman.* London: Harper Collins/Harper San-Francisco.

Jakobsen, M. D.
1999 *Shamanism: Traditional and Contemporary Approaches to the Mastery of Spirits and Healing.* New York: Berghahn Books.

James, A, J. Hockey, and A. Dawson
1997 *After Writing Culture: Epistemology and Praxis in Contemporary Anthropology.* London: Routledge.

Kapferer, B.
1995 From the Edge of Death: Sorcery and the Motion of Consciousness. In *Questions of Consciousness*, edited by A. P. Cohen and N. Rapport, 134–52. London: Routledge.

Layton, Robert
1997 Representing and Translating People's Place in the Landscape of Northern Australia. In *After Writing Culture: Epistemology and Praxis in Con-*

temporary Anthropology, edited by A. James, J. Hockey, and A. Dawson, 122–43. London: Routledge.

Lewin, R.
1995 Stone Age Psychedelia. In *Peoples of the Past and Present*, edited by J.-L. Chodkiewicz, 109–13. Toronto: Harcourt Brace.

Maffesoli, M.
1996 *The Time of the Tribes: The Decline of Individualism in Mass Society.* London: Sage.

Marcus, G.
1998 *Ethnography through Thick and Thin.* Princeton, N.J.: Princeton University Press.

Merkur, D.
1992 *Becoming Half-Hidden: Shamanism and Initiation among the Inuit.* New York: Garland.

Meulengracht Sørenson, P.
1983 *The Unmanly Man: Concepts of Sexual Defamation in Early Northern Society.* Translated by J. Turville-Petre. Odense, Denmark: Odense University Press.

Pollington, S.
2000 *Leechcraft: Early English Charms, Plantlore and Healing.* Norfolk, UK: Anglo-Saxon Books.

Reed-Danahay, D. E., ed.
1997 *Auto/Ethnography: Rewriting the Self and the Social.* Oxford: Berg.

Schieffelin, E.
1996 On Failure in Performance: Throwing the Medium out of the Séance. In *The Performance of Healing*, edited by C. Laderman and M. Roseman, 59–90. London: Routledge.

———.
1998 Problematising Performance. In *Ritual, Performance, Media*, edited by F. Hughes-Freeland, 194–207. London: Routledge.

Shirokogorov, S. M.
1935 *Psychomental Complex of the Tungus.* London: Kegan Paul, Trench, Trubner.

Smith, D. E.
1987 *The Everyday World as Problematic.* Toronto: University of Toronto Press.

Taussig, M.
1987 *Shamanism, Colonialism and the Wild Man: A Study in Terror and Healing*. Chicago: University of Chicago Press.

Thomas, N., and C. Humphrey
1996 *Shamanism, History and the State*. Ann Arbor: University of Michigan Press.

Turner, E.
1994 A Visible Spirit Form in Zambia. In *Being Changed by Cross-Cultural Encounters: The Anthropology of Extraordinary Experience*, edited by D. E. Young and J.-G. Goulet, 71–95. Peterborough, Ontario: Broadview Press.

Wallis, R. J.
2003 *Shamans/Neo-Shamans: Ecstasy, Alternative Archaeologies and Contemporary Pagans*. London: Routledge.

Wallis, R. J., and J. Blain
2003 Sites, Sacredness, and Stories: Interactions of Archaeology and Contemporary Paganism. *Folklore* 114(4): 307–21.

Willis, P.
2000 *The Ethnographic Imagination*. Cambridge, UK: Polity Press.

Young, D., and J.-G. Goulet
1994 Theoretical and Methodological Issues. In *Being Changed by Cross-Cultural Encounters: The Anthropology of Extraordinary Experience*. Peterborough, Ontario: Broadview Press.

CHAPTER THIRTEEN

PAGAN STUDIES OR THE STUDY OF PAGANISMS? A CASE STUDY IN THE STUDY OF RELIGIONS

Graham Harvey

R eligious studies arose as a broadly phenomenological discipline. In distinction from theologians (allegedly), scholars of religion aimed to describe and discuss religions as "lived realities," "as they are" rather than "as they ought to be." Sometimes the origins myth and self-justification of the discipline begins with the claim that it is "unlike theology." Rightly or wrongly, the ology is understood to be the engagement of "insiders" or "believers" with the authoritative sources (God, scriptures, traditions) that define what their religion should be, what they and other "insiders" ought to believe, understand, or do. The contrast suggests that religious studies is a more objective discipline. Here "objectivity" rarely means that scholars of religion have no interest, involvement, or experience in a religion or religions. That kind of disinterest (lack of interest) would be hard to find among reputable scientists; even they have some enthusiasm for the raw subject matter with which they engage. Sometimes, however, objectivity is understood to be the attempt to state the absolute or scientific truth of matters, even if this conflicts with experiential knowledge (perhaps a little like rejecting the idea that the sun rises in favor of a determined acknowledgment of the Earth's turning). The fact that some scholars approach religious phenomena in this way is sometimes marked by their relatively enthusiastic acceptance of the label "reductionist," that might otherwise appear to be an insult. This positivist stance and project continues to be a challenge to and in the study of religions. Weber (1958), among others, problematized this understanding of objectivity while arguing that scholarly objectivity should really involve a kind of "public discourse" that speaks to a wide audience but takes subjects' views seriously. It is this understanding of objectivity that is the most acceptable currency in the discipline. Nonetheless, it does not solve all the problems or convince everyone about specific approaches to religions.

This chapter is interested in the self-definitions and self-understanding of scholars who study religions. It particularly focuses on Paganism but is addressed to those who engage with all and any religions or religious phenomena. Furthermore, it begins with a reflexive case study of how I, as a scholar of religions, entered into and was changed by the subject matter of my research. This continuing process provokes further reflection on the wide open but strongly contested space rhetorically identifiable as existing between theology and reductionism. Conclusions are drawn about more adequate understandings of what phenomenology might become as it learns from *and* resists the temptations of theology and reductionism. These conclusions, lessons, and temptations are entangled with notions of objectivity and subjectivity, made evident in the performance of and arguments about the discipline's primary field research method, namely participant observation. A third position (not to be mistaken for a resolution of all the problems and possibilities) for research and other scholarly activities is suggested, namely guesthood. This resonates with suggestions made by other contributors to this volume.

Serendipity: Entering the Field

Terry Pratchett (acute observer of Paganism and life) has written,

> And if you want the story, then remember that a story does not unwind. It weaves. Events that start in different places and different times all bear down on that one tiny point in space-time, which is the perfect moment. (2001, 6)

Although I am not writing here about any "perfect moment" (especially if anyone thinks I am about to provide a testimony of a conversion experience), the point is well made that stories weave together threads that begin in different places. The story of my entry into the field to study Paganisms is a tapestry of different motivations, provocations, invitations, serendipitous events, and encounters. The thread I choose to pick now enables the telling of a story that is not merely personal and idiosyncratic but resonates with the tale told about the discipline of religious studies.

Having completed a first degree in theology (that certainly entailed reflection on personal commitments and subjectivity), I went on to research for a Ph.D. concerned with ancient Jewish and early Christian self-identification. This introduced me to religious studies and Jewish studies. I became a convert to a more phenomenological approach to religions: attempting to say what the texts said to those who read them religiously, but not feeling addressed personally by these texts or polemics. (This is, of course, to oversimplify a process that reference to the published version of that thesis, Harvey 1996, reveals to have been more tangled.) All this changed because an academic experience (rather than a religious one) demanded revisiting and encountering religiosity that has become of great academic and personal importance to me.

In 1986, when the Religious Studies department of the University of Newcastle upon Tyne developed an undergraduate course on contemporary religions (possibly entitled "New Religious Movements" as so many are, but perhaps more broadly interested in "Religions in Britain"), I volunteered a session on "the Druids." Why? Because I had seen some Druids while participating in Stonehenge People's Free Festival. Neither then nor now was the festival a completely Pagan event. In the 1970s I am not sure that most participants were aware that it occurred around the time of the summer solstice. I suspect that knowledge of and celebration of that timing was disseminated primarily by the media, Stonehenge's "managers," and other opponents (to one degree or another) of the event. At any rate, I had been attending the festival, like thousands of others, for the music, the sociality, and the sheer pleasure of joining in what seemed like the last remnants of the 1960s "summer of love" (this in the mid-1970s to 1980s!). The summer before the university course was being developed I had been with the would-be festivalgoers ("pilgrims" or "travellers") being hounded around the English West Country. At one temporary resting place (before the police made life difficult for the landowner who had opened his gates to us), some Druids distributed blankets (it being a very English summer). I had not even spoken with them and only knew they were Druids because the word went around the meadow. Since my offer of a contribution to the course was taken seriously I had to do some very rapid research.

That which followed demonstrates that the entirely reputable process of fieldwork—involving semistructured interviews, participant observation, dialogue, and correspondence, leading to reflection—changed me. The changes were, however, not only in my religious orientation, worldview, and experience. They also changed me as an academic researcher, not only in the sense that without the Druids I may have remained a scholar of ancient texts. In the midst of academic and personal changes I have come to realize that change is (self-evidently once it is noticed) central to religiosity and thus requires further changes in academic disciplines and their methodologies and self-understandings. The two following sections expand on the "subjective" and "objective" changes and lead to reflection on scholarly methodology.

Subjectivity: Being Changed

In the process of research about this particular Druid group, the Secular Order of Druids (SODs), I interviewed, observed, and joined in ceremonies with Tim Sebastion, their Chosen Chief or Arch-Druid, and others. At no point was I expected to be initiated or to assent to any aspect of their worldview. Researchers with more initiatory groups have had different experiences (as demonstrated by other contributors to this book). Indeed, the Secular Order only offers ceremonial initiation to those who demand it, usually those unfamiliar with this Order's broadly anarchist flavour. The few ensuing ceremonies I have witnessed clearly fall under the heading of carnivalesque or ludic (threats of kippers down the trousers are typical). However, another serendipitous thread of the tapestry involves my moving to a cottage in Northumberland near a wood that became of considerable importance to my subjective commitments and passions. In this location, removed from fieldwork, my reflexive consideration of dialogues with Druids were interrupted by strange encounters in the woods. After some time I even found myself facilitating local Pagan celebrations of the seasonal festivals. My long-standing pleasure in the countryside met my new-found pleasure in Northumbrian ecology, and both found meaning in the kind of stories told by Druids and the other kinds of Pagans I had begun to meet. Eventually I realized, slowly but after a number of significant "extraordinary" (Young and Goulet 1994) and "ordinary" (Turner 2003) experiences, that I was now a Pagan of some kind. I "came home" to the acceptance that various other threads of my life story made more sense to me if I named myself and them "Pagan." The next time I spoke about Paganism in an academic context I believe I heard myself shift from saying "they" to "we" and realized I had just "come out" as Pagan.

Nonetheless, while enjoying participating in Pagan rituals, festivals, and other events, I have steadfastly refused to join any group that has membership requirements or ceremonial initiations. I have also tried deliberately to avoid being an advocate for Paganisms. This does not evince any hesitation about my Pagan identity nor about the value of Pagan groups, belonging, and so on. Nor is it a position I hold up as necessary for all scholars. I have attempted to speak about Paganisms (the plural here is vitally important), happily including myself in a "we" rather than mislead-ingly pretending distance by saying "they." But I have written very little about "my" Paganism and do not offer it as the way Paganism "should be." I participate in Pagan events as a Pagan and as a scholar, but I think I have succeeded in not indicating that I know how Paganism should be (because I don't). Of course, all scholars now recognize that "the act of observation changes things." I hope, therefore, that when I have spoken at Pagan gath-erings it has made some difference. But when I write about Paganism, and other religions, I consider it important to recognize everything that "insid-ers" (to use a broad term) mean when they speak and act as religious peo-ple. Simultaneously, it has become increasingly important to me to avoid universalizing particular Pagan experiences as definitive of Paganism. This "warts and all" phenomenology of particularities is fundamental to any properly academic view of religions. Happily for scholars, this is only rarely contentious among Pagans, most of whom are happy with the notion that there are different ways to be Pagan and that diversity is essential to life.

This is not to deny that some Pagans do draw a line beyond which they are unwilling to recognize someone or some activity as Pagan. For exam-ple, the epithet "New Age" is often used by Pagans as an insult suggesting that someone, some event, or some act is too "nice" or "fluffy" to be worthy of the label "Pagan." Similarly, the epithet "bitchcraft" has gained currency as a recognition of a low level of sectarian sniping among Pagans (not only Witches) in the last decade. Worse things have been said. However, unlike some of my colleagues, I have generally encountered a considerable degree of openness and pluralism among Pagans. The exceptions allow me to use the rather thin joke that Paganism is a now "real religion" like other divided and divisive religions. That people are sometimes willing to construct boundaries is part of their story, just as much as the fact that boundaries and differences shift and change. Once again, real phenomenology is about real particularities, including any murky undercurrents.

I also want to acknowledge that my Pagan worldview and perfor-mance have been changed by my other research interests and other expe-riences of encounter and dialogue with religious people of many kinds. This is especially true of dialogues with indigenous peoples (e.g., Maori, Yoruba, and Native Americans and Aboriginal Australians of various groups). I have, for instance, found it of considerable importance to seek local, indigenous ways in which I, as a visiting (nonsettling) European, can offer respect to ancestors, land, and (other) local people. The suggestions that I make below about a third position to the duality normally offered researchers (participant or observer) is completely rooted in guesthood among Maori in Aotearoa and in London.

I recognize that I may have failed in some of the things I have said (above) that I have tried to do. The point I am trying to make, however, is that while I am happy to have been changed, happy with the subjective results of research and my position vis-à-vis academia and Paganisms, I wish to insist that this does not remove me entirely from some kind of objectivity or place me in some kind of theology. I want to maintain those distinctions, but with a difference that will emerge after a reflection on objectivity.

Objectivity: Public Discourse

Research among the Druids initiated me into how to do the fieldwork kind of research. From a background in theology and a solidly textual branch of religious studies, I had to find out how scholars engaged with the everyday and lived realities of religions. Students studying religious studies had advantages over me—at least they would have been introduced to the fruits of fieldwork research. Some would have had the opportunity to do a small research project about a particular religious group, event, or experience. I learned to do by doing. Thus, perhaps I should credit any skills I have in dialogue to the way Tim Sebastion and the SODs engaged in conversation with me about themselves. Only later on, when it became clear that Paganisms were of rising interest in academia, did I realize that my career had shifted. Then I realized how solid a foundation had been laid by my serendipitous initiation into fieldwork with this particular group, whose mode of discourse and performance dovetailed so well with the research methods that reading of "how to research" texts encouraged.

As a result, or at least in harmony with my new Pagan subjectivity, I situated myself in the lineage of religious studies scholars differentiating themselves from Theology. Therefore, in introducing my book on Paganism, I identified it as phenomenological, saying,

> I take seriously people's self-understanding and self-presentation. While I am not necessarily convinced or enthralled by everything that Pagans do or say, I consider that what they do and say is what Paganism is. (Harvey 1997, vii–viii)

I find the assertion that religious people cannot study their own religions academically foolish. Not only are there plenty of examples of religious people producing critically valuable, scholarly discussions of their own religions, but the claim denigrates the ability of scholars to train and encourage others. Processes of mentoring and peer review (among other training and evaluation schemes) demonstrably improve the ability of all scholars to engage in the kind of public discourse that Weber was willing to recognize as objectivity. If what I write is recognizable to Pagans as a reasonably accurate reflection on their religion and to scholars as an interesting contribution to critical reflection seeking understanding of religiosity, then my work is scholarly. If, on the other hand, I portray a religion in a way that baffles or offends its adherents and misdirects academic attention from matters of critical importance to them (perhaps regardless of whether *these* matters matter to religionists themselves), then I do not deserve acceptance in either community.

Participation: The Claim on Scholars

Field research is difficult in any discipline. Religious communities provide extra challenges. Paganism offers a particular version of these challenges. If religions are aspects of cultures that invite or require a response or commitment, or promise some significant return to those who respond positively or make some kind of commitment (intellectually or performatively), the attempt by researchers to remain apart is made difficult. If phenomenological research encourages a high degree of empathic engagement, it usually steps back from full participation. It seems acceptable to "walk in the shoes" of those among whom one researches, but only so long as it is clear that the shoes are borrowed. All of this is difficult enough when one is faced by communities that preach or teach the desirability of a response. But the difficulties are significantly enhanced when, as in the most typically Pagan events, there is no position from which to observe what is supposed to a fully participative event. Admittedly, Pagans are generous in not expecting everyone to "believe" or go along with the whole story, especially when they tell comic rather than cosmic stories. Pagans are usually pluralist, rarely having trouble with "outsiders" joining at least some of their circles. Nonetheless, there is often no place for a camera or notebook. Paganisms are far from unique here, but they do make the issues obvious. This may be one reason why the study of Paganisms has generated so much reflexivity, the other reason being the pervasive view of many of our academic colleagues that we have in fact gone native and lost our ability to think and talk critically. On the contrary, however, as colleagues included in this book demonstrate, even those who have been initiated—and, indeed, initiators—in Pagan groups and movements have produced academic work of considerable importance, not just in elucidating facts about Paganism but in critically engaging with the contemporary world.

At any rate, the call of religious groups (among others) and, in a particular way, Pagan activities encourages a more-than-"outsider" view. They invite, where they do not require, experience and levels of participation that some academics consider beyond acceptable boundaries. But if these invitations and demands are integral to the religions we study, how are we to study these religions without acceding to or accepting them? If it is not enough to say that we know such things are required, but we need to participate in order to understand—as a foundation for critical reflection and discussion—what are we to do? These questions are addressed to all scholars. Of course, those of us who find ourselves entranced, enthused, convinced, included, and committed to particular religions, ideologies, activities, and so on, face similar challenges in even stronger terms. One common answer is the evolution of "participant observation," in which trained scholars observe by participating. My point in this section has been that the participative part of this equation is rarely allowed the strength "insiders" would wish.

Observation: The Claim of Scholars

Terry Pratchett has written, "For something to exist, it has to be observed" (2001, 6). But he has also written,

> One of the recurring philosophical questions is: "Does a falling tree in the forest make a sound when there is no one to hear?" Which says something about the nature of philosophers, because there is always someone in a forest. It may only be a badger, wondering what that cracking noise was. (1992, 6)

If these propositions are true, as I suspect they are, events and "things" (actually persons) require observation, but that is fine because there is always some kind of observer. I realize this demonstrates how deeply I have become immersed in a kind of Pagan world, specifically an animist one. Here all actions are, probably, events (cf. Pflug 1992) in which persons reveal and construct themselves relationally and performatively (see Harvey 2004).

Elsewhere, Pratchett observes, "if it is true that the act of observing changes the thing which is observed, it's even more true that it changes the observer" (1994, 8). Happily, because academics are unlikely to take the word of a storyteller, other voices are raised in support of the possibility, desirability and/or necessity of "being changed" (to cite the title of Young and Goulet 1994). As Howard Eilberg-Schwartz writes,

> Twentieth-century anthropology has insisted that we have a great deal to learn about ourselves from the study of the other. . . . This is the myth that justifies the anthropological enterprise, a myth that says that the study of the other leads to enlightenment. (1989, 87)

Nonetheless, voices are raised more loudly against this dangerous possibility. There are those who argue that religious studies must be not merely "methodologically agnostic" but avowedly atheist. Scholars should, according to this kind of "social *scientist*," observe other people being religious, doing religion, or expressing religiosity, but they should not completely join in. Like the anthropologists of an earlier generation, they should avoid "going native," converting or becoming an "insider."

The purpose of scholarly activity is more than the collection of facts. If it takes some training, at least, even to present an acceptably "public discourse" about a religion (satisfactory to adherents and scholars), it takes more to go beyond description. Jim Cox (1998) has offered an invaluable guide to the processes and protocols of phenomenological participant observation. Undoubtedly, what he makes possible is the ability to engage with religious and other people and to return to the academic community to say something not only "about them/others" but also something reflexive. Nonetheless, there are critics of the way phenomenology has been practiced.

Beyond Phenomenology

Despite the severity of their challenge to phenomenologists, I am less interested in the work of avowed reductionists than in some other critiques. Certainly, phenomenology should not be about "simply" attempting to collect and state facts about a religion, culture or whatever. Just as biologists do not just count the legs of spiders, but discuss the significance of a species being in, or absent from, a particular place (perhaps as a sign of ecological health or degradation), so facts about religions are only foundational. It is, of course, important to get facts right, and the kind of facts that phenomenology gets right (when done well) are significant to any further academic activity. For example, it is not enough to list "facts" about religions such as these: Jews do not eat pork, Christians don't believe in reincarnation, and Pagans don't believe in Jesus. For a theologian or a preacher of these religions there may be cogent reasons for such assertions of how things should be. Of course, a scholar of religions accepts that these elite claims and essentialisms too are facts of a particular kind about religion(s). But if the subject matter of the study of religions is religions as they are lived, then it is important to note that there are many Jews who eat pork while continuing to consider themselves good Jews, there are plenty of Christians who do believe in reincarnation and fit that into their eschatology and soteriology, and there are some Pagans who do acknowledge Jesus' importance in some way within their Paganism. It is not only that boundaries are permeable, or that they are transgressed. It is that the boundaries are less factual than theologians or other nonphenomenologists might wish. They are polemical assertions not observable realities. This and similar points are important results of a broadly phenomenological approach.

Gavin Flood (1999), however, argues that we need to go "beyond phenomenology" in a quest for and application of metatheory. He argues, cogently, that too much of the study of religions collects "facts" and then globalizes or universalizes them. The temptation provided by theology is enticing: some scholars of religion are still attempting to describe the truth about a defined or fixed religion or religious phenomenon. This is evident from the number of religious studies departments that continue to offer courses on "World Religions," "New Religions," and (less commonly) "Indigenous Religions," let alone "Christianity," "Judaism," "Hinduism," and so on. Labels can be helpful, and it can be difficult to speak without recourse to some shorthand terms. However, Flood's metatheoretical approach (informed by dialogical and hermeneutical practices, and responsive to postcolonialist and feminist critiques) promises to enrich debates about human activities and intuitions as they relate to other factors in their ever-changing environment.

If this is a challenge to phenomenology, it could be treated as analogous to the encouragement to be "true to oneself." The foundational purpose of phenomenology was always to engage with the realities that present themselves and those discernible to the contemplative or reflexive. On reflection it becomes obvious that the "phenomena that present themselves" keep changing. The primary reason why academic and elite "insider" constructions of religions (whether Christianity, Paganism, or whatever) have been largely inadequate is that they ignore or denigrate change instead of seeing it as (paradoxically) essential. That is, the phenomena studied by the study of religions are changeable processes, made evident in particular local temporary specifities. Why then have scholars been so concerned not to change that which they study? While it may be creditable not to deliberately cause change (e.g., telling people how they should act or what they should believe), it has never been possible to avoid being part of the changes consequent to acts of scholarly observation and/or participation. Change is, processes are (to paraphrase Carol Christ 2003). In contrast with both those religionists and academic reductionists who seek the meaning of religion in the past or in single explanations (e.g., Boyer 2001 or Pyysiainen 2001), a more adequate, change-aware phenomenology will focus attention on the messy everyday entanglements of actual religious experiences, acts, and commitments as they emerge from and are embedded in wider social and cultural realities. It will immediately grasp the significance of the argument of Philip Carr-Gomm (Chief of the Order of Bards, Ovates and Druid) that the "real" Druidry should not be sought for in the past because its fullest expression is in the future (Carr-Gomm 2003, 19).

So, if the study of religions, including Paganisms, invites rich multi-disciplinary dialogues, it also requires something better than the research positions inherited from more "objectivist" or "positivist" scholars. It is to one such possibility that my final section points.

Guesthood: A Possibility

In the end, I argue, being objective or entirely subjective is impossible. Observers change that which they observe and are changed themselves. Participants who speak about their experiences have to find a language that others can at least begin to understand. There may be a gap between the full experience of an "insider" and the participation of a phenomenologist or, importantly, even of a fully reflexive dialogue partner. It is this space in which I am interested. I realize that the previous (possibly pedantic or grammatically anal) sentence can be read in two ways and I am happy to explore both possibilities of that accident. Firstly, my critical and intellectual interest is focused on the meaning and possibilities of the space between those kinds of relative objectivity and subjectivity that I continue to recognize as valuable, necessary, or inescapable. Secondly, in the space between those positions (but not in either a remote objectivism or a solipsistic subjectivity) I can enthusiastically engage in dialogue and participate in events inspiring emotional and intellectual responses. That space is thus an inviting one.

Pagan ceremonies most often take place in circles (per)formed for the purpose and with a central space that is usually empty. Or, more carefully, it is only entered for specific purposes by ritualists leading the event. It may, however, be seen and treated as crisscrossed by relational interconnections between participants, and therefore as being full of that which makes us persons. In the spaces between people new possibilities emerge and unfold. I have avoided taking a leadership role in Pagan groups, and only rarely take temporary roles in Pagan events. My research tends to have been conducted within the circle and across the dialogical space(s) between people. In Pagan terms, the events that serve best to enable such processes are the less formal but similarly participative times of story-telling and other bardic performances in which to observe and otherwise pay attention is to fully participate (as Andy Letcher argues in his chapter). My own contribution is a further reflection on the dualities that threaten to engulf academia.

By not becoming an advocate for a particular kind of Paganism from within that Paganism, but reflecting on the diversity of Pagan worldviews and lifeways, I have become more rather than less convinced that the study of religions should not be theological. Far from insisting that researchers must experience that which they research, I have come to understand that a "third position" is possible. This became clear to me both in reflecting on what Pagans might mean when they tell stories, and when they insist that trees or rocks communicate, and in reflecting on my (Pagan and academic) relationship with indigenous people. This third position is part of a broader contestation of the powerful dualities that undergird so much of Western culture (including academia). "Participant observation" is compromised by its dichotomizing of participation versus observation, and threatened by its temporal and spatial boundedness. That is, researchers typically engage in participant observation only while "in the field." The "critical" work of value to many academics is that done back in the study and lecture theater. Happily, more experiential and dialogical approaches (such as those also advocated by others in this book) challenge this separation of the field research phase from the reflexive and dissemination phases. Scholars are becoming people who continue to talk to those among (no longer "on") whom they research even after they have returned to the academy.

In the hope of further encouraging such relational, ethical, and anti-colonial engagements, elsewhere I have offered some reflections arising from Maori protocols of meeting and actively constructing guests as a model for rethinking how we perform academic research (Harvey 2003). These Maori protocols provide an opportunity, involving the crossing of a space not too dissimilar from that formed in Pagan ceremonies, in which strangers can become either enemies or guests. I am not asserting that "guesthood" is a space between objectivity and subjectivity, nor that it resolves all the problems of participant observation (still less that it is a more acceptable way to envisage and introduce ourselves while we engage in "participant observation"). The old dualities diminish the academic value of our work as much as they diminish its human value. Objectivity and subjectivity are not, in fact, separable and only considerable effort enabled the self-imposed schizophrenia (cf. Holler 2002) in which scholars attempted to divorce one from the other. Similarly, observers are necessarily participants (and participants commonly observe, albeit in ways that do not generate the kind of "public discourse" recognizable as academia). Concomitantly, "religion" labels particular aspects of people's lives, and these are always changing. If so, "guesthood" can label a truly phenomenological approach, acknowledging that the researcher engages with particularities, makes a difference just by being there, and should accept the responsibility entailed in dialogue and relationships. This latter prescription arises from dialogical, post- and anticolonial endeavors. It recognizes that while guests are not "natives" (or "family," "insiders," etc.), they are already involved and will be expected to say something respectful. It does not necessarily mean that what academics say is merely a parroting of what their hosts and/or informants say. In Maori events, at least, guests are expected to speak about differences and particularities arising from their perspective and interests. Guesthood research, then, does not "walk in the shoes" of the "other"; it sits across a fire and engages in mutually enlightening conversation.

Some of my colleagues prefer to name our discipline "study of religions" rather than "religious studies." By this means they aim to indicate that "religions" (whatever they are) are the subject of our academic enterprise rather than our home territory. Simultaneously, they wish to avoid the suggestion that what we do is done "religiously" or for religious purposes. It is commonplace for people to study the religions that they consider themselves members of. That Paganisms are often, but not always, studied by Pagans does not vitiate the value of that study. It does not make the study of Paganisms "Pagan studies." On the contrary, as this book seeks to demonstrate, the various positions from which scholars approach Paganisms contribute significantly to the improvement of academic approaches, methods, understanding, and critical reflection. My suggestion for the application of "guesthood" approaches is intended to further enhance scholarly participation in the world now that it has, largely, withdrawn from its ivory towers. Those who continue to inhabit the towers are contributing significantly less to the world and even to the academy than they seem to imagine. Researchers are guests and should live up to their hosts' expectations as they engage in dialogical relationships in the field, study, and lecture theater.

References

Boyer, P.
2001 *Religion Explained: The Evolutionary Origins of Religious Thought*. New York: Basic.

Carr-Gomm, P.
2003 *The Rebirth of Druidry*. London: Element.

Christ, C.
2003 *She Who Changes: Re-Imagining the Divine in the World*. Basingstoke, UK: Palgrave Macmillan.

Cox, J.
1998 *Rational Ancestors: Scientific Rationality and African Indigenous Religions*. Cardiff: Cardiff University Press.

Eilberg-Schwartz, H.
1989 Witches of the West: Neopaganism and Goddess Worship as Enlightenment Religions. *Journal of Feminist Studies in Religion* 5(1): 77–95.

Flood, G.
1999 *Beyond Phenomenology: Rethinking the Study of Religion*. London: Cassell.

Harvey, G.
1996 *The True Israel: Uses of the Names Jew, Hebrew and Israel in Ancient Jewish and Early Christian Literature*. Leiden, The Netherlands: Brill.

———.
1997 *Listening People, Speaking Earth: Contemporary Paganism*. London: Hurst.

———.
2003 Guesthood as Ethical Decolonising Research Method. *Numen* 50(2): 125–46.

———.
2004 *Animism*. London: Hurst.

Holler, L.
2002 *Erotic Morality: The Role of Touch in Moral Agency*. New Brunswick, N.J.: Rutgers University Press.

Pflug, M. A.
1992 "Breaking Bread": Metaphor and Ritual in Odawa Religious Practice. *Religion* 22: 247–58.

Pratchett, T.
1992 *Small Gods.* London: Gollancz.

———.
1994 *Soul Music.* London: Gollancz.

———.
2001 *Thief of Time.* London: Doubleday.

Pyysiainen, I.
2001 *How Religion Works: Towards a New Cognitive Science of Religion.* Leiden, The Netherlands: Brill.

Turner, E.
2003 A Visible Spirit from Zambia. In *Readings in Indigenous Religions,* edited by G. Harvey, 149–72. London: Continuum. First published in *Being Changed: The Anthropology of Extraordinary Experience,* edited by D. E. Young and J.-G. Goulet. Peterborough, Ontario: Broadview Press, 1994.

Young, D. E., and J.-G. Goulet, eds.
1994 *Being Changed: The Anthropology of Extraordinary Experience.* Peterborough, Ontario: Broadview Press.

Weber, M.
1958 Science as a Vocation. In *From Max Weber: Essays in Sociology,* edited by H. H. Gerth and C. Wright Mills, 145–56. New York: Oxford University Press.

INDEX

ABOUT THE CONTRIBUTORS

Jenny Blain is a senior lecturer in the School of Social Science and Law at Sheffield Hallam University, UK, where she leads the MA in social science research methods. Much of her teaching is on qualitative methods, discourse, and critical ethnography. Research interests include constructions of identity within Western paganisms and neo-Shamanisms, gender and sexuality, sacred sites, spirituality, and marginalized groups, and she is a director of the *Sacred Sites, Contested Rights/Rites* project. Major publications include *Nine Worlds of Seid-Magic: Ecstasy and Neo-Shamanism in Northern European Paganism* (Routledge, 2002) on Heathen neo-shamanism, and various articles on seidr, Paganisms, and sacred sites, investigating contestations of "rationality," interpretation and the "ownership" of knowledge, in addition to contested Pagan identities and their relation to site and place. Her own spirituality is based in Heathenry, shamanisms, and landscape.

Chas S. Clifton teaches in the Department of English and Foreign Languages at Colorado State University, Pueblo, where he is codirector of the writing program. He has been intrigued by issues of nature and religion as long as he can remember. Currently, he edits *The Pomegranate: The International Journal of Pagan Studies*. His book *Her Hidden Children: The Story of American Neopaganism* is forthcoming by AltaMira.

Douglas Ezzy is a senior lecturer in sociology at the University of Tasmania, Australia. His research is driven by a fascination with how people find meaning and dignity in contemporary life, and in particular the shaping of contemporary spirituality, ethics, and society by consumerism, power, and individualism. He is currently researching contemporary Witchcraft. He is on the editorial board of *The Pomegranate: The International Journal of Pagan Studies* and his books include the edited collection *Practicing the Witch's Craft* (Allen & Unwin, 2003). His other books and articles examine contemporary spirituality, illness experiences, identity theory, the meaning of working and unemployment, and research methodology. He has a deep sense of affinity with Tasmania and he is trying to discover what form of Pagan spirituality might describe a human who prefers the company of trees, wombats, and mountains.

Wendy Griffin is a professor of women's studies at California State University, Long Beach. One of the first to publish scholarly fieldwork in Goddess spirituality, she is particularly interested in women's rituals and the spiritual construction of gender in contemporary Paganism. She is the editor of *Daughters of the Goddess: Studies of Healing, Identity and Empowerment*, and the author of numerous journal articles and chapters in other anthologies. She is also coeditor of AltaMira's series in Pagan studies and on the editorial board of *The Pomegranate: The International Journal of Pagan Studies*. Outside of academia, she is a published novelist, a frame drummer, and a koi keeper.

Melissa Harrington is a postgraduate student in religious studies at King's College, London. She is currently writing her psychosocial dissertation on conversion to Wicca, with particular reference to Wiccan men. She has published various articles on Wicca and related topics. Her particular interests in this area include the growth of modern Paganism, the psychodynamics of ritual, and the technology of magic. She is an initiate of a number of esoteric paths, including Wicca, Thelema, and the Western mystery tradition.

Graham Harvey is lecturer in religious studies at the Open University, UK. He has published books and articles about the composition, performance, and contestation of identities among Jews, Pagans, and indigenous peoples. He is currently intrigued by the implications of both animism (living in a world known to be a community of persons only some of whom are human) and monotheism (the notion that it is sensible and valuable to honor only one deity). He has been a member of the Secular Order of Druids for many years and wonders what matters most to hedgehogs.

Ronald Hutton is professor of history at the University of Bristol, UK. His research interests include the history of the British Isles in the sixteenth and seventeenth centuries, ancient and medieval Paganism and Magic, and on the global context of witchcraft beliefs. He also has a particular interest in the ritual year in Britain and the history of modern Paganism.

Andy Letcher, trained initially in ecology and evolutionary biology, and completed his Ph.D. at Oxford in 1991. He left academia to protest against the building of new roads and spent six months practicing Eco-Magic and living in a tree house during the Newbury Bypass campaign. He pursued a second doctorate in religious studies at King Alfred's College, Winchester (awarded 2001), for which he examined the nature of Eco-Paganism. He works as a freelance teacher, writer, and musician, and is currently researching and writing a book on the use of entheogenic mushrooms in contemporary spirituality, drawing extensively upon his own experiences. A reluctant Druid, he prefers to think of himself as a Pagan Animist.

Ruth Mantin is a senior lecturer in teacher education and theology at University College Chichester, UK. Her research is focused on the power of religious imagery and her thesis explored the role of "Goddess-talk" in feminist spiritualities. Her passionate interest in this area is the result of her conviction that the means by which communities name and define the sacred have far-reaching, sociopolitical implications for the ways in which power and oppression operate. She has also written about the consequences of this for approaches to religious education in schools. She would not identify herself with any spiritual tradition but finds sources for her Goddess feminist spirituality in narratives that express the sacred as female, immanent, and embodied.

Sarah M. Pike is associate professor of religious studies at California State University, Chico, where she teaches courses on religion and ethnicity, Native Americans, new religious movements, nature and religion, and apocalypticism. She is the author of *Earthly Bodies, Magical Selves: Contemporary Pagans and the Search for Community* (University of California Press, 2001) and *New Age and Neopagan Religions in America* (Columbia University Press, 2004). Her current research is on art and mourning rites at the Burning Man Festival and teenagers in alternative religions.

Jone Salomonsen is assistant professor in theology and social anthropology at the University of Oslo, where she teaches contemporary religion, ritual, and gender. She has specialized in neo-Pagan and Christian traditions—including their interrelatedness—and has conducted long-term fieldwork in spiritual communities in California, Connecticut, and Norway. Currently she is involved in a bilateral research project on AIDS–Broken Bodies and Healing Communities in South Africa. Her first book published in English is *Enchanted Feminism: Ritual, Gender, and Divinity among the Reclaiming Witches of San Francisco* (Routledge, 2002). She has published two volumes in Norwegian on contemporary feminist spiritualities, and is currently finishing a book on young people's ritualized paths toward adulthood in church and society. Her work is anchored in a deeply felt vision that religion in Western society may possibly mean (public) relinking and (personal) transformation, not a set-apart community of spiritual siblings, not a puritan search for the perfect society within society.

Sylvie Shaw teaches environmental sociology in the Department of Fisheries and Marine Environment at the Australian Maritime College. When she returned to university in the late 1990s and discovered a subject called ecopsychology her academic life changed dramatically. She found that the way she lived with earth in mind and the spirituality she practiced could be embraced as part of her university studies. She was ecstatic. After completing her Ph.D. she came to the Australian Maritime College to teach environmental sociology. Here she has learned that the ocean and the creatures that inhabit it are under severe stress and she's realized that she needs to engage more with the marine environment as well as the land, to do ritual in a grove of seaweed, to cherish the shark and manta ray, to pray for the dugong as well as the lion, and to revel in saltwater spirituality.

Robert J. Wallis is associate director of the MA in art history at Richmond University, the American International University in London, and associate lecturer at the Open University. He previously coordinated the MA in archaeology and anthropology of rock art and lectured in art and representation at Southampton University. His research interests include the re-presentation of the past in the present, specifically narratives by neo-shamans, and the interpretation and sociopolitical contexts of archaeological and indigenous arts, particularly in shamanistic communities. He is the author of *Shamans/Neo-Shamans: Ecstasy, Alternative Archaeologies, and Contemporary Pagans* (Routledge, 2003), and codirector of the *Sacred*

Sites, Contested Rights/Rites Project (www.sacredsites.org.uk). He first identified himself as a "Pagan"—and like many pagans felt that he had been on this path throughout his life—at the age of 16. Having explored Celtic mythology, Wicca, shamanism, and Thelemic Magic (the latter two continue to be influential) from 1988–1994, he arrived at Heathenry ("Northern Traditions"). *Galdrbok: Practical Heathen Runecraft, Shamanism and Magick*, is due out with Mandrake Books at the winter solstice 2004.